Introduction
to
Social Solipsism

Fourth Edition
Rev.3.4.11
© 2011 Jack Dunietz. All rights reserved.
ISBN 978-1-257-09684-8

Contents

June 12 - Prologue

I'm horrified. I've been planning this trip for months. Two years of intensive philosophical education were designed to climax exactly on June 12th. Now it is June 12th, *Swissair* is faithfully carrying me to the carefully selected European destination where I will spend the next three weeks writing my MA thesis, and there is no climax in sight. Not only is there no climax, my mind is completely blank. It's not that I didn't anticipate this feeling. It's perfectly natural to feel 'as if' one's mind is blank five minutes before the test begins. In fact, I told myself a thousand times over the last months: Do not panic! It will come. If not on the first day, then on the second. Now I am on the plane, still closer to Israel than to Holland, and already in deep, genuine panic.

Panic was due only after long hours of futile stare at the empty white screen of my laptop. But if panic is inevitable, the sooner the better. I might as well resort to the pre-planned antidote for the dreaded predicament of mental drought: writing a diary. This was my premeditated solution to any attacks of muteness I may suffer from. This diary is to serve a dual purpose: First, it was to keep me writing. Like sex, drugs, and rock 'n roll, writing enhances and intensifies writing: Making it invokes more of it, and the more you do it, the more you want it. But keeping a personal diary in parallel to the main project, an MA thesis in philosophy, would also serve a second purpose: It could serve as a monitoring device - a place of reflection. In it, I could write **about** the thesis, besides writing **the** thesis. I could record my doubts, hesitations, feelings. It could serve as a logbook, a notepad into which anything may be scribbled.

And there is also the issue of the audience: On one hand, I'll be writing a formal document: a professional paper that has to conform with certain academic standards and include a multitude of footnotes, endnotes and bibliography. It will be read by a handful of professional academics that have the authority to entitle me with (or deny me) an academic degree. On the other hand, I also have a promise to keep: Two years ago I embarked on this philosophical adventure and practically deserted several social circles and many dear friends, leaving behind me this solemn promise: To write a thesis, a book, they will **understand**. Academic dissertations are usually written for very limited audiences and are notoriously unintelligible. They are hardly ever read, nonetheless understood, by laymen. This, I promised, will not be the case. I am out to acquire knowledge, and when some is acquired, I will not only share it, but will make it intelligible.[1]

---

[1] The first to emphasize the obligation of a philosopher to share his findings with his fellow humans was **Socrates,** in the simile of **the cave**[1]. Socrates deserves the first footnote not only because he is considered the forefather of western philosophy, or because he is the first philosopher I heard of as a child, but because of his legacy to philosophers to follow; The simile (or, rather,

Can it be done? Is it at all possible, within a period of three weeks, to write a paper that will qualify as a legitimate academic MA thesis, and at the same time be intelligible (and hopefully, to some extent, interesting) to the general public?

Here is the trick: The diary is the text you are reading now. the text above the line (down there, about three quarters of the way down this page). This text should be intelligible to everyone, in particular my friends. It requires no philosophical background. In this text I keep my promise, in accord with Socrates' directive: Share your findings! (with your fellow non-philosophers). But this text alone will not satisfy the second, academic audience; It will not qualify as an MA thesis. Therefore, the academic text lies below the line - as footnotes.[2] These footnotes, taken collectively, are meant for professional philosophers, for academics. This does not imply that ordinary people must ignore the footnotes. It just means that the footnotes are optional. In fact, I believe that even professional philosophers may prefer to ignore the footnotes on a first reading.

I feel a little better now: I managed to extract from my blank mind a whole page of general and administrative babble. I still don't know how to write, be it above or below the line. At least I have decided on the format: I know **where** to write **what** - and I hope the **how** will follow. This may sound a bit vague, but it shouldn't: The same problem arises every time something needs to be articulated. Think, for instance, of the American soldiers returning from Vietnam: They know exactly what they have been through, but very few of them found the way to explain, describe, articulate. Knowing something does not guarantee its successful communication to others. **Telling** is a skill in its own.

---

allegory) of the cave stresses the duty of the philosopher to his un-enlightened fellow men: *"We... shall be quite fair in what we say when we compel the [philosophers] to have some care and responsibility for others... You must therefore each descend in turn and live with your fellows in the cave."* The narrow context of this allegory concerns the **political** duty of the philosopher: His obligation to lead, despite his dissent. But the force of this claim transcends this narrow context: It is also a general directive, an imperative that is a central principle in Socratic thought. It is a commandment to every philosopher: ***"Share thy knowledge"***. He who had seen the light, is required to advertise his findings. Well, I have (to some extent), seen light. This is a conscious effort to convey, in two distinct **languages** in parallel (One above the line, the other here, below it) what I have discovered. For a "scientific" paper this may seem a fuzzy target. But hopefully things will get more focused soon. At any rate, Socrates provides me with the justification for the unorthodox attempt to write a philosophical thesis that is both significant (in the sense of "meaningful") and nevertheless intelligible to the non-philosophical ordinary reader.

[2] Here in the footnotes, superscripts refer to endnotes, mostly bibliography. E.g., in footnote 1 there appears a reference to endnote 1. Footnotes and endnotes are numbered independently and continuously.

Knowing what to tell is a necessary condition for telling, but it is far from sufficient. Successful **telling** is a project of interpretation, or translation: **From** the unarticulated "mode" of this knowing, of **what** is known, **to** a sequence of words: to **text**. This translation is considered successful if the reader (or listener) to the text seems to have captured the same "**what**" that was translated to text. This is what writers do: they translate, or convert, those "**what**"s to **text**. (Writing) philosophers are no exception: Some are better **translators** than others, and some are more talented translators than original thinkers.[3]

We are about to land in Amsterdam. About 20 Kilometers north of it lies a picturesque little village called **Edam,** world famous for its traditional cheese industry. In its center sits a small guest house called *De Fortuna* - "The Fortunate". When I accidentally encountered this magnificent place last winter, I immediately chose it as the ideal location for a concentrated effort of writing. Were I a novelist, or poet, I would probably devote the next few pages to a detailed description of the beauty of the place. But I am not.

Holland seemed a good choice not only because of the tranquil setting, but also for its traditional tolerance towards philosophy, writing, and freedom of expression in general. Not that it makes any difference nowadays, but there were times when Holland was one of the few, if not the only, place where people could not only think what they thought, but also print and publish these thoughts. It is the Dutch liberalism that enabled immortal thinkers such as Descartes and Spinoza[4] to operate in (relative) peace.

My laptop's battery is running low and the seat-belt sign above my head just came alive. I doubt whether I'll have the chance to write any more today. But tomorrow morning I shall try to tell you something about the thesis itself.

---

[3] The tradition of *analytic philosophy*[2] has brought this business of **translation** to the highest peaks: As **language** is identified as the means to grasp (and describe) reality, the clarification of language became the focus of philosophical endeavor. If it is clearly put in words, it is (must be) **understood**. Or is it? More to come.

[4] Spinoza lived in Holland all his life.[3] How ironic is it, that Spinoza suffered mostly from his fellow **Jews**, and hardly from the Christians around him! Spinoza's philosophy, to which I shall return later, was just as offensive to Christianity as it was to Judaism. If Spinoza happened to live (and express himself) in Italy, for example, He would most likely have joined Socrates in paying for his thoughts with his life. Incidentally, I believe that extreme acts such as Socrates' acceptance of his death sentence and Spinoza's excommunication from the Jewish community make a significant contribution not only to understanding those thinkers, but also to taking them more seriously. If the early Platonic dialogues genuinely portray the historical Socrates (and they are so commonly considered), then his conduct strongly supports his enigmatic claim that there is **really** something extraordinary outside the cave, or that there **is** a cave at all.

June 13 - Existence

Ok, I'm in business. Everything is up and running: The computer, the portable bubble-jet printer, an *Internet* link from a local number, and an *Email* hookup with my office. The place is even more beautiful than I remembered it. The people are friendly and helpful, the sun is shining, and the ducks are swimming in the narrow canal just outside my window. I checked into a lovely little room, Mtv is playing in the background, and I am evidently stalling now, until I think of something to say. Short break. Stop. Think. How to start? Above the line? Below the line? Ok, Ok. I got it back together now. The reader of this may know nothing about me. So now, a few introductory words. My friends may skip the next paragraph.

Two years ago I made a decision. Financially well off, with an extremely comfortable and undemanding executive position in a large company I founded many years ago, I decided to change my life; Or, rather, change the priorities in it. Close to the age of forty I declared a premeditated mid-life crisis, kissed everybody goodbye and enrolled in the Tel-Aviv University, to find out what has been said about the meaning of life. I had an ancient degree in computer science, and a very limited philosophical education, based mostly on S.H. Bergman's excellent *History of Philosophy*[5]. I studied like crazy: Five days a week, full days, and loved it. How refreshing was it, to constantly do stuff I really enjoy! How refreshing, to study something you love! I read, listened and wrote. First in Hebrew, than in English. And I really discovered things. I found out very important information.

As I said before, I promised to return and tell. I'm not really "returning", but I intend to tell - even as an interim report. Hopefully there will be more to follow. This first report is on the border zone between three philosophical domains: the

---

[5] Bergman's *History of Philosophy*[4] describes 500 years of modern philosophy, from Nicholas of Cusa to Phenomenalism (app. 1440 to 1940). The two last volumes (out of a total of four) of this excellent book were published post-humously. The first volume was first published in 1970, when Bergman was 85 years old. In the introduction to the first volume, Bergman mentions only one philosopher out of the whole cannon: He mentions **Spinoza**. He does so because Spinoza is a unique crossroads between (general) philosophy and Jewish philosophy, which Bergman knew and cherished. Spinoza is a victim of gross misunderstanding, of poor translation. Spinoza's motivation, as are his conclusions, and as the title of his most important book[5] indicates, is **Ethical**. Spinoza is an ethical man, an ethical philosopher, who took himself as dealing in nothing but morals. The severe criticism directed at Spinoza by his contemporaries, Jews and Christians alike, grasped the determinism he advocated as dangerously **immoral**. Spinoza was a mental giant, but a terrible writer. The "geometric method" in which *Ethics* is presented is, I suspect, not due to the mathematical precision with which his system is endowed, but to Spinoza's self-recognized limitations as an intelligible writer.

philosophy of Language, Logic and Epistemology. Although my primary motivation in taking to philosophy was **ethical**, I decided to postpone the important stuff, the ethical, real-life implications of philosophy, to the end: To my Doctoral dissertation perhaps. For now, I thought, I need to find out what it is to **know**, to **understand**, to **mean**. These seemed like necessary foundations of every philosophical quest. Well, you can probably guess what I found: **Nobody knows**. Really! They say, that research of the Human brain is still in its first steps - scientists know very little about the working of the brain (although each has and uses one). Well, about **meaning, knowing** and **understanding** we know even less. We don't really know the meaning of the word **truth**, nor if there **is** an 'objective' meaning at all. Or if there **could** be such an objective meaning. Or **what** it could be, if there is one. We don't even know what we mean when we say these last words in the preceding sentence: *if there is one*. We don't really understand the meaning of the verb *to be*. Sure, we all use it: We know what it is to *be* in any **particular** context; But is there something in common for all the different particular instances of *being*? Are there two kinds of *being*: *real being* and *just being*? And if so, what is common to the variety of distinct kinds of *just being*? and if they all do have something in common,[6] what separates the *real being* from all other kinds of being (aside from just saying that it is "real"). But even if I follow *Quine* and deny any "preferred" sense of *being*, still remains the question: What is it that is affirmed and denied in any particular context of **existence**? Consider the context of the game of chess: There **is** a rule that enables the pawn to make a first double step, and there **is no** rule that permits the pawn to step sideways. We all understand these two true existential propositions - the first being an affirmation of existence (of a rule in the game), the second a denial of existence of another rule. Note that there are here two distinct rules that are considered: The first exists, the other does not. But in some sense, they **both** exist, and even have a property in common: they are both rules! What we mean in the distinction between the existential status of these rule, has to do with their **validity**: The one is a real, valid rule, the other invalid. This

---

[6] *"To be is to be a value of a variable"* may be *W.V.O Quine*'s best known quotation.[6] Quine denies a "preferred" kind of existence, **real** existence (or "being"). He takes existence as always contextual. In his view, what we understand as **real** existence (say, **material** existence) is but another particular, scientific, or physical, context. There is no sense to "objective", or "transcendental" existence. This position is as metaphysical as any position could possibly be, and yet it is said about Quine that he has no metaphysical bone in his body.[7] How could that be? **(be!)** Is Quine's radical holist position **metaphysical** or is it not? If there is any objective sense to the term "metaphysics", Quine himself must be able to answer this questions. If posed to him, his answer would no doubt be, that it depends on the meaning of the word "metaphysics". He himself knows of no such objective meaning, so he cannot give an objective answer. Quine holds a holistic notion of meaning - a view with which I sympathize. In *Holism, A Shopper's Guide*,[8] Jerry Fodor and Ernst Lepore devote the first chapter after the introduction to Quine's *meaning holism*. More to come.

distinction smells of **morals**: It is **good** to follow a **valid**, rule, and it is **bad** to follow an **invalid** rule of the game.

In general, the distinction between rules that are "real", that "exist", from rules that do not, is clearly a moral distinction. It has to do with ethics, rather than ontology.[7] The case is similar (although less obvious) in other tokens of *existence*: Say one cosmological theory claims that *black holes exist,* while another theory denies this existence. What the first theory is actually claiming, is: "The existence of black holes supports our theory", while the second maintains: "The existence of black holes refutes our theory". In any theory, scientific or other, existential claims carry a moral, normative load: They support the theory (to which they belong). When a theory affirms the existence of a term it employs, it simply iterates the validity of the whole theory; it means "The theory is good".[8] A last quick example of the moral significance of existential claims is the age-old dispute regarding the truth-value of the proposition *God exists* - clearly a moral statement.

---

[7]   The interplay between Ethics and Ontology is a major theme of this thesis. It will be claimed, although in a somewhat disorderly manner, that ontology is reducible to ethics. For Plato, this distinction did not **exist**. For him, Ontology and Ethics are one and the same. So is the case for Spinoza. Both made this point extremely clear in their writings. I propose to repeat and enforce this claim, so badly distorted by Aristotle.[9] It is he who is mostly responsible for the western notion of 'the' (one and only) **real, objective** *existence.*

[8]   Much has been said about "existence" in the context of scientific theory. Einstein's revolutionary theory of relativity significantly contributed to the swift development of the *philosophy of science.* **Carl Popper**[10] and **Thomas Kuhn**[11] are but two examples. For my purposes, it suffices to say that "existence" in the context of scientific theories is completely theory-dependent, and no theory asserts existence that prevails **outside** of its realm. Existence (in scientific contexts) may be reduced to a **predicate**: *The property of being a member.* When we say that something exists, we mean it **belongs** to a certain (well known) **domain.** Existential claims may thus be reduced to simple **predication**: *Pegasus's do not exist* is simply the denial of predicating "material existence" to "pegasus'", and *Quarks exist* is the predication of "participating in physical theory" to "quarks". As Quine said in footnote 6, "To be is to be a value of a variable" - to belong to a group - to participate. This sounds familiar: Being is participating - taking part. Sounds awfully **Platonic**, does it not? The worldly objects **take part** in the (Platonic) **Ideas.**[12]   To me, Quine is a deep Platonists; Plato understands **Ideas** as predicates, as "pure" **properties**. Plato understands the proposition *"This tree exists"* as *"This is a tree"*, or *"This takes part in the Idea of tree"*. Quine is different only in his professional jargon: He understand *"This tree exists"* simply as *"This belongs in the domain, the category, the class, of trees"*. Quine understands an existential proposition of a particular object as nothing but its **classification**, its membership in a certain class. Plato distinguished two distinct **modes** of existence: **Real** existence, of the **eternal** kind, the kind only **Ideas** enjoy, and a worldly state of "quasi-existence", attributed to objects in the phenomenal world. Quine, although not explicitly, shares this view: He also distinguishes two distinct ontological status': That of **domains**, or classes, or categories, the **range** of the variable, and a second, inferior ontological status of **membership** in the class. In this distinction, Quine follows **Gottlob Frege**[13] in what is termed *the existential import*: Laying an ontological premise as the basis of logic and epistemology. More later.

June 14 - Meaning

I got a bit carried away yesterday evening in discussing *existence* - all I meant to do was give a general idea on some of the contents of the thesis. As I have already mentioned, I did not mean to concentrate on ethics - I first wanted to lay some solid **epistemic** foundations: To fully **understand** what it **means** to **understand**.[9] This led me to the philosophy of language, and analytic philosophy in particular. I found that some of the most prominent contemporary philosophers openly admitted their (our!) ignorance as to the meaning of commonly used terms such as *understanding, meaning* and *truth*.[10]

---

[9] *Meaning* and *understanding* are mysteriously interconnected - there is no consensus as to the correlation between these two terms. *Meaning* is considered a key-term in the philosophy of language - in **semantics**, while *understanding* belongs to **epistemology**. But in ordinary language, they are practically inseparable: What **is** understood, is the **meaning** of a sentence (or an utterance), and what **has** no meaning cannot be understood. The prevailing paradigm in the (western) philosophy of language takes **meaning** as something that is **objective**: The meaning of a term in a language is "attached" to the term in the same way for all speakers of this language. This objectivist notion of *meaning* could be summarized as follows: A term of a language must **have** a meaning. If it doesn't, it does not belong to the language. If the term is properly constructed, then the term "exists" in the language. There is one, objective meaning associated with every term in the language. The **meaning** of *"meaning"* is still vague,[14] but it is taken as **objective**: shared by all (competent) speakers. *Understanding*, on the other hand, is something a speaker **does**: It is a **verb: to** understand. Therefore, its **objectivity** is much more questionable. On one hand, *understanding* is a **feeling**: A mental "click". The passage from a state of not understanding to a state of understanding may occur independently of the event of hearing or reading the term that is understood; It may occur at a later time, with no external prompting. The objectivist notion of *meaning* contends, however, that the term **is** actually *understood* if and only if this *understanding* resulted in grasping **the** one and only (objective) *meaning* of the term. But if *understanding* is a **mental act**, the act of **grasping** the *meaning*, then it must involve an **epistemic change** in the speaker who had understood. This epistemic change can in no way be **objective**, because different speakers (even competent ones) have different conceptual schemes, and the **changes** occurring in them are therefore particular to the specific scheme. When a blind person claims to have understood the sentence *"The cat is on the mat"*, the epistemic change he has undergone by hearing and understanding this sentence cannot be identical to the epistemic change in the conceptual scheme of a seeing speaker.[15] Yet, the objectivist notion of meaning takes these two clearly different instances of *understanding* to result in a single, **shared** meaning they now both posses. My point is this: *Meaning* cannot be **objective** if *understanding* is **subjective**. *Meaning* and *understanding* go hand in hand: Either they are both objective, (and than *understanding* needs to be explained as a process that is identical for all speakers for every given lingual term), or they are both **subjective**, (which is how I understand Quine's *meaning holism*), in which case the concept of **language** must be redescribed.

[10] One of the best examples of self-proclaimed ignorance regarding the solution of this problem is provided by **Stephen Schiffer**, in his 1987 *Remnants of Meaning*.[16] After having made what was considered significant contributions to semantic theory and the philosophy of language in general, (Schiffer's *Meaning*[17] is a standard text in basic courses in the philosophy of language), Schiffer has the intellectual courage to admit in the last page of his last book: *"I simply do not know what could* ***count*** *as a philosophical theory of meaning and intentionality.."* I first encountered Stephen Schiffer in a Hebrew translation of his paper *Meaning and Thought*[18]. It was he who has first drawn my attention to the astonishing fact that objective meaning is either meaningless or self refuting.

13

Truth is a quite mysterious term: Not only do we all understand it; Our understanding of it is clearly a condition for qualifying as a **speaker** of a language. Still, the argument is still open[11] on the right (true?) definition of **truth.** Truth is traditionally considered the subject matter of **epistemology** - the science of human thought and understanding. Simultaneously, it is also the subject matter of another science: of (formal) **logic**. Here I found myself in a territory that seemed familiar, due to my technical computer-oriented education. But I quickly realized I didn't know the first thing about what **really** counts: the **philosophy** of logic. I was urged by my teachers to take more logic, and discovered that logical theory, like any other science, requires **presuppositions**: ground rules, basic terms, axioms, that were considered **given**: They defined the terms and provided (or explained) the motivation of the theory: Its **goals**. I quickly understood that even if I concentrate on logic, I will not escape the ethical. Who is to provide me with the **right**, or correct, presuppositions of logical theory?

The sign of *De Fortuna* says the house was built in 1654. While slowly strolling in the colorful hand-paved alleys of *Edam*, I reflected on the unbelievable fact, that my room has been there for three and a half centuries. When this house was erected, Spinoza was 22 years old, and already an intellectual giant and a free thinker. Two years later, in 1656, the Jewish community of Amsterdam excommunicated him for blasphemy. How frustrating must it have been, to be so

---

This excellent article describes, in twenty pages, the logical course of Schiffer's conversion, from a physicalist, Gricean[19] pragmatics theoretician to a Quinean *radical translator*[20].

[11] Quine's notion of truth is *deflationary*, or *disquotational*: It has no **explanatory value**: There is no significant difference between **"P"** and **P is true**. "Truth", according to Quine, is an inessential feature of natural language.[21] Every language (may) have its own, internal notion of truth. Quine separates the notion of truth from that of **reference**. On the connection between language and what it is **about** – the reference - Quine takes the **whole** language to refer to the **whole** reference (also known as "world") *as a corporate body.*[22] The truth of a particular sentence in that language does **not** depend upon a referential relation between it and a portion of the external world. This position defies the atomistic view of Quine's teacher, Rudolph Carnap.[23] Carnap held a different notion of truth. For him, truth was closely linked with **correspondence**. A sentence in a language is true if it **correctly** represents the state of affairs. Quine's criticism of this position may be summarized into one question: How can a sentence "**incorrectly** represent" the state of affairs? Carnap believed that a sentence either **represented** (referred) or it **didn't**. He didn't distinguish "correct" representations from "incorrect" ones. The third prevailing view on **truth** concentrates specifically on this "correctness": Pragmatists such as Dewey[24] and Pierce[25] claimed that it is just this correctness that establishes truth: A sentence is true if it *pays its way*,[26] if it **works**, if the sentence's truth is **desirable**, or **good**. This view, advocated in recent years by Richard Rorty, revives the Platonic inseparability of truth from **morals**.

misunderstood! Spinoza was a poor translator. He had wonderful thoughts, which became, when articulated in Latin, so offensive.[12]

So, my present task is really just one of translation, or articulation. The question of "knowing **the** truth" is independent from the question of "successfully communicating one's thoughts". The former does not guarantee the latter. In fact, Parmenides, Socrates and Spinoza are not the only philosophers who communicated poorly. So was the case with Leibniz, Hegel and Heidegger, and **is** the case with Dummett and Derrida. Philosophers, being so obsessed with **the** truth, sacrificed the **clarity** of their texts. The great Kant himself admits, in the *Critique of Pure Reason*[13], to have sacrificed clarity for precision. I believe, that from a **moral** point of view, Philosophy should be clear and intelligible. Intelligibility does not rule out profoundness. Superficial and incoherent ideas may be as unintelligible as any. An unintelligible presentation may only prevent the public from finding out that nothing significant is being said. This explains the flourishing of **analytic philosophy** throughout the 20th century. For the first

---

[12]   It is uncertain, whether Spinoza wrote in Dutch and than had it translated into Latin. He probably wrote *Ethics* in Latin,[27] in which he was less than fluent. In Spinoza's reply to Belinberg[28] he complains over linguistic difficulties. He wishes he could write in the language he was educated in (**Hebrew**, or possibly Spanish), so he would express his ideas more intelligibly. Spinoza is aware of the limitations of his language, what may be perceived as an aching lack of eloquence. Spinoza's worldview is strikingly similar to that of **Parmenides**[29]. This great pre-Socratic philosopher claimed to have been divinely enlightened, and chose to advertise the content of this personal enlightenment in poetry, rather than the simple prose of his Milethean and Eleathean contemporaries. Parmenides is considered enigmatic, but was clearly a metaphysical **monist**, like Spinoza. The resemblance between them is explicit in his *"The Way of Truth": "There still remains just one account of a way, that it is. On this way there are very many signs, that being uncreated and imperishable it is, whole and of a single kind and unshaken and perfect. It never was nor will be, since it is now, all together, one, continuous. For what birth will you seek for it? How and Whence did it grow? I shall not allow you to say nor to think from not being: for it is not to be said nor thought that it is not..."*[30]. Spinoza's monism incorporates an inevitable dichotomy between the attribute of **thought** and that of **extension**, and so does Parmenides': His dichotomy is between "The way of truth", corresponding to Spinoza's **thought**, and "The way of seeming", which corresponds to Spinoza's (physical) **extension**. Where Parmenides parts from Spinoza, is in restricting the notion of **truth** to the **first** way, the domain of **reason**. This dichotomy, shared by both, is (in modern philosophical jargon) the distinction between **epistemology** and **ontology**. What is striking, is that **before** the dawn of recorded human thought, truth was already identified as an **epistemic** rather than ontological notion. For Parmenides, ontology (in the sense of **existence** of sensory perceivable objects) is **illusory**. He has been described as "the father of **idealism**" in that the reality of the "way of the truth" can be understood as a non-material reality. But for monists such as Parmenides and Spinoza, the distinction between idealism and materialism is insignificant anyway.

[13]   In the introduction to the first critique[31] Kant confesses to have written an extremely difficult book to understand. He considers this inevitable, as a more "popular" (intelligible?) writing would result in a much lengthier text.

time, **clarity** of the text became a **value**.[14] A philosopher needs to be **understood** by his audience, otherwise he is not making good philosophy. This, again, supports my decision to write two texts, in two languages, alongside each other. The alternative would have been to sacrifice one of the two audiences of this book.

Many philosophers I have read over the last two years gave me a clear impression that they have discovered very important information about the **world**, and/or about **life** (and its **meaning**) and/or about **God**. They were all extremely intelligent and learned human beings, some with admirable biographies. Still, they did not agree with each other. I was amazed to discover to what extent they were **different** - (seemed to have) said different things. The task I set to myself, to form my own philosophical worldview, first seemed as a problem of multiple choice: Shop around, pick the philosopher that you believe is **right**, and learn everything he has to say about the things you find interesting. I soon discovered that I agree **both** with Spinoza **and** Leibniz[15], both with Berkeley and Locke, Plato and Aristotle. I discovered that they were not **really** in disagreement; they were simply discussing **different things**. Gradually I realized, that forming a personal philosophical worldview was not a question of picking **one** out of the variety of systems offered by the philosophical canon. Rather, it was a question of **reconciliation**: The worldview that I would form (as my own) must "explain away" the differences between all great philosophers: It must show, **how they were all right!** In a sense, this was Hegel's[16] greatest achievement: He accepted **all** the philosophies that preceded his own as **true**,

---

[14] Hylton[32] considers **clarity** a basic characteristic of analytic philosophy. It is not just a question of the **style** of writing philosophy; it is elevated to the level of a requirement, bearing a moral directive: Be nice to your readers. Make it **easy** for them to understand you. This broad characterization is what keeps writers such as **Rorty**[33] and **Putnam**[34] within the domain of analytic philosophy. By denying the objectivity of **reference**, both have renounced the objectivist paradigm that characterizes analytic philosophy. If they still "deserve" to be called "analytic philosophers", it is due to their clear language and intelligible style.

[15] Leibniz[35] and Spinoza are considered two opposing versions of 17th century **rationalism**. They are both considered extremely **coherent**, yet in deep, fundamental metaphysical disagreement as to the proper ("real"?) worldview. Spinoza took the road of **oneness**: There **is** only **one**, whole **thing**: the *substansia*, also known as *God*, or *Nature*. Leibniz, on the other hand, took the opposite direction to extreme **pluralism**: There **are** only isolated, independent and impenetrable *monads*, primordially synchronized.

[16] Hegel's[36] dialectical philosophy claimed to have **settled** all preceding (and seemingly contradictory) philosophies. His notion of **synthesizing** a **thesis** with its **antithesis** not only explained the **possibility** of (**true**) contradictions, (in this context, of different contradictory philosophies, all **true** at the same time), but is **supported** by this fact. The multitude of (seemingly) inconsistent philosophies counts as **evidence** for the validity of Hegel's system.

16

and by doing this, **reinforcing** the coherence and credibility of his **own** philosophy, which embraced all its predecessors under its wings.[17]

If I am to arrive at my own, personal philosophical *worldview*, it must be able to do exactly that: To show why, or **how**, all philosophers were exactly **right** in what they were saying. This worldview must be capable of producing, for every great thinker that ever lived, a certain **context** in which he should be understood, and **explained** to have been **right**. This requirement (from my *worldview* to-be) was not limited to metaphysicians, or even to philosophers in general. It pertained also to the three most influential systems in the history of the western world: Judaism, Christianity and Islam. Having been brought up in a traditional (although non-orthodox) Jewish environment, I always had a strong belief in the transcendent existence (!) of a morally **good** super-being, which I conveniently thought of as "God". In a way, it was this God, alongside several other age-old metaphysical open questions, that led me to the realm of philosophy. Most other confused 40 year-olds seek the truth with Jesus, Buddha or the holy bible; I went to the Tel-Aviv University.

Holland is a wonderful example of human coexistence. It (alongside several other west-European countries) is the closest thing to *Utopia* that mankind has reached since it was disgracefully thrown out of *Eden*. Centuries of peace (excluding two misfortunate episodes in the 20th century that didn't really concern the peaceful Dutch) molded a harmonious society, that is both as modern as any place (On the 500 year old church tower in the center of town, I spotted satellite antennae), while still preserving nature, modesty, humor and friendliness. I was walking the streets of Edam this morning with my wife, Esti, who joined me for the first three days to make sure I'm comfortably settled. She pointed out the fact that all street-level apartments had large glass windows facing the street, like a shop-window. Through those large windows, the interiors of the apartments were practically on display for the people walking on the sidewalks. These interiors were amazingly tidy, like little museums. It is no wonder this was pointed out by her, since she is known for her insistence on **privacy**. We have many times discussed the question whether her inclination for privacy was a normal human feature, or a weakness, a product of life-long conditioning. She said: "Can you imagine, living on display like that?" I sensed an opportunity to drag her into a quick philosophical discourse, and answered: "Why not? They probably have nothing to hide!" Esti was perfectly aware of the

---

[17] Another more recent writer who offers an explanation for all preceding philosophies, is *Jacques Derrida*.[37] His *Langue*, the monstrous "arch-language" on which we speakers and our corresponding little worlds (or conceptual schemes) float, propelled by the power of *Differance*, encompasses all philosophies: past, present and future.

implied criticism, and patiently replied: "You must admit that my obsession with privacy had faded lately." To this I had to agree. But this short exchange sent me thinking of the question that was still open: Is privacy a value? When we returned to the room, I opened the Bible that was lying beside my bed, and read about the **discovery** of privacy: *"...and he did eat. And the eyes of them both were opened, and they knew that they were naked;"*.[18] The second display of privacy comes two verses later: *"and the man and his wife hid themselves from the presence of the Lord..."*. The need for privacy, the awareness of having private parts, of secrets and hiding, emerged immediately after the sin was committed. Could (the need for) privacy be the necessary consequence of sinning?

On the central wooden ceiling beam of the dining room of *De Fortuna*, a Dutch sentence is inscribed in heavy gothic letters: *"Dan het Concert des Levens, krijgt niemand een program"*. although my Dutch is a perfect example of something **inexistent**, I believe to have understood its meaning: "In the concert of life, no one receives a program". I am not a competent speaker of Dutch; I'm not even an **in**competent speaker of it. I am nevertheless absolutely sure I understood this Dutch sentence. I happen to deeply disagree with what I understood in this inscription.[19] The problem with (the concert of) **life** is not that there is no

---

[18] The story of *Eden* is a fertile source of philosophical contemplation, even in non-theological contexts. I believe it is even relevant to issues in the philosophy of language. It was Eli Allon who drew my attention to *Umberto Eco*'s 1971 article *"On the Possibility of Generating Aesthetic Messages in an Edenic Language"*[38]. Eco's motivation in this article is primarily aesthetical, but it is an excellent exercise in semantics. He devises a thought experiment, taking place in the Garden of *Eden*. Adam and Eve have a simple, basic *Edenic* language with a limited vocabulary which enables no contradictions to be phrased. When the pair discovered that God's command can be violated, the first **contradiction** was introduced into their hitherto innocent language: A **command**, even from the highest authority, is a self-contradicting term: It is something that **must** be obeyed, and still it is something that **may** be disobeyed. What a shocking revelation must it have been! The exposure to the first contradiction in history had a strange effect on the first two **speakers**: They hurried and **got dressed**. The clothes mankind has been wearing ever since symbolize the human contradictory state: They mark the contradiction by acting as the barrier, the **separator** between what is **"I"** and what is **not**.

[19] We take it for granted that a speaker may understand an utterance of another speaker, and still deny the truth of the uttered proposition. I shall later strongly argue **against** this contention. But for the time being, I still employ a loose, "fuzzy" understanding of the verb *to understand*. When I claim to have understood a sentence P uttered by a fellow speaker S, I don't claim to have captured **the** objective meaning of P. It is not yet established (as far as I am concerned) whether *meaning* is something that **can**, in principle, be objective (shared by all speakers). By claiming to have **understood** I just declare the fact that **I** have attached **a meaning** to P. I could later discover (possibly with help from S) that the meaning I attached to P does not cohere with the meaning I (similarly) attached to another sentence, Q, also uttered by S. In such a case, I will find myself compelled to revise the meaning of either P or Q (assuming I care to make sense of S's utterances). But if, for instance, S happens to be dead (as is the case with the author of the Dutch inscription), it

instruction manual; on the contrary: There are **too many**. Every holy script was designed as exactly that: As a guide to proper living. The same holds for the writings of most philosophers throughout history. In the multitude of trees, one does not see the forest. So I come up with a somewhat revised meaning of the inscription: "In the concert of life, there is no **official** (objective) program. There are many, and every one is free to write her own".[20]

---

is up to me alone to decide on the meaning of P. If P and Q are two distinct sentences uttered (or written) by a speaker who utters no more, the only criterion for proper understanding of P and Q are their being **consistent** with each other: If they are **not**, I cannot say I have understood either of them correctly. But if they do not contradict each other, I consider them properly understood.

[20] We cannot **really** understand and **disagree** at the same time. Consider the following example: My little daughter Keren says to me: "There is a witch in my closet". I open the closet, and there is no witch. Keren says: "She left. But when you close the door, she will return". I am tempted to say to her: "I understand what you mean by saying there is a witch in your closet, but I disagree; you are **wrong**: There is no witch in your closet". But before I do, I wonder: Do I **really** understand what **she** means by her claim? Is it possible for me to grasp **her** understanding of this witch, who can hop in and out of young girl's closets? **My** understanding of "witch" must be significantly different from Keren's. Therefore, the way **I** understand the sentence "There is a witch in my closet" must be significantly different from her's. The fact that I **disagree** with the (meaning of the) sentence as **I** understood it, is the **evidence** for my **not** having understood!

19

June 15 - Language

I had a strange and wonderful dream last night. I just woke, and shall quickly tell my faithful word processor about it, because for some reason it has a much more accurate and reliable memory than I. The dream was a lucid dream: I knew I was dreaming. I was aware of the fact that I was here in Edam, but I was sitting at something that seemed like a control-panel, or control room (I must be spending too much time with computers). I had several screens in front of me. I was not alone in the room. There were others, all behind me, looking at the displays over my shoulders. I did not see their faces, as I was facing the controls, but I was speaking with them. They seemed like friends or family, judging by the easy manner of the conversation. I was sitting in this "control booth", watching the screens that showed the events of the last few days here in Edam. I don't remember seeing **myself** on the screen; It was as if it was **my** point of view that this "movie" showed. I was simply "reliving", with many *rewinds* and *fast-forwards* (and an occasional *pause*) my real life experiences, only this time from an **external** point of view. It would not have been so odd, if it were not for the fact, that I was fully aware not only of dreaming, but also that I am dreaming that I am watching things that **really** happened.[21]

---

[21]   The phenomena of **sleep** and **dreaming** are not receiving enough attention from philosophers. Nowadays, they are practically ignored by the philosophical community, and are left exclusively to the attention of psychologists and cognitive scientists. **Sleep** is a mysterious phenomenon, and no *worldview* is complete without some explanation of it, one that fits with the whole picture. The problem is this: If sleep is nothing but a physical, natural phenomenon, why do we have to **lose our consciousness** in order to rest? Why must our **awareness** be "cut off" from existence **every day**? Something must be **going on** while we sleep; and dreaming proves it: Something is definitely going on. Only it is quite incomprehensible.

An unorthodox attempt to investigate the phenomenon of sleeping and particularly of dreaming, was made by W. Dunne in *An Experiment with Time*[39]. Dunne is using dreams to explain **time**, another amazing phenomenon (which I plan to discuss later), while using time to explain **dreams**. Dunne must have been strongly influenced by Einstein's contribution to a new understanding of the concept of time, because he treats time as a fourth spatial coordinate. As human perception is limited to only three spatial coordinates, the fourth must be perceived **sequentially**, slice by slice. Dunne's *worldview* is, in a sense, *Parmenidean*: A huge, eternal, fixed four-dimensional *substansia*. We humans are of course part of this stationary universe, each of us receiving a partial picture of it: Throughout our lives, we are exposed to a series of temporal three dimensional "slices" of reality. This is clearly a deterministic, *Spinozist worldview*, one that immediately invokes questions regarding the concepts of **free will** and **possibility**. Dunne is not concerned with modality, ethics or free will. He explains dreams as experiences from "slices" that are outside the regular sequential flow of time. After having received (**real**, although displaced) sensory impressions from the past or the future while sleeping, our flexible and resourceful conceptual schemes manage to put these "irrational", time-displaced impressions into some intelligible framework: "create a story" of the dream; One that can be articulated in the context of the **present** - the time of being awake. I first came across Dunne's book by accident many years ago, and was deeply impressed.

It was a pleasant experience, since the last few days here in Edam were extremely enjoyable. I vividly remember watching the short visit Esti and I made to the local Museum. We walked through a reconstruction of a typical Dutch family house in the 16th Century. The house looked just like a doll-house, with low ceilings and tiny multi level bed benches. The "video" of this visit was played several times, and paused in various points. It was a wonderfully odd feeling, and it is quickly fading away as I am now trying to describe it. I'm trying to cling to it – but it quickly fades away, like a falling from heaven. While trying to describe this experience, I am drifting into a feeling of loss and frustration at my inability to reproduce, or at least properly **remember** this dream. All that now remains from the experience are my conceptualized memories. But on the other hand, I am strangely satisfied by the quiet knowledge that such a great feeling **exists**, that it is **possible**. It may be evasive, hard to reproduce, but it is **out there**.

Esti and I just returned from a long post-breakfast walk in Edam. I am slowly forming a detailed picture of the place in my mind. We walked alongside the southern border of town, alongside a wide canal filled with water lilies and ducks. While walking, I thought of the constant evolution of the concept *Edam* in my conceptual scheme: Only three days ago, It was just a beautiful Dutch village, with a picturesque guesthouse called *De Fortuna* in its center. In three short days, this concept changed dramatically: It now has particular streets, shops, bridges. It is becoming more detailed, a **fuller**, more **particular** concept. Only three days ago, the concept *Edam* and the concept *Marken* (another, similar village not far away) were almost synonymous![22]

---

[22] On second thought, different concepts cannot be synonymous. There is no agreed **definition** of the concept *concept*, and it is often considered **primitive, irreducible** (inexplicable in other terms). It is also questionable what discipline is to deal in *concepts*: Epistemology? Semantics? (Formal) Logic? **Bergman** takes concepts seriously; In his *Introduction to the Study of Logic*[40] he devotes a whole chapter (out of a total of six) to **concepts** and **names**. Traditionally, there is a clear distinction between the two, based on a distinction between *Autosemantic* (or *Categorematic*) expressions and *Sinsemantic* (or *Sincategorematic*) ones. This distinction, first pointed out by Aristotle's late disciples, assumes that some expressions in language have an **intrinsic** meaning, independent of other expressions in the vicinity (in the same sentence, or its implicit presuppositions). The *Autosemantic* expressions, which have a concrete **reference** that directly provides them with **meaning**, are the terms of language known as **names**. *Names* are characterized by the fact that they **refer**, to something **outside** of language. *Names* are names **of** something. At the same time, when a speaker utters a name, he has, **internally**, a mental representation of whatever he takes the name to refer to. This mental representation is the *concept* associated with the *name*. The key problem in the philosophy of language, is how could a *name* refer to two distinct entities at the same time: To an external reference, and to the mental representation of its utterer (or listener).

What is the connection between these two distinct things the *name* refers to, and the **meaning** of the *name*? The meaning is a **third** thing associated with the *name*. It is not (necessarily) the reference, as in *Moses*[41], and it is not (necessarily) the mental representation, as in *atom*. The reference of a name is something external: independent and objective, regardless of speakers (or their existence). The mental representation, on the other hand, is completely subjective: It is internal, and cannot be communicated (except by using the *name*, which does not help in eliminating the subjectivity of the mental representation). The **meaning** supposedly bridges the gap between the completely objective (and directly inaccessible) reference, and complete subjectivity of a particular speaker. Language **assumes**, that there **is** something called **meaning**, which is **intersubjective**: Shared by all speakers, objective, yet accessible by subjectivity. **Meaning** of *names* in a natural language plays a similar role to that of **force** in physics: Physics **assumes** there **is** something objective called **force**, and uses this concept, which was **posited** and defined by physical theory itself, to explain physical phenomena.

When we speak a natural language, we come equipped with a pre-installed presupposition that enables us to participate in the language game[42]: <u>Names have a shared, intersubjective meaning</u>. This presupposition explains the possibility of **mistakes**: Should I realize that my mental representation of a *name* is **different** from its (intersubjective) **meaning**, this mental representation constitutes my **mistake** in (properly) **understanding** the *name*. The meaning of a name must therefore be **comparable** to a mental representation: They are made of the same "stuff". Mental representations are **private**, but **meaning** is **public**. This public meaning, when grasped by a speaker, has the form of a mental representation; One that may be compared to other, **private** mental representations (to determine whether I have the **right** mental representation for a particular *name*). This *worldview* of what happens in natural language hypothesizes an objective domain, a "realm" of objective meanings. This objective realm is easily perceived in the case of **mathematical** *names*. The meanings of the *names* "1" or "=" are considered as objective (or, rather, intersubjective) as *names* could be, but the debate in the philosophy of mathematics, regarding their ontological status, is still open.[43]

Be us formalists or Platonists, in using **language** we are presupposing some sort of **objective** domain of meanings. This timeless domain strikes me as very similar to Plato's *world of Ideas*.[44] Now we have a three tier structure: A *name* uttered (or heard, or thought of) by a speaker, has **three** denotations, in three distinct and exclusive domains: It has a **reference**, in the ordinary, material ever changing world; It has a **mental representation** in the mind of its speaker, and it has a **meaning**, in the presupposed, intersubjective domain of meanings.

Gottlob Frege made a well-quoted distinction between sense and reference[45] – a distinction I find problematic. Frege takes *sense* once as **meaning** and once as **mental presentation**. If all speakers were competent in the same language, and shared the same conceptual scheme, there would be no possibility of **mistakes**: The mental representation would always be (identical to) **the** meaning of every *name* in the language. But we **do** make mistakes, and the dichotomy between the objective (reference) and subjective (sense, or mental representation), becomes a **trichotomy**: alongside those two domains lies a third world: **Popper's** *"world three"*[46], also known as Plato's *world of ideas*, Parmenides' *way of truth*, Derrida's *Langue*, etc. etc. As far as **"reality"** is concerned, this third domain is much more **"real"** than the two others: One is completely private, subjective and inaccessible to more than one speaker; The other is inaccessible to **any** speaker, and also hopelessly time-dependent: Before one has a chance to say something about it, it has already irreversibly changed.

But *names* are the **easy** part. What are **predicates**? presumably, they are **groups** of things that have names. but than, **groups** may (and do) have names too! So predicates are also names, but names **of** things that are different in nature than the things that have (simple) *names*. The difference between the two kinds of things denoted by *names* and by names of groups (predicates) is traditionally

22

Walking along the canal, a man passed us walking his dog. It was the ugliest dog I ever saw. The man was repeatedly throwing a tennis ball for the dog to fetch, and the dog seemed to enjoy the game. But how **ugly** it was! I said to Esti: "What a nice man - he probably volunteered to keep this ugly dog, because nobody else would!" Esti looked at me, mildly surprised: "Do you really think this man thinks his dog is ugly?" She was right, of course. **My** concept, my mental representation of this dog was so much **poorer**, so extremely **different** from that of its owner. Esti said: "You want something to think about? Imagine yourself now conducting a conversation with this man **about** his dog, without the dog around. Tell him why you think his dog is ugly, and learn from him why his dog is beautiful". I smiled and said: "He says the dog is not only **beautiful**, but extremely loyal and smart. He says the dog has wonderful, deep brown eyes. He says the dog has the smoothest fur. He says..." Esti interrupted me and said: "Don't get carried away - next you will make him an offer to buy the dog.."

The interesting point about this trivial incident is not the evident relativity of **taste**. It is that while speaking, I **really** changed my taste regarding the appeal of the dog, with no "external" help. I started out with a poor, general concept of **an** ugly dog, one that was (presumably) the product of my senses, and quickly transformed it into something **else**, something of which **ugliness** is not a main characteristic. It has been said (although I cannot remember by who), that *understanding something is understanding why (or how) it is **good***. No doubt, the dog's owner **understood** *his* dog in a much better, **deeper** sense than I

---

considered **ontological**: Things with (simple) *names* (the things that *names* denote) are *objects*: They have the ontological status of **existence** (whatever that means), while **groups**, the things that predicates denote, do not "exist" in the same sense of "existence". Our ontology-laden subject-predicate oriented natural language is operational: It has two kinds of terms, *names* and *predicates*, corresponding to (the) two aspects of reality, or "the world": The things that **exist** in it, **objects**, and the **properties** of the objects; namely, the **potential** diverse **groupings** of these objects. That is how the subject-predicate structure of language provides the **ontological basis of reality**; the distinction between what there **is** and what **is not**. All it takes for an objectivist, ontological *worldview* to form, is to think in a subject-predicate based language.

Or, the situation may be viewed in reverse: Ontology, **existence**, is presupposed. To provide for this primitive notion, the predicate 'existence' has been granted a preferred status: It was declared (by Kant[47] and others) as a **non** predicate, and endowed with special symbols: (∃), the existential quantifier, and (∀), the universal quantifier. Thus language was made **to fit** reality. But, as Parmenides has so long ago pointed out (and his pupil, Zeno[48], so vividly demonstrated), It was inevitably a self-refuting language to describe a self-refuting *worldview*; From Zeno to Russell[49], no one in the history of western thought, has conclusively solved what is known as "the great antinomies"[50], or paradoxes that follow from the objectivist *worldview*. **self reference** is a sheer contradiction: If **referring** is to something **external**, If this is the **essence** of referring, than it is meaningless to speak of **self** (hence internal) **reference**.

understood *mine*. In what sense, then, am I here speaking of **the** dog of **the** man? In the last paragraph, I discussed several distinct concepts all qualifying as **the** dog: The concept the man has of his dog; the concept I initially had of the dog, when it was still (mainly) ugly; The revised concept of a loyal, smart brown-eyed dog. I am describing a variety of **subjective** concepts. But to be (myself) understood by (my) reader, the whole incident is portrayed in an **objective**, intelligible setting, a context which I and the reader (and maybe also the man and his dog) **share**. I could now possibly tell you that the incident never happened (although it **did**), and everything would remain as it was; The physical existence of **a** dog is not at all required to understand the story. All that is required, is the **notion** of an objective **setting**, a shared context. (Did this last paragraph belong below the line?)[23]

My teeth ache; No, it is my gum. I have an inflamed gum. Strange. I've had no problems with my teeth and gums for years. Why now? Don't give me your worn down scientific explanations; "because you didn't brush thoroughly; because bacteria are feasting on food remains; because the statistical frequency of inflamed gums in western males is once every 18 months". I'm not looking for sentences containing the term 'gum'. I'm looking for the **reason**. I want to **understand why** I have a gum-ache (Please, don't tell me that it is because I have an inflamed gum. I know that). Do **you** understand what I mean when I want to understand **why** I have a gum-ache? No, probably not. So let me explain: I want to know **what good it will do**. I wonder, **what purpose** is served by my gum ache. Considering gum aches **in general**, can they be considered something that is intrinsically **bad**? I believe not. I could easily make up a story in which a gum ache served a definitely positive purpose. Gum aches **ache,** but they are not necessarily **bad**. Some pains may, in some circumstances, be good and desirable. I will spare you the examples. Back to **my** ache. Why **gum** ache, of all possible pains? and why **now**, here in Edam? This will be a good exercise in **understanding**. Hang on and find out.

---

[23] Let us, for now, accept the fact that **objective meaning** is a necessary presupposition of language. This affirms "**existence**": the existence of a domain, that is **shared** by all (competent) speakers of the language. This necessary presupposition is responsible for the subject-predicate nature of our language. This is a **logical** consequence, not an empirical observation of the nature of natural languages, (e.g. Chomsky[51]), which takes **existence** (handled by the quantifiers) as a special, "elevated" super-predicate. This is how the **objective world** came into existence, together with language. But alas! before we realized what was going on, we had **two** "objective" worlds on our hands: The everyday material common-sense world constituted by everyday common natural language, and another, Platonic world that contains **meanings**, made of the stuff mental representations are made of ("concepts"). No speaker has a full picture of **either** of these worlds; He does not know everything that **is**, and he does not know everything that **could be**. He only has a full picture of **his**, subjective world - his *worldview*.

Esti is leaving tomorrow. I am really very well organized (except for my gum ache...). I'll have to shift into high gear: So far I have written 16 pages in three days. The pace will have to double, if I am to accomplish anything. And I still haven't really explained what my thesis is about. All I have managed to say thus far is that I was led to formal logic, only to discover that it, like any other discipline, requires prior presuppositions and stipulated definitions. I found that philosophical debates are often about what the truth **ought** to be, not what it **is**. Pay attention to this distinction: We **do**, intuitively, primitively **understand** the claim "It *ought* to be so". We do **not** have the same, internal understanding of "It **is** so". The first statement is **ethical**: It claims that something is **good**. This is a notion as primitive as a notion can be. Desire, preference, inclination, is in our nature. The second statement is (supposedly) **empirical**: A statement of **fact**: It **is** so. I believe that "ethical" statements, **value** judgments, are something **universal**: Every speaker **means** the same thing when he says "I feel good". This is **not** the case with the statement "This object is red". But I seem to be putting the carriage before the horse. I took a variety of courses in Logic, all with Prof. Ruth Manor, who showed extreme patience in tolerating my constant interruptions. My thesis is on the point of intersection between Logic, epistemology, ontology and ethics, and it makes the following claim:

> *Human conceptual schemes are governed by the simple rules of propositional calculus. The more complex predicate calculus is but a special case of propositional calculus, modeling the phenomenon known as natural language. This special case is characterized by the stipulated notion of objective **existence**, a notion of a public world. Every **theory** has, in principle, such a primitive notion, if it is to be **discussed**. For this joint enterprise (a public world) to succeed, Speakers do not only have to be assumed to be similar in their logical structure (propositional calculus), but also in their **intentional** nature: In their capacity to be attracted or repelled, to distinguish the good, the desirable, from the bad, or undesirable; a **moral** perception. These two characteristics constitute the basic structure of a **speaker** of a natural language. As to the **world**, it is a mere **product** of language. The structure of the world is a reflection of the way we understand our language. I propose a sort of 'Copernican revolution' regarding the essence of language: Language does not employ subjective moral terminology to describe an objective, factual reference; It does precisely the reverse: It employs subjective ontological terminology to*

*describe an objective **moral** reference. In short: What there **is**, is what we, in employing language, eventually decide **ought** to be.*[24]

This last paragraph clearly belongs below the line. Ignore it. Its nice indentation almost ruined the whole text I've written so far. I must be careful using features of *Word* I am not fully acquainted with. If it weren't for Esti, who took a formal course in *Word* and helped me reconstruct the original format of the text, I would have been in trouble. And my gum is getting worse. And I feel I'm running a fever. And Esti is leaving me in the morning. I will be **completely** alone. I and my gum ache.

---

[24] This indented paragraph is important, so if you are just reading the footnotes, read it now. I propose there is a consistent, truth-preserving **reduction** of predicate logic to propositional calculus. Also, I shall propose a sort of new semantic interpretation to propositional calculus. Instead of a domain that has nothing but two truth values, T and F, my interpretation will consist of a domain of **properties**, once known as Platonic Ideas.

June 16 - Gavagaya

The alarm clock we bought just for this single ring, rang at five o'clock in the morning. Esti is leaving. The Taxi is picking her up at five thirty. I opened my eyes, and in the dim morning light I realized that the population of the room had doubled during the night: The two beautiful furry cats that belonged to the guesthouse have chosen my room to spend the night. Esti said with a smile: "I guess you won't be **completely** alone after all. They probably sensed you love cats." It was a comforting thought, for some reason. Also, my gum was much better. Yesterday evening I had the manager of *De Fortuna* call the local dentist, and made an appointment for eight thirty this morning. Should I cancel? I kissed Esti good-bye, and dosed back into what was left of this night's sleep.

At eight the new alarm clock hit again. Esti must have set it before leaving. I woke, immediately conscious to the state of my gum. Should I cancel? This business with the dentist is really out of place. Had it happened when Esti was still here, I would not have minded a visit to the dentist, with her. But alone.. Even yesterday, when I was really aching, I was reluctant to ask for a dentist. I'd **much** prefer the infection to pass without professional intervention. What eventually compelled me to get up during dinner and talk to the manager about a dentist, was *Heidegger*[25]. As he had taught me, I **cared** about my situation, and did what the rules prevailing in my *worldview* prescribe in such cases: I got up and asked the manager for a dentist. Simultaneously, I also applied a second rule; the rule against *haste* (which is a variation of the rule against *fanaticism*), and added that I don't insist on an immediate appointment; If it is inconvenient, tomorrow morning will do. Thus, I ended up with an eight thirty appointment with Dr. Schaap (*Sheep* in Dutch).

It's eight o'clock. Should I cancel? I am definitely much better. Maybe the gum problem was just a physical manifestation of my fear of being left alone. I have never been alone for two and a half weeks. In fact, I have never been alone for two and a half **days** (I am not kidding!). Or maybe my faithful exercise of *care* about my health has already born fruit, and **making** the appointment already solved half the problem? Well, even if I decide to cancel, I need to tell the manager. So I went to the reception, and shared my doubts with Mr. Dekker, the

---

[25] Heidegger[52] contributed two important concepts to my *worldview*: The concept of *Dasein*, the subjective awareness of 'I', which will be discussed later, and the concept of *Sorge*, or *care*. He maintained, that an important characteristic of being a **subject**, (the *Dasein*), is the intentional nature, which he understood as **caring**. I, as a (human) **subject**, *care* about things. Heidegger offers an original angle to describe the **moral** nature of rational creatures. Instead of saying that they have the capacity to distinguish between good and bad, he says they have the capacity to **care** (about what happens). **Care** is the opposite of **indifference**.

manager. I could have guessed his reaction: "Go to the dentist. If you don't, you are bound to hurt again tonight". He must have read Heidegger. He was right, of course. What excuse did I have for **not** going? Just an instinctive and unjustified aversion from doctors in general and dentists in particular.

So I went, thinking about Heidegger. I entered a large waiting room, that served several doctors' clinics. One of the doors said *Huisarts*, another *Tandarts*. I bet on the latter, (it wasn't much of a bet, because I spotted another sign, saying *Dr. Schaap*), and joined several other patients waiting by it. Every few minutes a hidden speaker mumbled a name, and one of the waiting patients would rise and enter the inner office. I felt the urge to enter unannounced, to make sure I am on some list. But it was exactly eight thirty, so I decided to wait. Fifteen minutes (and two patients) later, I contemplated on leaving. My gum felt just fine, and I didn't feel like entering the clinic and complaining. Heidegger's grip on my decisions must have faded, because it was *Kant* who sent me in to tell the doctor I exist (outside in the waiting room). Apparently, I wasn't on the list, because Mr. Dekker called Dr. Schaap at **home** last night. I could have waited outside forever. I was immediately accepted, and treated by Dr. Schaap's associate, a friendly young woman called Dr. Verhoef.

Why **Kant**[26]? Because Kant's deontological ethics supply an extremely **simple** method for leading a **good** life: Abide by the rules of **your** world. **If** in **your** world gum aches result from gum‾infection, and dentists cure gum infections, then the general rule applicable in case of gum aches is "see the dentists!". If it was not **me** sitting in the waiting room, but someone else, I would **definitely** have advised him to see the dentist, even if it means barging into the inner office, and even if the gum seemed to be getting better. So this was the advice I gave to myself, and found myself in Ann-Mary Verhoef's chair. She gave me two shots and treated me for twenty minutes. I had a bad infection.

I returned to *De Fortuna*, childishly proud of myself. I decided not to have breakfast, and drank two cups of thick Dutch coffee. I was sitting near the

---

[26] Kant is all over the place: He was a revolutionary **epistemologist**, contributed to Logic, Aesthetics, and metaphysics. But it is Kant's **ethics** that, to me, make him the most important thinker in the history of modern philosophy. Kant's epistemological Copernican revolution does not come close to the revolution in his original conception of **deontological** ethics.[53] Here is how I understand his position: *Worldviews* are governed by *rules*. These *rules* are constituted by no other than the particular **holder** of the particular *worldview*. *Rules* have the odd nature of being **breakable**: It is **possible** not to abide by the *rule*, but to break it (see footnote 18 above). When a rule is accepted (or, rather, **constituted**, which is in this context synonymous) by someone, and also **broken** by him, a **contradiction** occurs (is manifested): The *worldview* is incoherent: Its holder does not abide by the rules of his own system.

28

reception desk of the guesthouse, observing Mr. Dekker receive a phone call. He seemed to get excited, mumbled a few Dutch words, hung up and hurried out, grasping his coat. I wondered what happened. I looked out the glass window and saw Mr. Dekker start his car and drive away. I remained seated for another ten minutes, and as I was getting up to go to my room, I saw Mr. Dekker parking his car. Next to him sat an elderly oriental looking lady, laughing at something Mr. Dekker was saying to her in English. Mr. Dekker ran out of his car, opened the trunk and retrieved two identical suitcases. As I was walking to my room, I got a good look at the lady, who was entering the guest house with Mr. Dekker. She was Japanese, probably in her sixties, with a pair of light blue eyes and smooth, white skin. She was very beautiful, despite her age.

I am now sitting here, just finished telling you this morning's events, thinking of my thesis. How to start? I need to go below the line, and get organized there. I've been writing scattered thoughts, dropping names of philosophers here and there - don't even bother going there, unless you must. Nothing important happened. Maybe I should read the last few footnotes, see if I could pick up on anything there.[27] I managed to squeeze out a half decent footnote, so I can reward myself with a small lunch, as I've skipped breakfast.

---

[27] We shall return to Kant and Heidegger later. Let me now elaborate a little on my temporal semantic interpretation to propositional calculus. My **domain** consists of objects of one kind: of **properties**. Every propositional variable (such as P,Q etc.) in (the syntax of) propositional calculus refers to a corresponding **property** in the domain. This interpretation is based on *Alonzo Church's*[54] **P₁** language. Every simple well-formed-formula (*wff*) in **P₁**, i.e. an **implication** (P⊃Q), constitutes a claim regarding a relation which may or may not prevail between two properties. A domain must contain **at least** two properties, hereafter denoted by the propositional constants **F** and **T**. The relation prevailing between any two properties is called **"inclusion"**: If Q includes P, we'll express it with P⊃Q (for example, P is "being a dog" and Q is "being an animal", then "being an animal" includes "being a dog". This relation can also be expressed in the opposite direction: The property of "being a dog" **entails** (i.e., is included in) "being an animal". As for the two necessary properties F and T: F entails T, T does not entail F. The relation of entailment is transitive but not symmetric. The properties in the domain may each be in one of two states: "on" or "off". The truth value of each propositional variable corresponds to the state of the corresponding property at any given point in time. The domain is dynamic (changes over time) in two ways: The properties in it change their state (from "on" to "off" and back), and new properties are born, according to a mechanism to be described later.

Some *wff*s in P₁, are contradictions (e.g. P⊃~P). All *wff*s that are **contradictions**, refer to property F. Some *wff*s in P₁, are theorems (e.g. P⊃P). All *wff*s that are theorems, refer to property T. The *wff* (P⊃P)⊃F is (syntactically) a **contradiction**, and therefore refers to 'F'. Out of the infinity of *wff*s in P₁, some are **contradictions**, therefore refer to F, some are **theorems**, referring to T, and some are neither theorems nor contradictions; e.g., P⊃Q. These *wff*s are **contingent**. Contingent *wff*s refer to the relation between its two corresponding properties. Propositional variables correspond to a property. The truth value of the propositional variable corresponds to the state of the property.

29

Returned from lunch. It seems I will not have a chance to be lonely after all; Mr. Dekker noticed me on the way out and invited me to join him and his new oriental guest to lunch. I was strongly attracted to her quiet, impressive appearance, and gladly accepted. Mr. Dekker introduced her by her first name only. He said: "Please meet **Gaya**. She has been a regular guest here since before I was born". Gaya did not seem nearly old enough to satisfy this statement, but I said nothing, assuming it was just a figure of speech to stress how faithful a guest she was. I asked politely: "How long will you be staying?" and she spoke for the first time. She smiled and said: "It depends." Dekker interrupted: "She never tells me how long she plans to stay. I suspect she is just trying to make my life miserable". Gaya smiled again and said: "You know better than that. I promise to tell you as soon as I know." Dekker sighed: "I know, I know. Do you mind if I leave you two alone for a while? I have a lot to do." I didn't mind. Gaya and her smile intrigued me. I asked her: "Was he serious in saying you have been coming here since before he was born?" "Sure" said Gaya. Her English was much better than mine. "This place stands here since 1654." "I know," said I. "But Mr. Dekker does not seem **nearly** young enough for this to be true". I figured a sophisticated, implied compliment would not hurt an old lady. Gaya smiled again. "It is not Dekker's youth, but my old age, that makes it true. I am an old friend of the family. I was very close to his mother and grandmother." I was **dying** to ask Gaya how old she was. Her smooth oriental face provided no clue. Neither did her hands, which were as smooth and white as her face. She said: "I understand you came here to write?" I was flabbergasted. "Yes. When did Dekker have the chance to tell you this?" She smiled for the third time: "I saw you before, when I came in. I asked Dekker who you were, and he said that you came here to write some book. Are you a writer?" It was **my** turn to be flattered. Why on earth should she ask Dekker about me? But I didn't dare to ask. instead, I answered: "No. I am trying to write my MA thesis. In philosophy." She seemed interested. "How interesting!" she said. "What about?" I have been asked this question endlessly over the last months, and hated it. I never know how to answer. This time I tried a new approach. "I'm not sure. I hope it will come." Gaya came alive. Her blue eyes (I have never before seen a Japanese person with blue eyes) were shining with interest. She leaned forward and said: "**Really**? How splendid!" Before I had the chance to ask her what was so splendid, the waitress came with our order, and a moment later Dekker rejoined us. The remainder of lunch was uneventful, and before I got up to leave, I said to her: "I

Now, let us get an intuitive feel for this newly constructed domain. It contains a multitude of **properties**, two of which we already know: F and T. Whenever a **contradiction** appears in language, we recognize it as such, and this encounter teaches us something new. Say at a given moment, property P is on and Q is off, and the *wff* P⊃Q is encountered. The logical mechanism then settles the contradiction by creating a new property, R, which is the property of being P but not Q.

hope to have the chance of speaking with you again." "But of course!" said Gaya. "I insist!". I left.

I am back in my room now, reliving this last hour. I don't know what got me so excited. She is an extremely nice old lady, with beautiful eyes and a warm smile, but this is hardly a reason for my strange feeling of infatuation. What **is** it about her I find so appealing? I know: She showed **real** interest. It seemed she **really** cared about who I am and what I do. Hopefully I will meet her again at dinner. If I'm lucky, we might even eat together again. Time to return to my footnotes.[28]

I just had a horrible experience. I must be plagued - first my gum and now this. I smoked some grass I bought in Amsterdam on my arrival. I thought it would help me put some sense into the implications, negations and contradictions below the line. Instead, I became nauseous and felt so bad I thought I will die. I drank a

---

[28] The syntax of P_1 has a single operator: '$\supset$', also known as 'implication'. This operator has two function: Firstly, it states a relation that supposedly prevails between the properties which correspond to the antecedent and consequent. Secondly, it is a connective, used to create a new *wff* out of two *wffs* which compose it: If P and Q are *wffs*, $P \supset Q$ is also a *wff*. Any two properties in the domain may compose a third property: When a speaker of P_1 encounters an implication $P \supset Q$, he understands it as "P entails Q", which means that if P is on, Q **must** be on too. This is **modus ponens**. If P is on and P entails Q, then Q must be on too.

The best way to grasp the nature of these properties populating the domain of such a language, and the relations of entailment prevailing amongst them, is **not** as **sets** as in set theory, whereas our domains contain no **objects**, no **members** of such sets. The property *red* requires no red **objects** to have meaning, and neither does the property *pegasus*. A property derives its meaning not **extensionaly**, as in predicate logic, but **intensionaly**: through its entailment relations with other properties. The property *red* derives its meaning from all the other properties which entail *red* (like *tomato*), and from those which *red* entails (like *color*).

Now, consider two speakers, S1 and S2. The **only** thing they have in common, is that they are speakers of the language P_1. As speakers, who use P_1 to **communicate**, they know (or, rather, they **assume**) each other to be speakers of P_1. That is, each knows that the other's *wffs* refer to properties in a domain, which necessarily contain F and T. They may have never spoken before, and therefore are not acquainted with each other's *wffs*. Now, S1 utters the expression *Gavagay*[55]. S2 never heard this word before, and contemplates: By saying *Gavagay*, S1 cannot mean the contradiction F. S1 knows that S2 is a speaker, and pointing to F which is apriori known to both, would serve absolutely no purpose. S1's uttering a **contradiction** alone does not constitute **communication**, a conversation (unless they are *Zen-Buddhists*, to which I shall refer later). So, S2 assumes *Gavagay* refers to another property in S1's domain. S2 knows almost nothing about this property, but his repertoire of properties has increased by one: The new property *Gavagay* was added to it. Besides the name of this new property, S2 only knows that it came from S1's domain: The property *Gavagay* is included in S1, reasoning that can thus be phrased as *Gavagay*$\supset$S1. Next, S2 wishes to learn more about the newly acquired property *Gavagay*. He exchanges *wffs* with S1 to find out more about *Gavagay* and more of S1's *wffs*. This process was termed by W.V.O. Quine *radical translation*[56].

bottle of water, took a shower, a walk, but nothing helped. I crumbled on the bed, swearing at my own stupidity. I should know better! And just after I so clearly (?) explained why one should obey his own rules... I begged forgiveness from Kant, lying on my bed with the whole of Edam whirling around me. I could not believe the intensity in which I was receiving signs in this place. Two lessons in one day?! I seemed to have **understood** the gum ache. I admit that it was **good** that I had it - It taught me a lesson, and no harm was effected. Need I now **understand** this horrible feeling in order for it to pass? I swore never to let it happen again, dragged myself to the bathroom and returned the lunch I so enjoyed having with Gaya. Relieved, I returned to bed and carefully paid attention to my quick recovery.

After playing with *Gavagay* in the footnotes, I went for dinner. I must have done **something** right today, because Gaya was sitting alone at a table for two, and offered me to join her. She said: "I asked Dekker whether you have already eaten, and he said you have not. So I took the liberty of saving you a seat. I understand that you are alone, like me. Would you?" I was delighted, and made no effort to hide it. I was genuinely intrigued by this lady. I sat down across the table from her, and said: "This is **awfully** nice of you. I am really flattered." "Flattered?" She asked. "Why flattered?" I did not know how to reply, so I said so. "I don't know. That is how I feel." Gaya seemed pleased. "You keep giving the right answers" she said. "Are there **wrong** answers?" I questioned. I was starting to regain my self confidence. "By 'right' answers I mean answers that **I** like. Yes, there **are** answers which I dislike. These, for me, are wrong."

After having ordered, Gaya asked me: "Are you the western man?" I was not sure I understood her question. "**The** western man?" I accented the first word. "Are you not familiar with this expression?" She wondered. "I Think I am" I replied. "Did you mean to ask me whether I was **a** western man?" She smiled, as if she knew something I did not. "What is the difference?" "The difference between **a** western man and **the** western man?" "Yes." Said Gaya: "I often fail to see **the** difference between using the indefinite article and the definite article." "I see" said I: "You remind me of my masseuse, Michael. He is a new immigrant from Russia, and he does not understand the **definite** article; In Russian there is no such distinction. He always says 'If cold I close window'[29] or 'How is

---

[29] **Conditionals:** A conditional proposition of the form A⊃B is the basic unit of **communication** between speakers; the basic **sentence**. When speaker S1 says to S2: 'A⊃B', he provides S2 with information about properties A and B. If S2 already knows one of these two properties, this propositions provides information about the other, using the one he already knows. If S1 assumes S2 already knows A, and based on this acquaintance, he 'describes' a second property, B, which includes A (and is therefore the consequent of the implication). The implication acts as a connecting link between properties, enabling speakers to direct their fellow speakers through **chains** of properties, each property entailed (implied) by its predecessor. When S2 recognizes something S1

pain?'". Gaya asked: "Do you speak Russian?" "Not a word" I replied. "I do. I always thought that in Russian, **Every** noun **automatically** carries the definite article. By asking you 'How is pain?', I believe your masseuse **meant** to ask you 'How is **the** pain, did he not? He **must** have meant **your** pain!" This was news to me: "You mean that by saying 'Coffee is hot' Michael actually, **always**, means '**the** coffee is hot?" "Precisely!" said Gaya. "How, then, would a Russian say 'coffee contains caffeine'?" She answered: "He would **say** 'coffee contains caffeine', because there is no definite article in Russian, but he would **mean** '**the** coffee contains **the** caffeine', of course. Do you find any difference in **meaning** between the two? Would you understand him **differently** if he said so, or, for that matter, '**the** coffee contains caffeine', or 'coffee contains **the** caffeine'?" I paused for thought, pretending to be busy chewing **the** first course of **the** meal that was just served. I was trying to think of an example where the evident difference between the definite and indefinite was indispensable. Finally I spoke: "You mean that the distinction is redundant? How about the need to distinguish between **this** coffee and coffee in general? for example, '**this** coffee is good coffee'?" Gaya had no problem with my counter example: "Michael would probably say 'Coffee is good', and nothing would be lost in the translation. Look, don't try to find counter examples. The Russians have survived for a long time without the distinction. If the distinction was indispensable, their language

---

uttered (verbally or otherwise) as a proposition (as an **implication**), he takes it as a 'request' to focus his attention on its antecedent and consequent. If S2 recognizes the antecedent as a contradiction, he uunderstands that S1 is directing his attention to the special property F, shared by all speakers.

This explains the great significance of the contradiction in communication; It is not something obscure, inexplicable, meaningless (whereas everything follows from it). On the contrary: It is the clearest, most evident, the **only** term in language that **everybody** understands (has a specific corresponding property which is denoted by it). That is how *Zen* priests stay in touch with each other, although they are in completely separate worlds: They realize that the only thing they have in common is F (and the syntax of P_1), and they constantly say to each other: "contradiction!", "contradiction!" and know (for sure) that they are properly **understood**.

This is how speakers help each other create new properties. Supposing S1 and S2 each have a property, P, each assuming that his fellow speaker means 'the same' property (whatever 'same' means) by P. Let us further assume that S1 has a second property, Q, which he wants S2 to share with him (to have a 'similar' Q in his system). In order to achieve this, S1 needs a 'hinge', a sort of 'hook' on which to 'hang' Q, which is new to S2. He needs to 'define' Q for S2. For this he needs P: a property that entails Q, and known to S2. (1) If he can find no such P, such as the case of two speakers who know **nothing** of each other, except for the fact that they are speakers, (a situation of *radical translation*), then he must start with F, which he **knows** his fellow speaker to posses; In this case he simply 'asks' him to create (their first shared) concept (property). (E.g., *Gavagay*). But in case (2) they already have some property they considered shared (e.g. P), then S1 can communicate a property Q that is **new** for S2, by saying P⊃Q. S2 than creates a new property that includes the property (denoted by) P, which he thereafter refers to as Q.

would have provided for it. Everything that can be said in English could also be articulated in Russian. Different languages have different ways of expression. Before dinner I was leafing through the bible I found in my room. There exists a Hebrew preposition that has no English translation; The fourth word in the book of Genesis?" "Yes - the word את" I replied, and added: "The man who declared the independence of the state of Israel and was its first prime minister, David Ben Gurion, maintained that this word was redundant, and made a point of never using it!" "How interesting!" Said Gaya. "I wonder why he picked this poor little preposition. I would have started with eliminating the distinction between the definite and indefinite".[30]

---

[30] **The** definite article is an unessential, although a convenient convention in many languages. It signals, that the noun in question is **particular**. This particularity has nothing to do with material existence, nor with uniqueness. It just signals that the noun following it **should** be familiar to the hearer of the expression containing it. Let us assume, that S1 and S2 **share** their understanding of the term *the*, and let us further assume that S1 uttered *the Gavagay*. Would S2 now be in a better position to understand S1's utterance? It seems not. The definite article is useful **only** for past reference; When it is used, as in *the Gavagay,* the hearer should understand that the speaker means **the same** *Gavagay* that was mentioned (or implied) **before**. For the definite article to be effectively used, a **shared context** is already assumed. The nouns in this shared context are entitled with the article, to identify them as such.

But before our two speakers could establish an agreed term to specify properties that are already **shared**, that belong to some **shared context**, such a shared context needs first to be established. The first name that enters this shared, **objective** domain, is of course *Gavagay*. Within S2's domain of properties, S2 creates a "sub directory" of properties that he takes S1 to **share** with him. Next, S1 utters a second name: *Managay*. (This exercise is conducted from S2's point of view, and demonstrates the evolution in S2's conceptual scheme. It is assumed, that S1 undergoes a similar process, which I will disregard). *Managay* is added as a second property to the special sub-domain S2 created in his scheme, devoted to properties which they both share. S2 may thus accumulate a multitude of shared, "objective" properties, and gradually discovers the entailment relations prevailing between the newly acquired "objective" (shared) properties. The objective domain, **shared** by both speakers, is developing, becoming **richer** not only with (names of) properties, but also with relations prevailing between them.

Let us now somewhat revise the circumstances of the conversation between S1 and S2. This time, let us add **another** *apriori* property that is shared by both; that is **objective**. Let us call this property **existence**, or in shorthand, x. This time, the speakers not only assume each other to be **speakers**, namely, to master the syntax of P_1 (and its **innate** properties, F and T), but also to (both) have the *apriori* property x; the way they (both) understand this property is as follows: It is the property of **all** the properties belonging to the shared, objective sub-domain ("all the properties that exists in the shared world": - "objective properties"). Every property that belongs to the objective sub-domain, entails x. In any particular domain ("scheme"), some properties entail x (they belong to the objective sub-domain; they "exist"), and some do not (they "don't exist" – they don't belong to the objective sub-domain). This special property x lets us make existential claims in **propositional calculus**: Consider this Predicate-Logic proposition:: "For every (x), Px". We understand this claim as "Property P applies to all objects in the domain". For example, let P be the property of "composed of atoms". If this property applies to all things "existent", then this property P **includes** property x: $x \supset P$.

I watched Gaya finish the first course. She seemed older than this morning, but even more beautiful. Her silky white hair was woven into a neat plait that was hanging loosely on her shoulder. After the waitress cleared the table for the main course, I asked: "So what did **you** mean by asking me whether I was **the** western man?" "I was asking a question **about** you. I was asking whether the description 'the western man' applies to you." I did not know what the right answer to this question was. Gaya was Japanese, definitely **not** "the" western man. But how could I possibly deny it of myself? "I'm afraid I am", I finally answered. "**Afraid**? That is strange!" She seemed surprised. "Is being the western man not considered a compliment by the western men?" I decided to take the initiative. "Or the western **woman**?" Gaya was surprised again. "The western woman? I have never heard this expression, except in the context of the American wild west. Is there such a thing as 'the western woman'?" "I don't know. I thought you could tell me." I replied. "Well, I don't think so. I think that the western man has made a point of his being the western **man**, not western **person**." I thought I understood. "Do I sense some gender-based criticism?" "I make it a point never to **criticize**" said Gaya. "But I must admit, that I do resent the age-long discrimination against women in the history of western civilization." "Only **western** civilization?" I wondered. "I understand that women were not better off in any **eastern** civilization!" Gaya became more serious. "Well, maybe. But in eastern civilization, women were usually considered something **very** different from men. In the east, they could hardly be **compared**."

After the main course, Dekker joined us for coffee, and the conversation concentrated on "what's new in Edam". I learned about a local music festival a week from today, and that Gaya planned on staying at least until then. Dekker was pleased to receive **some** information about her plans - he was obsessed with not getting stuck with empty rooms. Before returning to my room, I gathered some courage, and offered Gaya to join me on tomorrow's morning walk after breakfast. She accepted, provided it would not rain. I went to sleep wondering whether Gaya didn't have anything better to do than spend time with me.

35

June 17 - Logic

I woke up late. I think I spent the night at the control-room again, but I am not sure. All I remember, was that Gaya was in the dream. I had her on my mind as I awoke, and was afraid I would miss her at breakfast. I got fully dressed, so I wouldn't have to return to the room before the walk, and hurried to the dining room. Gaya showed up five minutes after me. I said: "What a coincidence! I just came in myself!". Gaya smiled, as usual: "It is not a coincidence. I asked Dekker to call me down when you arrive." Diplomatically, I tried to retrieve some information: "What do you usually do when you are here? don't you have plans?" What I meant to ask, of course, was how did she make herself so available to someone she just met. "Nothing. I walk, I talk to people." "Do you have many friends around here, besides Mr. Dekker?" "I know quite a few people that live here, if that is what you mean. But I have no plans. Don't worry, you are not imposing."

We had breakfast and went for a walk in Edam's quiet streets. I let her lead, as I assumed she knew her way much better than I. We were walking along the centuries-old traditional Dutch houses, with their large windows facing the street. Many of the houses had fat, lazy cats stretched on the window sill. In one window, there was a porcelain cat in a sitting position, and next to it, a real live cat, in the exact same position. They looked like twins. We stopped and looked at the two almost identical cats, when the real cat quickly jumped down, and quickly came outside. The cat started humming, rubbing itself against Gaya's legs. She knelt and gently patted the animal. A moment later, the cat left and resumed its position at the window, next to its porcelain twin. I spoke[31]: "Can you repeat this trick with the **other** cat?" Gaya smiled, but said nothing.

---

[31] Both speakers, S1 and S2, assume **each other** to possess a special, objective subdomain. It **should** be exactly identical for both, but there is no way of telling, except by **speaking** to each other: By constructing sentences (*wff)s*, transmitting them to the other speaker, and receiving *wffs* in return. What they are trying to speak **about**, is the properties which belong to their shared subdomain. When two speakers converse in their natural language, they typically have a large shared subdomain, which can be visualized as the intersection of their respective conceptual schemes. A key property which belongs to such a typical shared subdomain, is **x** - existence - the property of being an object. This creates a dichotomy into two classes of properties: The ones that **exist** (included in x), often called *objects*, and the properties that do not exist, *predicates*. They also invent a special notation, they call **predicate logic**[57]. This new, advanced, sophisticated notation, is based on the (primitively understood) distinction between properties that exist (objects) and properties that do not (predicates). This newly devised notation is applied every time the special property x ("existence") is involved. x may take part in an implication in one of four ways: **(1)** The *wff* (x⊃P) becomes (x)Px: *objecthood entails Phood* (if it's an object, it's also P) becomes "for every object, P is true". **(2)** when S1 wants to convey the fact that a predicate P is **not** entailed by all objects (that there **is** at least one object that does **not** entail P), he constructs (instead of ~(x⊃P)) a *wff* that is the negation of the previous one: ~(x)Px. This is the **denial** of (1), but at the same time, it is an **affirmation** of existence: Of the existence of **some** object (included in x), that does not include

36

Many people in Edam have cats (I had two, temporarily), but **every** house in Edam has beautiful plants, everywhere: In the window, in and around the house. We passed several plant shops, with an incredible assortment of plants. I said to Gaya: The people here have a thing with plants; almost an obsession, don't you think?" "You make it sound **wrong**," she answered. "On the contrary. I think it is wonderful. But there are many beautiful things. why **plants**?" Gaya smiled. "Because they **live**!" "You mean they are more beautiful because they live?" "No," she answered. "Plastic or silk flowers can be no less beautiful. Plants **live**, so they need **care**. It is the **care** that plants require, that makes them so appealing to humans; To **some** humans." "Plants and cats" said I. "And kids" added Gaya with a smile. "Do you have kids?" "Three daughters" I said proudly. "How nice!" She seemed delighted to hear that. I changed the subject: "You are a very

---

P. Taken as an affirmation of existence of some (unspecified) object, an alternative notation is used: $(\exists x)\sim Px$: *There **exists** some property (included in) x, an **object**, which is not included by (**does not entail**) P*. Naturally, $\sim(x)Px \equiv (\exists x)\sim Px$. In the next case **(3)**, $x\supset\sim P$ (or $P\supset\sim x$) turns into $(x)\sim Px$: The (inexistent) predicate P entails a contradiction ($\sim x$). But this is also a **denial** of existence: of **any** object that entails P: $\sim(\exists x)Px$. Again, naturally, $\sim(\exists x)Px \equiv (x)\sim Px$. Finally, **(4)** $\sim(x\sim P)$ (or $\sim(P\supset\sim x)$) is an affirmation of existence of some object, which includes P: $(\exists x)Px$.

This concludes the basic transformation from propositional calculus to predicate logic, based on an *apriori* understanding of the property **Existence**. Let me summarize:

$$\underline{\text{Predicate Logic}} \quad \underline{\text{Propositional calc.}}$$
$$Pa \Leftrightarrow a\supset P$$
$$(x)Px \Leftrightarrow x\supset P$$
$$(\exists x)Px \Leftrightarrow \sim(x\supset\sim P)$$
$$(x)(Px\supset Gx) \Leftrightarrow x\supset(P\supset G)$$
$$(x)\sim(Px\supset Gx) \Leftrightarrow x\supset\sim(P\supset G)$$
$$(\exists x)(Px\supset Gx) \Leftrightarrow \sim[x\supset\sim(P\supset G)]$$
$$(\exists x)\sim(Px\supset GX) \Leftrightarrow \sim[x\supset(P\supset G)]$$
$$(x)(y)Pxy \Leftrightarrow x\supset(y\supset P)$$
$$(x)\sim(y)Pxy \Leftrightarrow x\supset\sim(y\supset P)$$
$$(\exists x)(y)Pxy \Leftrightarrow \sim[x\supset\sim(y\supset P)]$$
$$(\exists x)\sim(y)Pxy \Leftrightarrow \sim[x\supset(y\supset P)]$$
$$(y)(\exists x)Pxy \Leftrightarrow y\supset\sim(x\supset\sim P)$$
$$(y)\sim(\exists x)Pxy \Leftrightarrow y\supset(x\supset\sim P)$$

Equipped with the newly acquired notion of **existence**, our two speakers and their (mutually assumed) shared objective subdomain may proceed to invent **mathematical objects**. All they need, is an agreed (shared, objective) **object** hereafter called **the empty set**. The empty set **exists**.[58] The primitive relation prevailing between properties (objects and predicates alike) provide the notion of **membership**, which, together with another presupposed existent property, the **object** 'the empty set', is enough to construct the whole realm of **objective** mathematics. This view supports a Platonic, **realistic**[59] view of mathematical entities. (Whereas in the terminology employed here, 'objective' is synonymous with 'existent'.) This discussion will be developed further in footnote 42.

interesting person", I said courageously. "Believe me, everyone is interesting. Unfortunately, hardly anyone knows this fact. I think **you** are interesting. Tell me about yourself." I said: "But it has to be a fair exchange. You will tell me about **your**self". "Naturally," she said. "It does not work any other way. You will tell me about your world, and I will tell you about mine." I hesitated, but encouraged by her completely uninhibited behavior, I asked if I could ask her a personal question. "But of course!" She said. "How come you never tell Mr. Dekker how long you are staying?" "Because I never know whom I will meet. My plans are flexible. I always stay as long as it is **interesting**. and it always is. Sometimes for a long time. When it is over, I know it is over. Never before. But don't worry about Mr. Dekker. I always pay for the room until the next guest occupies it. He is just carrying on."

I returned to my footnotes. I find it hard to concentrate. What an amazing lady! I try to focus on *radical translation* and *existence*. Down there, I already have two **speakers** in place, in the process of creating a **joint world**. In a way, that is what Gaya had offered to do with me. I don't know much about her, aside from my **presuppositions**. What would be the best approach to **really** understand her? A standard subject-predicate natural language hardly seems **enough.**° I skipped lunch. I knew that if I looked for Gaya, she would be there, and my footnotes would suffer. Maybe it will be a good idea to tell her about the thesis. Maybe she will surprise me again, and I will combine business with pleasure. We'll see. Still, it can wait until dinner. Apparently, she's not going anywhere.

I spent the rest of the day in my room. The dining room was packed because of the weekend, and Gaya said she had to spend the evening with some local friends (She **did** have friends in Edam). Mr. Dekker was relieved to find out that I have no objection to having dinner served in my room. I finished footnote 31 and printed today's crop. Only three pages! at this rate I'll need three **months** in Edam, not three weeks! While getting ready to go to sleep (don't forget to brush your gums!), I was planning tomorrow's conversation with Gaya. Even if nothing significant happens with my footnotes, at least Gaya might provide me with an interesting story to tell. If she allows herself to be pushy, so can I: Tomorrow I will ask her about her religious, or metaphysical inclination. I wonder if she is a Buddhist or something. I know next to nothing about eastern philosophy. May be she will enlighten me. Good night.

°Our two speakers continue to enhance their expanding joint objective world. They invent a variety of abbreviations, to improve the efficiency of their communication. For example, instead of saying "B implies (or entails, or is included by) A, **and also** ~B implies ~A", they say "A is the **cause** of B", where A and B are **objects**. When A and B are not objects, but predicates, they say "B is the **reason** of A". (See footnote 46 below).

June 18 - Art

Good morning. The sun is shining through my window. It is Sunday, and the first nice day since I arrived here. One of my two adopted cats (or am **I** the adopted one?), the red haired one, was occupying my chair. I carefully carried it to the second chair, and it didn't even bother to move or open its eyes. maybe it is a porcelain cat... I decided to write a little before breakfast, because I still feel guilty for yesterday's poor achievement, as far as my writing is concerned. Before I fell asleep, I thought of basic concepts such as *number, reason* and *cause,* which I touched in the end of footnote 31. It occurred to me, that these concepts, alongside several others, are what Kant termed *pure concepts of understanding,* or *categories.*[32]

Speaking of Kant, I cannot resist quoting one of his pupils, Johann Herder: *"I have had the good fortune to know a philosopher... In his prime he had the happy sprightliness of a youth; he continued to have it, I believe, even as a very old man. His broad forehead, built for thinking, was the seat of an imperturbable cheerfulness and joy. Speech, the richest of thought, flowed from his lips. Playfulness, wit, and humor were at his command... He was indifferent to nothing worth knowing. No cabal, no sect, no prejudice, no desire for fame could ever tempt him in the slightest away from broadening and illuminating the truth. He incited and gently forced others to think for themselves; despotism was foreign to his mind. This man, whom I name with the greatest gratitude and respect, was Immanuel Kant."* What a role model! It is much, much easier to **believe such** a man!

I just remembered that Mercury came out of *retro* yesterday, and is back on its forward course. No wonder the world seems so much brighter. I wish I knew more about Eastern philosophy, so I could conduct a reasonable conversation with Gaya about the deep abyss separating it from western thought. I only know a little about *Zen* and *Tao*. Both emphasize the role of **contradiction**, or the

---

[32] Kant's twelve categories of the mind[61] were considered by him as the basis for understanding any **experience**. Kant considered these concepts **innate**. As **conditions** for understanding, of being human, rational creatures. The claim that emerges from the preceding discussion, is that these categories may be **reducible** to a simpler structure; That concepts such as negation, quantity, cause, contingency etc. can be **constructed out of** the syntax of P_1, coupled with a presupposed notion of **objectivity**, taken as membership in the subdomain especially constructed by the speakers for the purpose of communication. Another category, that of identity, is nothing but the relation of **mutual entailment**: When two properties entail each other, they are considered **identical**. I am not yet sure whether this reduction of Kant's categories is in fact possible, so I shall, for now, settle for a weaker claim: Each of the speakers S1 and S2 **assume** each other's domains to include properties that correspond to the categories, regardless of **how** they were (originally) constructed.

principle of **polarity**, as the basic building block of reality.[33] When I was sitting down at my favorite table at the window for breakfast, I saw Gaya standing outside, on the small bridge over the canal that was flowing by the guesthouse. She was talking to a small group of people, standing or sitting on the bridge, and painting the scenery. They were all oriental, like Gaya. before the waitress had the chance to come to my table, I got up and joined Gaya outside. She was speaking what must have been Japanese. The painters were facing different directions, some were drawing with a pencil, some in water colors. Gaya greeted me with a smile and said a few words in Japanese, probably about me, because the men smiled at me and nodded. I nodded back, and a moment later Gaya and I entered the house and sat down for breakfast. Gaya said: "They came for the day; A large group of Japanese amateur painters. They are scattered all over Edam." "This place must have a world reputation" I said. "Although I never heard of it until a few months ago." "You never heard about Edam cheese?" "No, I haven't". "Well, I agree that this place **should** be world famous for its beauty, not the cheese" said Gaya. "It is a lot like some beautiful place in Japan. Strange, but Dutch people share many aesthetic values with the Japanese." I tended to agree. Many charming corners in Edam very much resembled Japanese gardens. "Do you know what these people are doing?" I hesitated before answering. They were evidently drawing or painting, but apparently this was not what Gaya meant. "What?" I asked. "They are **speaking**" said Gaya with an enigmatic smile. She knew she had to elaborate: "You must be aware of the fact that **language** is not limited to verbal or written words and sentences. If I approach a stranger and offer him an object I am holding in my hand, without uttering a word, he would no doubt understand my gesture as, at least, an offer to

---

[33] Now our two speakers already converse freely, talking **about** the objective world they take to be shared by both, and about inexistent properties that are not objective, but can nevertheless be discussed with the help of predicate logic, or the subject-predicate structure of their *wffs*, or **sentences**. S1 and S2 each have (in their respective conceptual schemes) a subdomain they consider shared. Each of the two believes the other holds an identical subdomain. Still, there is ample room for **mistake**: The two supposedly identical subdomains may be different: a **discrepancy** between what S1 and S2 consider the objective world: S2's objective subdomain includes an object, C, which is **not** in S1's objective subdomain. This incident is the paradigm of the concept of **mistake**: a misunderstanding between two interlocutors. What was hitherto considered **the** objective subdomain, **is no more**: There are two, **different** subdomains: One in S1's conceptual scheme, and another in S2. They are not aware of this fact, whereas if they were, they would no doubt try to mend the situation, to avoid further misunderstandings. S1 and S2 are aware of the **possibility** of such mishaps, and may even suspect that such discrepancies may prevail, but they nevertheless continue to **assume** (what choice do they have, except for loneliness?) that their objective domains are **isomorphic**.[62] It is irrelevant who of the speakers is "responsible" for the discrepancy, for the occurrence of the **mistake**; whether S1 did not articulate properly, or S2 did not receive the message properly. It is also meaningless to claim that one of the speakers is "right" and the other "wrong", because there is no external criterion by which this could be determined. S1's and S2's objective worlds are just **different**.

pay attention to the object I am holding. There exists a 'universal' language, based on the senses of sight and sound. A language that is based on the well known fact, that almost all humans see in three dimensions and hear sounds." "I understand. Please go on" I said in anticipation. "When we are in the vicinity of what we take to be another normal **person**, we already have a whole lot of things we **know** about him." "Naturally." I agreed. Gaya continued: "We know, that if we suddenly feel an itch or a pain, the other person will not share this feeling. On the other hand, if we suddenly see lightning and hear a thunder, the other person would share our experience. We know, in advance, what is **private** and what is **public**. Everything that we take as the **public** things, is nothing but a **language**. I once knew a Frenchmen that built a career on this simple fact." I tried a wild guess: "Do you know *Jacques Derrida*?" "Gaya smiled. "The one and the same. Quite an arrogant fellow; but brilliant!" I got excited. I didn't know much about Derrida, but I read some of his, and admired his flamboyance and temperament. "You know him **personally**?" Gaya laughed at my excitement. "I am an old woman. And Derrida wasn't always as famous as he has become. In the sixties I was teaching in the *Sorbonne*, and I met him quite often." I took a mental note to return to this surprising piece of news later, but I still had to find out how the Japanese painters were **speaking**: "So all humans 'speak' an *archlanguage[34]*, which they take each other to understand." Gaya continued: "We have **private** things: Feelings, thoughts, ideas, and in using language, we make them **public**: We articulate them, phrase them into something another person can understand. These painters are admiring the beauty of Edam. Their feeling, their sensual experience is completely private. The way **you** articulate this private thing, is by uttering sounds; sounds I heard you utter yesterday: 'How beautiful, how pretty, how nice'. You intended to convey your private feeling, or private thought, just to **me**. And you were successful: I understood. You translated your private thought to public language, when this **public** included just you and me. If you wanted another person to understand, you would have to phrase it into language **again**. The nature of the sound waves you produced by speaking is such, that it is accepted as **inaccessible** to any person out of hearing range. Audible, verbal speech is very practical if the audience is to be **limited**. If you wanted to make your articulation more public, you could have shouted it, or used a megaphone, or posted a billboard..." I interrupted: "Or written a book!" "Precisely. What

---

[34] Derrida's *archlanguage* or *archwriting*[63] is a key concept in his *worldview*. Although he is considered a relativist, of the 'continental tradition' (if there is such a thing), I prefer to understand him as a radical objectivist. It is my version of "mini-deconstruction", applied to Derrida himself. I think of him as an objectivist, because he only accepts what is included in the (arch)**language**, the **objective** subdomain of human speakers. Like Gaya, he considers all **objects** as *wffs*, turning the whole (objective) world into one great **book**. Where he differs from Gaya, is his disregard for anything **else**. Or maybe it is not disregard, but just **keeping quiet**, as Wittgenstein so eloquently said: *What we cannot speak about we must pass over in silence.*[64]

these Japanese painters were doing, is to **create physical objects**. They are very aware of the fact, that physical objects are the most universal means of communication. They are accessible, durable, and are even easily duplicated." I interrupted again: "This is exactly what the concept of **book** or **document** is all about!" Gaya lost her smile: "Don't be so obsessed with your book! **of course** books are a paradigmatic example of this principle. No one contests the fact that books are composed of, or are **part of**, language. My point is, that a drawing is **exactly** like a book: It is a physical object, hence **public**. When viewed, it is **understood** as an expression; like all expression, it is an expression of something **private** - something that privately "belonged" to someone, and he **wished to make it public**. When these painters return to Japan, they will show their friends the pictures they painted. It is their way to share with others the experiences they had here. They could write a book, like you, but it would be much more imposing, to expect a friend to read prose in order to understand what they have been through; what private experiences they encountered. They could, of course, do a variety of things: They could write **a poem**. A poem is usually short, less imposing than prose. They could write **music**; Or they could write a long book. It has been done, sometimes successfully." Gaya stopped speaking, and we ate in silence.[35]

"I am sorry to have criticized you. I hardly ever do this. But you **really** are obsessed with this book of yours" said Gaya. "It's all right" I replied. "You are perfectly right. Besides, I am delighted you feel free to criticize me. Please don't stop." Gaya seemed relieved. We finished breakfast and went for the morning walk, that was hopefully to become routine. The sun was peeking through the clouds, and it was much warmer than yesterday. After fifteen minutes of walking, we sat on a bench facing the main canal. In less than a minute, we were surrounded by a dozen ducks, some of which approached Gaya and rubbed their necks against her leg. Gaya patted their feathers gently. I said: "They behave like cats." Gaya replied: "They want to be fed. Tomorrow we'll bring some bread from breakfast and feed them." She had a thing with animals. They seemed to love her.

---

[35] Painting, poetry, (some) prose, music etc. are not just different manifestations of language; They are all known as **art**. The question "what is art" is still wide open, and Gaya basically offered a broad definition: **Art is** *the creation of an* **object** *out of a* **predicate**. ('object' and 'predicate', of course, as defined in footnote 31). The artist has a property, a predicate, that is of course **not real**, not in the objective subdomain. In order to communicate it, he needs this property to become **objective** - to become an **object**. He therefore **constructs**, using objects like paint, canvas or magnetic tape, an object that is his **artwork**. This object **includes** all the objects that were used to compose it. An artwork is nothing but an object, as is every other property in the objective subdomain. What makes it **art**, is the fact that it is the **creation** of a particular speaker: As an articulation of his **private** properties.

On the way back, I was looking around me, observing all the beautiful *objects* that were everywhere, and wondered which of them qualified as **art** and which did not. Some of the objects were the creation of nature: cats, ducks, storks and endless vegetation. Some were man-made, but still not art: The intentions of their creators were clearly not to convey a feeling or a thought: cars, boats and the like. On the other hand, many objects were pure art: pictures, statues, sculptures. But I concentrated on the objects that seemed to be on the border between 'art' and 'non-art': Things that seemed artistic, but also had another purpose, such as houses, walls, windows furniture etc. I asked Gaya: "You said that art is nothing but a **word**, or **sentence**, in the language of **objectivity**. right?" She replied: "Yes. This is a nice way of putting it." "But people **create** many things that are definitely **not** considered **art**. Do they not?" "Of course" said Gaya. "Does every sound you utter constitute a **sentence**? An object can be considered a part of **language** only if it used for **communication**." I wasn't satisfied. "But looking at the objects around me, how do I determine which is, or was, used for communication, and which were not?" Gaya stopped walking and looked at me. "How do you **determine**? How do you determine **anything**? You **decide**, of course!" She resumed the walk. I thought of what she said. I have already learned to take her seriously, not always at face value. If it is a part of language, if it is an articulation of someone's feelings or thoughts, it is **art**. But if everything around me, **the world**, is **the** shared human context, it is **all** language! could **everything** in it be considered **art** by Gaya? I was ready with a question. I made a wide gesture, pointing at everything around us. "All of this is *Derrida's archlanguage*, right?" She smiled: "Not his. **ours**. I doubt that he has ever been here. In **his** world, Edam is probably just a brand of cheese." I was surprised, and took another (then private) note to ask her what she meant by **his** world. "So in what way is the objective world **shared**?" Gaya gave an unexpected answer: "Did you notice the name of this street?" I looked around, looking for a sign. I spotted one on the next building. It said *Kant Straat*. I couldn't believe the coincidence, but I was more interested in what she had to say. She said: "You must know Kant well enough to remember what he said about **space**. What is **considered** shared by all humans, is their **perception** of space, not the particular objects occupying it. It is an accepted feature of human *archlanguage*, that every speaker is only acquainted with a **part** of the totality of objects occupying space. What is (considered) shared and objective, is the spatial *form of intuition*."[36] I rephrased my rhetorical question, repeating the

---

[36] Kant considered the human spatial perception as an **innate, apriori** capacity. **Logically**, it is the **condition** of the **possibility** of our spatial sense data. I agree with Kant, that this *form of intuition* is a condition of spatial sense data; But I **disagree** with its proclaimed **apriori** nature. A human, rational creature **need not** have spatial perception. Picture a paralyzed, blind person: He is not in a worse predicament than Helen Keller, who could not **hear**. Our blind paralyzed speaker could still

wide gesture: "All of this, around us, is part of the language in **our** conversation, the one we are conducting now. Right?" "Right." Said Gaya. "Then, it qualifies as a **work of art**, does it not?" Gaya stopped and sat on a bench. I sat beside her, and she spoke: "I understand a work of art as something that was **created** by **someone**. Who created **this**?" She repeated my gesture, pointing at our beautiful surroundings. Now it was my turn to smile. I said: "I did." Gaya was as serious as I've never seen her before. She answered slowly: "In this case, it is a work of art. It is a **magnificent** work of art, and I thank you, from the bottom of my heart, for presenting it to me." She closed her eyes for a moment, took a deep breath of the fresh spring air, and leaned back, enjoying the indeed magnificent surroundings. I felt **extremely** proud - like I have just successfully performed a great achievement. After a few moments of blessed silence, she spoke again: "A work of art must be created with the **intention** of being a work of art - as an act of **pure communication**. A pure work of art is an object created by the artist for the **sole** purpose of **communication**, with no other motive. More often than not, works of art are **also** something else; A means to make a living, for example. In order to classify something as art, it must be assumed that it was created with the intention to share, present, **communicate** a feeling or a thought." Gaya offered a **criterion** for classifying (something as) art. If I am lucky, she might also produce a criterion for its **evaluation**. I asked: "Is there such a thing as 'bad art' or 'good art'?" Gaya answered without hesitation: "Is there such a thing as 'good articulation' and 'bad articulation'? again, I think it depends on the **receiver** of the communicated message. If the message is **understood**, it is a 'good articulation'. If the work of art is well understood, it is good art." I was a bit disappointed. 'Understanding' of art as a criterion for its value seemed like explaining the obscure with the more obscure. "How do you mean **'understanding'** the artwork?" Gaya looked around, searching an example. She pointed at a statue of a small baby angel: "What do you think about this statue?" "Nothing much" I replied. "Then it is not good art. If nothing 'happened to you' when you looked at it, you apparently did not get the intended message. There **is**, of course, an intended message, otherwise it wouldn't stand here on display like that. Besides, maybe it is a bad example. It is almost certain that the artist who created this object had more than **communication** on his mind. Can you give me an example of **remarkable** art?" I searched my memory banks for a good

---

be a brilliant musician, and live a full, **comprehensible** life. He would no doubt be very **different** from many others, but still completely **human** and rational. I don't believe space is an essential condition of perception; Just of **spatial** perception. I cannot say the same thing about Kant's **other** *form of intuition*: Time. Time, I believe (and contrary to both Einstein and Dunne[39]) is very different in **kind** from space. **Conceptualizations, deductions, take time**. The process of enhancing one's conceptual scheme, of acquiring knowledge, constructing new concepts (properties), receiving more *wffs*, **happens in time**. I can understand **awareness** without space; I **cannot** understand it outside the realm, the *substratum* of **time**.

example. Art wasn't my strong side. I picked something indisputable: "Beethoven's Fifth symphony". "Excellent example" said Gaya. "And I believe he had **nothing** but communication on his mind. Do you **understand** the Fifth symphony?" I didn't know if I did; Gaya helped: "What I mean is: **Is it beautiful**?" "Of course" I replied. "I would not have picked it as an example if I didn't think so!" Gaya summarized: "I think **beauty** is a measure of **degree of understanding**. If something seems very beautiful to me, it leaves a strong mark. I **remember** it. It invokes **feelings**, it leaves me **thinking** about it. When exposed to excellent art, one always has the feeling one didn't understand **enough**; that it is **loaded** with **meaning**. I believe that good art is nothing but a case of successful communication.

Walking back home, I noticed that I am clearly starting to get acquainted with the streets and alleys of Edam. It is a beautiful, **sunny Sun**day, and there are many tourists (some of them Japanese painters). But they are all **very** quiet. How nice! It is the time of Sunday services, and faint harmonious hymns were flowing out of the churches we passed. On my first day, the village seemed like a labyrinth of streets, alleys, canals, pathways and bridges. They were all slowly 'falling into place' in my mind. I smiled to myself, remembering the last time I thought of the expected evolution of my concept (of) *Edam*. Gaya said: "It is wonderful to discover and learn new things, is it not?" I didn't know what she meant: Was she reading my mind? I repeated her words in my mind, and considered the possibility that she meant our mutual discovery of each other, or at least **my** discovery of **her**. But before I had a chance to check which it was, she continued: "It is up to you, you see." I was flabbergasted. Is this a **conversation**? but then again, she might simply have continued the preceding sentence - nothing mysterious. The strange moment was not over. She spoke again: "Do not look for the answer **outside**. It doesn't matter, or rather, **meaningless**, to ask yourself what I **mean** by what I say. Rather, ask yourself **what you understood**. You must force yourself to accept the fact that it is **you**, no one out there, that endow the sentences with **meaning**. When you are in a mystical mood, mystical things happen." I exhaled. The air must have gotten stale in my lungs. I knew better than to say anything. It was one of those rare, but unmistakable **magical moments**.

Gaya went to her room and I remained outside, in *De Fortuna*'s exquisite blooming garden, watching the two cats bathing in the sun, and was **happy**. A while later I started coming down, and examined the state of my thesis. Maybe I should start getting to the point. So far, I deliberately refrained from touching the concepts of **truth** and **falsity**.[37] I took another walk, alone, and had a late lunch.

---

[37] Let us start with **falsity**, rather than **truth**. The last significant contribution our speakers S1 and S2 made to the proposed understanding of **language**, was to **tell a lie**. In footnote 33 I considered it

I already know my way quite well; In the first few days I deliberately got lost, just to find my way back. I cannot get lost any more. Edam is acquiring clearer shape and form every day. The same seems to be the case with my footnotes. They are still confused, but a vague picture is starting to emerge. I find strange pleasure in making the analogy between those two completely unrelated and distinctly different processes. Or are they? I am walking slowly, looking people in the eye and nodding a friendly Hello. I once read a sci-fi story by Larry Niven, about an extremely advanced civilization of creatures called **Puppeteers**. The Puppeteers had two small heads, mounted on thin, long necks, like that of an ostrich. Their brains were not in the heads - they had large brains safely secured under a bony hump on their back. They had three strong legs, and each head was equipped with two human-like eyes and a strong beak, acting as a hand. What reminded me of the Puppeteers was their habit to hold their two heads opposite each other, and stare **themselves** in the eyes, in moments of amazement, puzzlement or reflection. I had a strong attraction to the Puppeteers, and was intrigued by their ability to look **themselves** in the eye. It is not looking at your own eyes in the mirror. The image in the mirror has no separate presence (at least not according to the *worldview* I own these days). It is like looking at **yourself** and **not** at yourself at the same time. The two heads functioned independently, although governed by the same brain; As a kind of 'very connected' Siamese twins. I remember the visual picture I constructed in my mind while reading this book, of the Puppeteer's two heads turned towards each other, looking each other in the eye and **sharing the same thought**. This is how I felt after lunch, looking the friendly Dutch in the eye and mumbling "Good day!"

---

a **mistake**. But if we assume that, for some reason, S1 **deliberately** uttered the misleading *wff*, it is a plain and simple **lie**. Be the source of this mishap intentional or not, it results in the creation of a discrepancy between the objective subdomains, the corresponding "objective worlds" of S1 and S2. After this breach, one of the speakers still considers his objective world an exact replica of the other's. Now, if he should suddenly discover that it is **not**, he may consider the other speaker as **having a mistake**. Were he an undogmatic liberal, he might admit the possibility that it is **he** who is having the mistake, not the other. In any case, a need would arise to reconcile the *worldviews* and converge them back into identity, or isomorphism. Now, who should be the one to change **his** system to make it conform with the other's? Who will win this battle between two *worldviews*?

At this point, let us enhance our vocabulary a bit. Hereafter, *wffs* or sentences will sometimes be called **propositions**, and *wffs* denoting **objects** will be called **beliefs**. Beliefs are therefore speaker-dependent. And so is falsehood: a proposition cannot be "objectively false". It can only be false with relation to some speaker, that has a system of properties with an objective subdomain. if the proposition in question is not one of his **beliefs**, it is **false.** Now, **truth** comes naturally: If a proposition is not false, it is **true**. The paradigmatic case of a false proposition is the affirmation of existence of a predicate, or the denial of existence of an object. Traditionally, it was viewed as the paradigm of **contradiction**: To say that a predicate exists, is to say that it is what it is not, and to say that an object does not, is to say that it is not an object.

I took the liberty of calling Gaya on the phone, to ask her if and when she wants to have dinner with me. She was surprised about the **if**, and we agreed to eat at eight. I came prepared, and before she had the chance to take the initiative, I said: "I am now writing about the concept of **truth**." Gaya was as unexpected as ever: "Now you have a new kind of article? A truth, **the** truth, and **the concept of** truth?" Before I had a chance to reply, Gaya added, smiling: "No, no. I'm just kidding. I understand. Are you writing about anyone in particular?" Good question. "Well, I'll probably have to mention a few. Tarski[38], Davidson, Quine..." Gaya interrupted: "In your book the history of truth starts in the 20th century?" Bingo. She's right again. "You didn't let me finish; I was listing them backwards." She was teasing me: "No you were not. If you were, Davidson would have been first!" I was surprised, for the nth time: "You seem to know quite a lot about quite everything" I said bitterly. She was pleased with herself. "Come on, I simply had very many years to accumulate all this stuff. Besides, I hardly know anything about neither Tarski nor Davidson, except for the fact the

---

[38] No discussion of **truth**, however superficial, is complete without **Alfred Tarski.**[65] I will start with him. Tarski's truth theorems make explicit the connection between meaning and truth: Between a language and what it is **about** (what its terms refer to). Contrary to some interpretations of Tarski's writings, his T-sentences do not "connect" *wffs* with "the world", neither does he advocate an objective reference. There is nothing of the **world** on the right side of a T-sentence. Just another sentence, expressed in meta-language. This sentence is taken to carry the **meaning** of the *wff* that appears on the left side of the T-sentence. The *wff* on the left is a proposition, that can be either true or false. If (or when) it is **true**, its **meaning** appears in the right side of the T-sentence. Tarski has elegantly spelled out the connection between meaning and truth.

Tarski's truth is theory-dependent - "internal", as is Quine's.[66] No theory-transcendent "objectivity" is claimed for it. He limited the scope of truth to a particular theory, while only its **nature** is considered universal, due to the universal **structure** of T-sentences. a Tarskian T-sentence has the following form:

Proposition P is true **if and only if** fact P obtains

The right side of this equation supposedly carries the **meaning** of P. This explicitly spells out the situation of our two speakers of P_1: The **correspondence** between a *wff* and a property in the objective subdomain. Three terms participate in this equation: An **object** or **relation** (on the right), a **proposition** (on the left) and **truth**, acting as the equal sign in the equation. Note, that according to such a notion of truth any two of the three terms determine the third: Given a proposition P and the fact that it is **true** determines its meaning, namely, the denoted object; Given an object and the requirement that the resulting proposition should be **true**, determines the proposition; and thirdly, a pair constituted by a proposition and an object, determines the **truth** or **falsity** of the proposition. If **truth** be understood as I suggested in the preceding footnote, it is **speaker dependent**. I.e., the identity of the speaker **determines** the truth value of a given proposition. According to my interpretation, Tarski's T-sentences demonstrate a three-term relationship: Between an **object**, (a fact in the world), a **proposition** (a *wff* in language), and a **speaker**: Any two of the three determine the third. This exposes the **speaker** for what he **is**, in the context of truth: A speaker (or specifically, the content of his objective subdomain) is nothing but a living **truth theory**.

former preceded the latter by several decades. I know more about ancient philosophy. Don't you think you should start there?" I already had the answer ready. "Plato is my **destination**". She seemed interested: "Really? You are a Platonist?" Was I? "Not in the common sense of the word. But in some respects, I am." Gaya was proud of me. "Well, I guess if one is confined to western thought, he might as well be a Platonist. He doesn't belong in the western tradition anyway. Charming fellow, Plato. Second only to his master." Gaya spoke as if she knew them both personally. I was beginning to doubt whether she really knew Derrida. Maybe she is just playing games. I decided to be more skeptical towards her. I asked innocently: "Did you know them too?" Gaya examined me suspiciously, probably reading my mind. Then she said seriously: "What does it take to decide that someone was a charming fellow? Do you think that Albert Einstein was a charming person? Kennedy? Paul Newman? No. for you I have a better one: Wouldn't you say that Immanuel Kant was an **extremely** nice man? Do you necessarily need to have dinner with someone to establish that he is charming? Don't you think that by reading **everything** that someone wrote you get to know him much better than by having dinner with him? Or did our long conversation from this morning already evaporate? And the answer to your impolite question, taken literally, is: **yes**." This time it hurt. And I deserved it. She did nothing to deserve my skeptical attitude. She really put me in my place. I hope I didn't irreversibly damage the relationship. And on top of all, she **had** to imply, at the end of this strict rebuke, she couldn't resist implying that she **did** know them personally... and yet, not conclusively. I didn't know how to react, so I waited patiently until she spoke again. She defused me with her bright smile: "It's over. You may come out of the bunker." We both laughed, and I regained my pulse. I said: "I agree about Socrates. He was **really** a charming man. Plato was a divine writer, but I am not sure he was **charming**." "Good point" said Gaya. "But compared to **his** pupil, he was an angel." "Aristotle?"[39] I wondered. "Who else? He was a mean..." She hesitated. "No. I am exaggerating. But Aristotle was definitely **not** a nice guy. Plato knew him very well. No wonder he refused to nominate him as his heir in the academy. And Aristotle was so

---

[39] Aristotle was the founder of (or, at least, the most significant contributor to) the objective subdomain of what is known as western civilization. His writings, especially the *Organon*[67], are a detailed description of the content and prevailing rules of **reality**. In a manner of speaking, he was obsessed with **existence**. He literally changed the meaning of this word, as Plato before him denied the **real** existence of things that **change**. Aristotle introduced a **truth** that was **a-moral** - that had nothing to do with **good**, with human interests. By doing so, he significantly enriched the objective subdomain he shared with his fellow speakers, but in the process, he sacrificed morality. He maintained, that **good** things and **bad** things existed side by side in the objective world. Speakers from him on were forced to accept into **their** objective subdomain, things that they did not **wish** to exist. Needless to say, his contribution to the contents to this world was immeasurable, but by enriching it he imposed heavy restrictions on human **freedom**. A speaker could no longer decide, if he wished to communicate, what to accept as having objective existence. It was **forced** on him by the growing community of speakers.

arrogant he couldn't bear it. He left. It was clear that he would become a fierce competitor as soon as Plato died. He was a coward, too. He fled his trial, because 'he didn't want the Athenians to commit the same crime twice'. Much did he care about the purity of their souls" she sneered. After a moment's pause she added: "His biggest achievement is educating the greatest conqueror in history. The guy had absolutely no conscious." Gaya seemed personally disgusted with Aristotle. I'm not a great Aristotle fan myself, but for different reasons: "He is the one who first separated ontology from ethics." I said. Gaya shrugged. "Isn't that what I said?"

June 19 -Truth

Before breakfast, I was going over some of my old notes regarding **truth**. I came across a two-page piece I wrote soon after I started my re-education. It was something I wrote especially for my 14 year old daughter, Maya, to give her an idea what this new education is all about. It was already a quarter to ten (Breakfast is served until ten), so I put the two pages in my pocket. As I was leaving my room for breakfast, I saw the maid outside. We said 'Good morning' with a wide smile (we always do) and she asked whether she could make up the room now. I approved, and went to the dining room. Gaya was not there, but as it was close to ten o'clock, and I wasn't the one to bend the **rules**, I started eating. I don't eat much in the morning (or ever), and when Gaya joined me a few minutes later, I was already having my post-breakfast coffee. Gaya noticed the pages on the table beside me, and asked what they were. I explained, and she became very interested: "How nice! this is what I call pure communication: A work of **art**!" I blushed (or, at least, that's how I felt) and said: "Far from it. It is naive, childish. I knew next to nothing when I wrote this". "All the more fascinating" said Gaya enthusiastically. "Can I read it?" I could not refuse. "Sure, why not? But you cannot: It is in Hebrew." Gaya was banging at her soft-boiled egg and said: "I have an idea. You finished eating, right? It is only two pages. Why don't you translate it for me? I will eat and listen." In spite of my instinctive reluctance, I took the pages in my hand, leaned back and translated while reading:[40]

---

[40] The traditional trichotomy between *correspondence, coherence* and *pragmatist* theories of truth seems to be more an issue of **presentation** than of essence. Correspondence truth theorists[68] stand behind their Tarskian T-sentences, insisting there **must** be something out there our words **refer** to. They have loads of convincing arguments, which is a small wonder, because it suffices to say that in absence for something represented, the concept of **language** loses the best part of its significance. It is the **essence** of language to **represent**. But this nobody denies! Even radical anti-representationalists are well acquainted with the reference of **their** language: It is their own private **conceptual scheme** - their belief system. When Tarski said "Snow is white" is true if and only if snow is white, he didn't specify where one should look for (the) snow. Maybe he thought it was obvious; Where else to look for it, other from one's own **mind**, where the meanings of *wffs* are deciphered, where language and truth reside. No objectivism is implied by the notion of correspondence truth.

Coherence theories of truth, on the other hand, do not (necessarily) deny the existence of reference - not even of an **objective** one. They just deny that it determines truth. According to them, a statement is true if it is **consistent** with a **group** of statements it is compared with - a group consisting a **theory**. Truth is thus a relation between a statement and a (coherent) group of statements. A **theory** is a **consistent** logical system, and **consistency** is defined **internally**. When a new statement is examined 'against' it, if it contradicts any of the theory's statements, it cannot be accepted into the system; It is marked **false**, and its **negation** is accepted. Quine is a living example for peaceful coexistence of coherence truth and objective reference: He is a **holist** and an **empiricist** at the same time.

*"What is true is what exists!" Declared Maya categorically. "And if it is unknown whether it exists or not?" questioned Dana. "There are ways to find out" replied Maya. "Look it up in the encyclopedia, or ask mother". "Or maybe **you**?" Sneered Keren; "You are saying this only so you can decide what is **true** and what is not!" "How is this relevant?" asked Maya; "I did not claim that what is true is what I say. I just maintained that what is **true** is what exists in the objective world, and that there are ways to find out what exists in the objective world and what does not. The fact that you are too lazy to look it up, and instead you ask **me** if something really exists or not, does not imply that I just make up the answers." "Really? and when I asked you whether cats like to **swim**, and you said that they did? 'Till this day,* Pinky *escapes every time I come near him, ever since I threw it in the pool!" "That's different" replied Maya; "The question what cats like or don't like is a matter of opinion. No cat ever officially notified what it **likes**, and to **my** opinion, cats like to swim." Dana immediately recognized the flaw in her older sister's reply, and attacked: "Ok. So the question what cats like is a matter of opinion. Can you give me an example of a truth that depends on **existence**, not on opinion?" Maya agreed to take part in the conversation, although my presence in the ring almost ensured the defeat of the correspondence truth she was trying to defend; "Sure, what's the problem? Here goes: It is **true** that we have a cat named Pinky. In fact, it is true that there **are** cats. It is true that cats are animals. Enough? Or do you need more examples?" Dana rubbed her hands with satisfaction. Maya must have voluntarily become an easy pray; "And if tomorrow morning Pinky will open its mouth and announce that it does not like to swim, will it still be true that cats*

After more than two thousand years of "divorce" between ethics and epistemology (or between morals and truth), *James*[69], *Pierce*[70] and *Dewey*[71] reintroduced **values** into the discussion of truth. Late 19th and 20th century **Pragmatism** is a fresh approach to truth, in that it relies on some or other notion of **good**, or **desirable**, or **successful**. Pragmatism is non-committal on the issue of **representation**; It has no **need** for a reference. Instead, it presupposes speakers to have not only **beliefs**, but also **desires**; This concept (or its variations: The 'good', the 'right', the 'correct') is closely linked to the concept of **intentionality**. Whatever the variation, the pragmatist premise, is that speakers share an (objective) notion of **desirability**. In an over simplified manner of speaking, pragmatism identifies **true** with **good**, and **false** with **bad**. The way **I** understand the essence of pragmatism (and of coherence), there is no conflict between them. Pragmatism simply employs an additional premise, and 'narrows down' the infinity of truths that coherence is willing to accept. The way I see it, pragmatism is a **species** of coherence truth.

Pragmatism takes the moral factor not just as an **important** factor in determining truth and meaning, but as **essential** factor, **constitutive** to truth and language. Participation in the language game requires some **motivation**: a **reason** to willingly import and export beliefs, to constantly compare one's own belief system with others. An **interest** is required to provide a **direction**. Without **desire**, without **will**, there would be no reason to exchange beliefs, to create language. Language is at all possible because all speakers **want**, and they all know what it is **to** want.

*are animals? and that Pinky is a cat?" "I should have known you are bound to start with your 'ifs'. I told you a thousand times that saying **if** followed by some nonsense, does not prove anything!" At this stage I interfered, whereas Maya broke the rule against applying undue authority. "Wait a moment, Maya" I said; "Your use of the word **nonsense** does not make you right. Incidentally, I forgot to tell you all, that this morning Pinky told me that it hated swimming."[41] Maya shrugged contemptfully; "If you start like **that**, this will never end." "Wait a moment" I requested; "Say it! You undoubtedly take my statement as **untrue**: That it is **not** true that Pinky started speaking this morning. Why don't you say what you think - that I am **lying**?" "Because I've seen this picture before" said the experienced Maya; "Nothing in the world can force you to admit this. It is simply **irrefutable**". "Right" I said; "We constantly rely on the testimony of **others** regarding what **exists** and what does not. Maybe you will agree to change your notion of truth just a **bit**: What is true is what exists, and what exists is what **credible** people claim to **certainly** exist?" "I accept the revised definition" said Maya; "Provided everyone here accepts the fact that **I** am **credible**." Keren, who listened to the exchange in silence, turned to Maya: "For me to accept your credibility, you must first prove yourself credible. Don't tell Dana that cats like to swim, and don't tell me that there are no dwarfs in the park across the street."*

---

[41] *The principle of charity* was defined by *Neil Wilson*[72] as a (logical) constraint on interpretation (hence on **communication**). This principle states that speakers **in principle** utter truths. That they generally behave **in accordance** with their belief/desire systems. The principle of charity, adopted in several variations by Quine, Davidson and others, seems **trivial** in one sense, but provides a deep and significant insight into the nature of truth. It is **trivial**, because **that is what we do**: In discourse, speakers are assumed to be sincere unless there is evidence for the contrary. Had this not been the case, attempting communication would seem pointless: If I allowed myself to assume that there was no **correlation** between someone's utterance and what she **believes**, I would not be able to infer anything from her utterances to her beliefs. Her utterances would just be a conjunction of true and/or false statements (for her), thus carrying no intelligible information. Even if this conjunction of statements seemed coherent, I would not have any way of determining whether this coherent conjunction is **consistent** with her belief system, or **contradictory** to it. (Her testimony as to which it is would hardly help...)

Although trivial, The principle of charity plays an important role in understanding the concept of truth. Without it, truth is meaningless. I said before that a speaker can be perceived as a 'living' theory of truth. When a speaker says that a statement is true, she is expressing a small portion of this truth theory. The words of this speaker are the only access anyone ever has to **her** truth theory. If it is not assumed that she is telling the truth, she cannot be regarded as **having** any such theory; She cannot be regarded **a speaker**. The concept of truth is based on the assumption that every speaker knows what (for her) is true (unless she knows that she does not know, in which case it is not a **belief**), and on the further assumption, that by "true" all speakers **mean** "What **I** believe in". The principle of charity exemplifies the basic nature of truth as a predicate of *wffs*: **A proposition is true** (for speaker S) if and only if **S holds it as her belief**.

*Maya, who does not like being reminded of her vices, retired. I stayed with the younger two, to continue the discussion on **truth**. Dana was still not satisfied, and gladly continued the discussion. "Dad, do questions of truth and existence really just depend on the testimony of others?" "Firstly, not **just** others. We said **credible** people. This is the crux of the matter: Who decides **who** is credible? This decision only **you** can make. Only you can decide what person, or what book, to **believe**." Dana paused for thought, and Keren looked at me silently. Finally Dana said: "Some sources I **know** are credible. I have no problem with those. But if what someone, who's credibility is yet unknown, tells me that something is **true**? In fact, **how** can I determine her credibility?" "This is not the only problem - determining the credibility of a source. Sometimes, **you** are the source that determines truth. Remember the tennis game we watched on TV yesterday? The line referee decides **himself** on the **truth**. He does not rely on any external source. **He** is the source!" Keren broke her silence and interjected a question: "And what if the second referee decides otherwise?" "That's impossible" I replied; "Every line has only one lineman in charge of. If he decided that the ball was out, even the ten thousand people in the audience, and millions of TV viewers cannot change this decision. What he decided is what **was**." Keren's moral instincts came alive, and she spiced the story up with an ethical angle: "Suppose two tennis players are having an important match. One of them is a very good person, and also the best player in the world, and the other is a mean person and not as good a player. But this match is **tied**, and they are playing the last ball. The last ball falls exactly on the line. Now the referee can decide **what really was**. He must determine who won the match. If he is also a good person, he can decide that the good guy wins!" Dana looked at Keren, still in thought. Then she said: "If only all the referees in the world were really **good** persons. But what if the bad player bribed the referee? It would be better if a **machine** was invented, to determine whether the ball was in or out." "Such a machine **was** invented" I replied; "But it is hardly ever used. It won't serve any purpose - letting machines decide our truths for us. The trick is to continue to let **humans** make the decisions - only they should be the **right** decisions." The clear emphasis of the word 'right' invoked an immediate reaction: "**Right**?" "Yes, right. What is the problem?" At this stage, Dana seemed to have reached some conclusion, and her words sounded almost like an announcement: "Before, you said that what is true is what I, myself, decide that is true; Or, what was said by someone that **I** have decided is credible: **I** have decided to believe him. This means, that in **both** cases **I** make the decision: Not Maya, not you, nor anybody else!" I was proud of her, but said: "This is not such a great revelation. Discovering that in the end, only **you** determine truth, is not such a great achievement. The important question is, whether you always know **what** to decide. If, to begin with, you always had a clear and strong opinion regarding what is true, this whole discussion would not have arisen. The whole thing* *started because more often than not, you do **not** have a definite opinion, and you need a criterion to help you decide."°*

*Dana is a pragmatist. For her, what is **true** has always been what **works**. The sudden implied freedom to decide her own truths only reinforced her instincts. She withdrew from the conversation, satisfied with the new authority the*

°I already mentioned that Quine holds a deflationary notion of truth. To him, it has no explanatory power, whereas it is determined **internally**, inside the theory, and not 'transcendentally', as **rationalists**[73] would have liked it. **Meaning**, on the other hand, Quine takes as **objective**: It is extensional, and determined for every *wff* by its truth conditions (i.e., its logical relations with all other *wffs*). Concurrently, Quine identifies a special, 'preferred' class of *wffs*: Observation statements. Their preferred status is based on the fact that they are not 'revisable': The rest of the theory has to 'accommodate' itself to cohere with them.

Donald Davidson is a Quinean in many respects, but he differs from Quine in these two points. He denies the preferred status of observation statements. He takes this preferred status to be already theory-laden: A product of a **specific** theory. Every theory may determine what **it** takes to be observation statements. More importantly, Davidson differs from Quine in his understanding of **truth**, and, consequently, also of **meaning**. Davidson does not accept the empty, disquotational notion of truth. Davidson believes that truth **does** have explanatory power. For him, truth is best exemplified by the principle of charity, as above. Davidson distinguishes between the **meaning** of a *wff* and the **belief** expressed by it. His strategy is this: To presuppose the belief (the principle of charity!) in the truth of the *wff*, in order to derive its **subjective** meaning: **Belief** acts as 'mediator' between meaning and truth: it can 'compensate' for a possible 'discrepancy' between the two, simply by **not** believing. A speaker may **understand** a *wff* as **true** (even if it is considered false by another), if he **believes** it is true. This, again, establishes the three-way connection between the proposition (*wff*), its meaning its and truth: any two determine the third (footnote 38): When a speaker understands (the meaning) of the proposition **and** believes it, than it **is** true (the principle of charity!). If the speaker understands (the meaning) of a **true** proposition, he must be holding it as a **belief**; And most important: Given a proposition P **and** the fact that it is **true**, determine its meaning.

Davidson's meaning, unlike Quine's, is **subjective**. This is a small wonder, whereas he embraced a different notion of **truth**. I don't think one of them is right, and the other wrong: I think they have different vocabularies: They speak (slightly, but importantly) different languages. What Davidson understands by the term "meaning" is clearly different from what Quine does, and the same applies to **truth**. Davidson's 'variation' on Quine's thesis of *indeterminacy of translation*[74], is an **indeterminacy of** (the particular) **language**. As of 1986,[75] Davidson adopted a more radical view as to what happens in human discourse: Every speaker, at any particular moment in her life, **is** a truth theory, or a **language**. In Davidson's language, an **Idiolect**. Meaning is therefore private, subjective, whereas it is 'determined' by the specific dialect, **idiolect** the speaker is competent in.

In Davidson's (personal) idiolect, the criterion to "identify" a language is its truth theory. Therefore, "falsehood" of beliefs is only possible when viewed from **outside**, considered by **another** idiolect. Davidson maintains, that each speaker speaks a different language from his fellow speakers; **Different** wherever they assign different truth values to a proposition, and **similar** wherever they agree on the truth value of the given proposition. The only thing that is **objective** in Davidson's *worldview* is the **proposition**: The *wff*. No two languages are **identical**. They can be only more (or less) **similar**. And similarity between languages is a question of **degree**.

*discussion vested in her. I remained alone with little Keren, who was not yet satisfied. Her first question was expected: "So now Dana may decide whatever she wants. What happens if she decides that kids don't have to go to school?" "Do you really think that anything significant changed in Dana's life today? Did I ever force her to go to school?" "No" replied Keren. "But up until now, she thought that it is **true**, in the real world, that kids should go to school. If **she** may now determine **truth**, she may decide that they need not!" "Do you know what Dana wants to be when she grows up?" I asked. "Of course - a veterinarian!" replied Keren. "And you think she knows that vet's need to study in the university, and that in order to be accepted to the university, one needs to graduate from school?" I asked. "Sure she knows" replied Keren; "She cannot **both** not go to school and **still** become a vet. She will have to decide: Either or!" "How true" I agreed. But Keren wasn't finished: "If so, than Dana **cannot**, after all, decide what is true and what is not. She **cannot** skip school **and** become a vet, like she cannot decide that now is daytime **and** night time at the same time! Some things she **can** decide upon, and some she cannot!" Keren was doing fine. So I decided to try one last step: "**Can** not? In what way? Do you mean **unable**, incapable?" Keren did not know how to answer, so I volunteered the rest of it: "It is not **prohibited** to hold contradicting beliefs; maybe they only **seem** to be contradicting. In your world, not going to school and becoming a vet are contradictory. In Maya's world, her beliefs in biology and zoology contradict the existence of dwarfs in the park. But it is not impossible, that Dana should decide to put it to the test: To check whether it **is** impossible not to go to school and still become a vet. Stranger things have happened. What one takes as a contradiction, is not necessarily a contradiction for the other. Your dwarfs will continue to live in the park, as long as you want them to. If, and when the day will come that you will find yourself forced to choose between your dwarfs and a bunch of other, (scientific?) beliefs, you may find the way to **settle** the apparent contradiction between dwarfs (or **God**, or Astrology) and science." I concluded with a sentence, that was directed more to myself than to Keren, who started to lose her concentration: "The requirement of **coherence**, the minimal requirement from truth, is not a heavy constraint: It can always be satisfied by an appropriate enhancement of the **theory**."*

I raised my eyes and looked at Gaya. She gave me a huge smile and said: "How marvelous! It was close to eleven when we left the dining room for our morning walk. Before leaving, Gaya said: "Don't forget to take some bread. We wanted to feed the ducks." I wrapped a few slices of bread in a napkin and put it in my jacket pocket. We went straight to yesterday's duck-bench, and sat down. The ducks approached us immediately. They were about ten in number, and I started ripping small pieces of bread and throwing it to them. They were fiercely fighting over every bit. One of the ducks was especially militant. He attacked

55

every other duck that managed to grab a bite, even if it was already swallowed. I resented its behavior, and deliberately deprived it of food. Consequently, the situation became worse. The hostile duck was constantly attacking the others. Some of them even left the scene, as it seemed to be the strongest bird in the flock, and they didn't feel like losing important feathers. I tried a different strategy: I ripped a large piece of the hard part of the bread, and threw it further away, to lure the mean duck away from the rest. It worked, it got busy with the larger piece, and the rest of the flock managed to consume the remainder of my bread in relative peace. The whole episode, that was supposed to be a nice, peaceful way to start the day, was quite unpleasant. More than anything, it was a clear display of the cruelty prevailing in nature. One of the ducks that suffered most from the beak of the cruel one, was a small duck with a broken wing. It was dangling on its side; It looked badly crippled. Naturally, I tried to prefer this particular duck in the feeding, and by doing so, turned it into the most frequent victim of the attacks. The poor crippled duck got the least food, and suffered the most. Right after the last bit of bread was consumed, I stood up and said: "Let's go. Feeding ducks is much less fun than I anticipated." Gaya watched the whole scene in silence. She was very much aware of what was going on, both outside and inside of me. After we started walking again, she said:° "No justice, ha?" I

°To know what a speaker **means**, we must assume that she is speaking the truth (expressing a belief). Were there a way to know **apriori** what she means, we could be the **judge** as to the truth value of her statement. But we don't! It is impossible to even **try** to understand what she is saying, if she is not **apriori** taken to be speaking the truth. This assumption is essential for us to be able to extract the **meaning** of the statement. Davidson criticizes the popular notion, prevailing in the philosophy of language, of **linguistic conventions** which constitute a public language. He rejects the 'definition' of 'language' as a set of behavioral conventions, whereas this view fails to explain anything **unexpected** that (often) happens in discourse; It fails to explain **mistakes**. No prior agreement between speakers is required for a conversation to develop. As Davidson himself so eloquently writes:[76] *"The need for conventions to explain meaning is another aspect of the reification of* (objective) *meaning. It is only if we see meaning as something to be **captured** in the words we use, and conveyed by them from one speaker to another, that we think there must be something connecting the speakers, something - such as* (objective) *language - they share, that bears meaning as a vehicle"*.

Davidson sees "language" as an **abstraction**, a generalization of the linguist, distinct from particular utterances: *"It is **not** the mastery of... language that permits communication... (It) is something like an **art**... of theory construction, in the form of interpretation."* When we **listen** to a fellow speaker, we continuously form, throughout the conversation, 'theories' regarding his intended meaning, when he utters a word, a sentence, or a group of sentences. If we assume him to speak an idiolect that is **similar** to ours, e.g., **his** version of English, the theory that we put together with the intention of understanding him shall be based on **our** past experience in what we take to be similar cases of English conversations. If we fail to construct such a 'mini-theory', (If, for instance, we were mistaken in identifying him as speaking a dialect of **English**), we swiftly replace the theory that is to explain the situation with another theory, more suited for the task. This alternative theory may include the belief "he does not speak English", and again we may try to understand him, this time with help of gestures and sign language that presuppose that he is, e.g., a member of western civilization, or just that he is a sane human being. Our ability to communicate is based on an

56

agreed. "No justice." I could feel a lecture coming. I waited in anticipation, but she started with a question: "You'd much rather have the ducks would stand on a line, each getting fed in its turn. Right?" "Yes." I said. "Especially in view of the fact that they are **Dutch** ducks. If they were American ducks, I would be less disappointed." Gaya continued: "And also, if possible, you would like them to be properly fed **every day**, right?" I agreed again. "Had you succeeded in achieving this," said Gaya, "You would have managed to ruin the whole duck civilization. If all the ducks were properly fed every day, they would lose most of their interest in life. You are making the age old western mistake: You try to eliminate the **bad**, not realizing that by doing that, you are also eliminating the good. It is the **problems** that ducks have, their hunger, their broken wings, the fear from a stronger animal, which make duck-life so wonderful, so worth living. You are not only trying to make them **human**, but make them **western** humans!" Frankly, Gaya didn't tell me anything I didn't already know. But it was a wonderful example. Still, it was too early to summarize; the lecture only started. "On the other hand, this is not about ducks, or about **the** ducks. As usual, this is about **you**. Nothing out of the ordinary happened to this flock of ducks this morning. For them, it was routine. The only one who introduced (the concept of) **evil** into

---

epistemic capacity to interpret situations, not a semantic capacity to interpret *wffs*. In other words: In pursuit of effective communication, each speaker is constantly trying to guess his fellow speaker's idiolect. There can be no **objective** criterion to determine the success of this venture.

Michael Dummett[77] shares with Davidson the following premise: *If the concept of objective language is meaningful, **then** it must be based on its linguistic conventions.* (in other words, on the meaningfulness of the term **'competent** speaker'). This agreement acts as the basis for their **disagreement**: Davidson denies the notions of linguistic conventions and competent speaker, and from the denial of the consequent he infers the falsehood of the antecedent: There is **no** meaningful notion of 'objective language'. Dummett, on the other hand, holds the antecedent as a premise of the discussion, and hence (rightly) infers the consequent. Like with Quine, this difference of opinion between Davidson and Dummett does not imply that one of them is **wrong**. It just implies that they understand their terms (slightly, but significantly) differently; They speak different idiolects.

Bjorn T. Ramberg[78] tries to resolve the disagreement between Davidson and Dummett, by denying the proposition they both share: He proposes to assume that language does **not** necessarily depend upon agreed linguistic conventions, **and** to further assume that such conventions **are** in fact employed. In other words, he proposes to separate the question of understanding the **meaning** of an utterance, from the question in **what language** it is. Ramberg's motivation in this maneuver is to demonstrate what he terms "Davidson's Copernican revolution" regarding language: The reversal of priorities between **language** and its **interpretation**. The Davidsonian concept of language is derived, extracted, from the particular occurrences of speakers' **interpretations**. Incidentally, this view nicely accommodates for the phenomenon of **metaphor**: New, original expressions that keep "the" language alive. Davidson does not reject the work of **linguists**, but takes their subject matter, "objective language", as a mere abstraction. Ramberg takes the middle road between Dummett and Davidson (employs yet a third idiolect): There **is** a theoretical notion of an objective language, an "idealization". No speaker in the world speaks it, but it provides them all with a convenient tool to use and enhance their own idiolect.

the situation, was **you**." I protested: "Could it have been perceived in any other way?" Gaya smiled. "It depends what you mean by **it**. You had an experience, and I had an experience. Do you want to hear about **my** experience?" Very much" I replied. "Here goes" started Gaya. "I don't mind my broken wing. It has been broken ever since I can remember. The problem is I am **hungry**. I can't seem to be able to lay my beak on anything edible. I am starved. Ho, Lord of the ducks, **please**, I need a miracle! and the miracle arrived. You came with **food**. I managed to get five large pieces. The bully duck bit me several times, but I am used to that by now. I don't really mind. The bread was **so** tasty! I don't remember ever enjoying a meal as I have this morning. Thank you, Lord of the ducks! Life can be **really** beautiful sometimes."

°In his essay *"The Structure and Content of Truth[79]"*, Davidson rejects the following two main approaches to the concept of truth: He rejects the notion that truth is "human", Epistemic - that truth depends on, is derived from a particular speaker's epistemology. Davidson also rejects metaphysical realism, positing the **world prior** to the concept of truth. He claims to have successfully avoided both horns of the dilemma. This achievement is based on Tarski's (Internal) Truth, acting as a "bridge" between **meaning** and **truth**. Davidson perceives truth as **primary** - something we are equipped with **a priori**. Based on this initial **gear**, like our speakers S1 and S2, we "create" a reference, something our sentences **correspond** to. **Meaning** and **reference** (the "facts") are the **product** of truth, not its **source**. But Davidson finds relativism hard to digest. He wants to discuss **everybody**'s truths, not just his own; I suspect that the **objectivity** of truth was, for Davidson, both an essential **presupposition**, as well as the *telos* of his inquiry: He explicitly declares himself to hold a **negative** view on coherence truth, rather than a positive view towards correspondence. Davidson criticizes the coherence approach by pointing out, among other things, that it provides no criterion of choice between many different consistent sets of beliefs. But a closer look will reveal this to be a "pseudo-problem": What **kind** of "choice" needs to be "made" between two (each consistent) theories? Such a "choice" can only be conceived to be made from "God's eye view", a point of view Davidson explicitly rejects. When considered from **within** (a particular) theory, it is perfectly intelligible to have a clear (although private) notion of truth, while **accepting** the fact that another speaker, equipped with a **different** Theory, also has (his own, private,) truth. Questions regarding truth and falsity, when **discussed** amongst speakers, are handled in an "artificial" **sub-Theory**, a special **context** "created" for the specific conversation: a sub-theory incorporating **the presuppositions** of the conversation. "True" and "false" are **not** predicable to **theories.** They are Relations between statement (or sentences, or utterances) and the **whole** Theory - the entire corpus of the speaker's belief system; (or, in a particular conversation, the 'mini-theory' - the **context)**. It is senseless to label a **theory** as **false**; What could possibly be the criterion for this falsity? What could be the **difference** between a false theory and a true one? Theories cannot be **compared**. The most we could hope for **between** theories is a kind of **logical isomorphism**, based on the **premise** of a shared Logical Structure.

Davidson takes relativism to deprive truth of its role as an intersubjective standard; He sees this as an inevitable consequence of relativism. But he overlooked human **will**: The implicit **stipulation** of every speaker before entering the language game: Truth is, **henceforth**, intersubjective. It is this **elective** stipulation of truth's **universality**, which makes language **possible.** Davidson regards statements, propositions, as **theoretical**, **unobservable** entities. They are **generalizations** of particular **utterances**. Utterances **always** have an "attached" **speaker**, equipped with an **intention**, which corresponds to the particular utterance. An utterance that is classified as belonging to a class "designated" by a certain statement, can be considered to have the truth value of that Statement

Nice. Very nice demonstration of relativism. Frankly, she made me feel better. But I wanted to get **more** out of this. I asked: "You experienced one thing, I another. I'd much rather have had **your** experience than mine. Do you have **control**, a **choice**, of what **kind** of experience you have? In other words, of how you **interpret** the situation?" She said: "Can't you see you are simply doing it **again**? What are you asking - If there is a trick of always seeing **the good side** of things? Don't you realize that if you succeeded, you would **lose** the meaning of 'the good side'? There would be only one **side**, and it would be neither good nor bad!" She didn't answer the question. I didn't let go: "But **can** you?" She looked

---

(e.g., "It is raining!", "'Tis raining", "Es regent" and "Drops of water are falling from the clouds" are all **true** utterances, all represented by the true statement "It is raining"). The truth conditions of an utterance must be **determined** by the utterer. Classification to **statement** (fixing the utterance's **meaning**) comes later: First there is a speaker with an **intention**, and a notion of **truth**. He combines the two to create a **true statement**, which in turn is translated into (true) utterance form, and **expressed**.

Davidson perceives all Speakers' truth theories to include one key concept that is considered **shared**: the concept **'truth'**, acting as the mediator between the different Idiolects. When a speaker makes an utterance, she assumes the interpreter's theory to "coincide" with her own regarding all **relevant**, or related, beliefs: She makes the utterance based on a set of presuppositions. This set acts as the substrata of the conversation - a kind of presumed **overlap** of the two idiolects. Davidson's speakers are not **aware** of the exact content of the truth theory which they **are**. This theory is no other than their whole Belief System, and no one is ever **aware** of all (or most) of her beliefs at a given moment.

In the abovementioned article, Davidson **identifies** a theory of truth with a theory of meaning. Such a theory **T** of speaker **S** is a long list of T-Sentences, acting as its "natural laws". He proposes a "unified theory", linking the speaker's intention (and meaning) with both her beliefs **and desires**: The extent of her **wanting** something to be true, plays a role in setting its truth value. Such a (hopefully quantitative) unified theory should take into account, in the process of determining the truth value of a proposition, all of the speaker relevant beliefs, **and** the speaker's **motivation** to accept the proposition as true (or reject it as false). In cases of a very **strong** motivation, the speaker may "sacrifice" another belief, **(A)**, in favor of a new, **attractive** one **(B)**. But here an interesting question arises: By sacrificing, abandoning, **A**, the system **changed**, in a way that could accept **B** as **true**. **B**'s **meaning** is now different from what it was **before A** was abandoned. This gives **B** a **different** meaning when it is **false**, than the meaning it has when it is **true**. By "setting" the truth value of a proposition (accepting it as a belief, or rejecting it), the speaker **influences** its meaning in an important way. Since the principle of charity requires (assumes) that speakers **tell the truth**, their utterances are interpreted as "carrying" their meanings **"as true"**, unless the interpreter has good reasons to assume otherwise.

Davidson is a self proclaimed pragmatist. He emphasizes the role of desire, attraction, interest, in the concepts of meaning and understanding. The **intentional** nature we posses, our *conatus*, is not only a significant factor in communication - it is a condition of its possibility. Being human, rational, a speaker, thus consists of (private) beliefs, (private) desires, objective *wffs*, and a **constitutively shared** concept of truth.

at me, with a thoughtful expression on her face. "If I want. But I don't. I like **living**. This is one of the reasons I enjoy spending time with you: You have **your** side of things, and you keep giving me fresh angles." I considered this an undue compliment, but said nothing. She must have sensed I was disappointed with myself, because she had more to say: "Don't get me wrong; Your point of view is indispensable. Do you realize, that my story about the duck **depended** on your story?" "How do you mean?" "Had you not **cared**, had you not exercised **care**, the poor invalid duck would have remained hungry, and I would have no story to tell. You saw injustice, you cared, and you **acted**! You had the bread; I, for myself, could not do anything to help - I could only **interpret**. It was you who supplied the **moral attitude**, and the **required** action. Because of your **western** point of view, the poor duck had the best breakfast in its life. I am not putting down the western point of view. I am just criticizing its often implied **exclusivity**. Feeling sorry for someone else is not always **right**, but it is not always **wrong**. The trick is to know when to do either. My rule is this: If there is anything you can **do** about it, then you **should** feel sorry for someone else: Help him. If there is nothing (you can think of) that you could do to help, don't even feel sorry for him. There simply is nothing to feel sorry about. And if you **do** feel sorry, consider it a sign that you could **do** something about it. You were right to feel sorry about the duck. You could help. And you did. But I was also right, in **not** feeling sorry about the duck: There was nothing I could do; There was simply no problem!"°

When I returned to my room, the maid just finished. We smiled at each other, but skipped the 'Good morning', a greeting that already got used up before. I thought about the extensive smiling I practice around here, and decided that it was nothing but an integral part of the local **language**: A kind of short friendly "Hello". Come to think of it, a smile is a part of other languages as well: Where I come from, it means: 'I am in a good mood', or 'I find the situation amusing', or 'I like you'. In some scary parts of New York or Los Angeles, it means 'I am not afraid of you'; But here in Edam, it simply means: 'Have a nice day' or something similar. I continued to think about this "body language" when I was sitting in the sun outside what has become my favorite cafe, on the main street. It was the same place where I had lunch yesterday. Yesterday, when the waitress cleared my table after I ate, I gave her a used napkin that I was holding in my hand, so it does not get blown in the wind. She didn't understand why I was

---

°Enough about Davidson. I got quite carried away writing about him, as I tend to sympathize with so much he has to say. In the relevant respects, our idiolects are "similar". I cannot resist bringing one last short quote in this context, by Dewey, who Davidson has the highest esteem for: *"...the profuseness of attestations to supreme devotion to truth on the part of philosophy is a matter to arouse suspicion..."*[80].

handing her a used napkin, but my gesture and my smile made her understand that I wanted her to take it from me. She was a friendly lady with a warm smile. She took the napkin and sincerely said "I accept". I understood this as an expression of wonder. I explained: "It gets blown off the table by the wind". She understood and laughed, probably at her own misunderstanding. Today, as I was sitting there in the sun, observing the tourists passing by and enjoying the sun, I saw her standing on the threshold of the cafe, also looking into the street. Our eyes met. We both broke a wide smile, and looked back at the street. Was this a **conversation**? I think it was. We were both saying to each other: "How **nice** is it all, is it not?"

It **was** nice. The world was beautiful (it still is). It is spring, I am in the most beautiful place in the world, I spoke with Esti this morning and everything at home is just fine; My writing pace has reached a reasonable 9-10 pages per day, and I met the most amazing lady in the world. I haven't seen her since our morning walk, and I managed to squeeze in quite a lot of writing since then. Gaya was nowhere in sight. She had a way of making herself disappear every time I had something else to do. She must be doing it on purpose, not to impair my writing by offering me too much of her time.

June 20 - Beauty

After two hours of predicate logic[42] before breakfast, I met Gaya in the dining room. "Come, I want to show you something" she said as we started our morning

---

[42] Let me now return to the discussion of **predicate calculus**, last discussed in footnote 31. There I maintained, that predicate logic may be constructed **out of** (which is another way of saying it is **reducible to**) propositional calculus. Here, again, is the proposed transformation:

$$Pa \Rightarrow a{\supset}P$$
$$(x)Px \Rightarrow x{\supset}P$$
$$(\exists x)Px \Rightarrow {\sim}(x{\supset}{\sim}P)$$
$$(x)(Px{\supset}Gx) \Rightarrow x{\supset}(P{\supset}G)$$
$$(x){\sim}(Px{\supset}Gx) \Rightarrow x{\supset}{\sim}(P{\supset}G)$$
$$(\exists x)(Px{\supset}Gx) \Rightarrow {\sim}[x{\supset}{\sim}(P{\supset}G)]$$
$$(\exists x){\sim}(Px{\supset}GX) \Rightarrow {\sim}[x{\supset}(P{\supset}G)]$$
$$(x)(y)Pxy \Rightarrow x{\supset}(y{\supset}P)$$
$$(x){\sim}(y)Pxy \Rightarrow x{\supset}{\sim}(y{\supset}P)$$
$$(\exists x)(y)Pxy \Rightarrow {\sim}[x{\supset}{\sim}(y{\supset}P)]$$
$$(\exists x){\sim}(y)Pxy \Rightarrow {\sim}[x{\supset}(y{\supset}P)]$$
$$(y)(\exists x)Pxy \Rightarrow y{\supset}{\sim}(x{\supset}{\sim}P)$$
$$(y){\sim}(\exists x)Pxy \Rightarrow y{\supset}(x{\supset}{\sim}P)$$

This transformation is **truth preserving**, whereas the four rules of inference of the syntax of predicate calculus are equivalent, under the above transformation, to theorems in P_1 (I am herein using the connective **conjunction &**, to avoid long, incomprehensible *wffs*):

(1) Universal generalization: Inferring $(x{\supset}P)$ from P: $\mathbf{P{\supset}(x{\supset}P)}$.
(2) Universal Instantiation: Inferring $(a{\supset}P)$ from $(x{\supset}P)$, when a exists $(a{\supset}x)$: $\mathbf{[(a{\supset}x)\&(x{\supset}P)]{\supset}(a{\supset}P)}$.
(3) Existential generalization: Inferring ${\sim}(x{\supset}{\sim}P)$ from $(a{\supset}P)$, when $(a{\supset}x)$: $\mathbf{[(a{\supset}x)\&(a{\supset}P)]{\supset}[{\sim}(x{\supset}{\sim}P)]}$.
(4) Existential Instantiation: Inferring B from ${\sim}(x{\supset}{\sim}P)$, provided $(P{\supset}B)$: $\mathbf{[(P{\supset}B)\&{\sim}(x{\supset}{\sim}P)]{\supset}B}$.

Following, are some examples of valid inferences in predicate calculus, and the corresponding inferences in propositional calculus:

(1) $\dfrac{(x)Px}{(\exists x)Px} \Rightarrow \dfrac{x{\supset}P}{{\sim}(x{\supset}{\sim}P)}$

(2) $\dfrac{{\sim}(\exists x)Px}{(x)(Px{\supset}Bx)} \Rightarrow \dfrac{x{\supset}{\sim}P}{(x{\supset}P){\supset}(x{\supset}B)}$

(3) $\dfrac{(\exists x)(y)Pxy}{(y)(\exists x)Pxy} \Rightarrow \dfrac{{\sim}[x{\supset}{\sim}(y{\supset}P)]}{y{\supset}[{\sim}(x{\supset}{\sim}P)]}$

(1) Let us take a closer look at $(x)Px$: It is the claim, that the predicate P applies (is true of) every object in the domain. Is this a claim **about P**? Traditionally, this is how it is conceived, whereas the domain is assumed to be "fixed", or "well known". This universal claim is understood as making the claim that **P is** universal: It has a certain logical relation with **every** object (that is) x, in the domain: (every) $x{\supset}P$. But just as the **domain** is here used to **describe** P, so P is used to describe the domain; The two terms here **explain each other**. If one is well acquainted with the domain, but knows less about P, by this *wff* he receives a piece of information about P. But if one is not so

walk. She led the way, alongside the southeast border of Edam. It was a street I didn't walk before, as it seemed to be leading nowhere. We walked in silence. I was thinking about possible topics of conversation, when we passed a small triangular cage, about two meters long, one meter wide, and knee-high. In it was a black and white rabbit. It was eating the grass that grew on the cage's floor. I have seen quite a few similar cages in other streets of Edam. I asked: "What do you think about this?" Gaya looked at the caged rabbit, and said: "Do you want to talk about it?" I smiled; "You sound like a psychiatrist." "I am" she replied. "You **are?**" My question mark must have been very accented; she seemed amused; "What is so hard to believe? Did any of our conversations imply the contrary?" Why was I surprised again? Gaya seemed perfectly equipped to be an excellent psychologist. "Are you a **doctor?**" She replied: "I have a Ph.D. in psychology. Hardly a cause for wonder." I returned to the rabbit; "Yes, I want to try to talk about it. Let me see if I can see things **your** way. This rabbit was born in captivity. Its world does not include physical freedom. It does not miss it, because for it, it does not exist. And regarding **my** attitude to the situation, there is nothing I can do about it. I will only get the rabbit killed if I turn it loose. Therefore, I do **not** feel sorry for the rabbit. There is nothing to feel sorry about."

Gaya listened, with a small content smile on her face. She said: "You have done your homework. Did you **write** about yesterday's ducks?" Bingo. "Yes I did." I thought she was now going to ask me about what I am writing, but she didn't. She stopped walking, and pointed to a small grass yard beside the street. It was a small grave yard. It seemed very old, most of the tombstones were missing. Only about twenty of them were left, scattered around. Suddenly I realized that it was

---

acquainted with the domain, but knows P, this *wff* tells him something meaningful about the domain, about x.

The same applies for the existential quantifier: $(\exists x)Px$ is the claim, that the predicate P applies to **at least one** object in the domain. Again, is this about P? I believe it is more about the domain, about x: It says something **about** x, using P: $\sim(x \supset \sim P)$, or $\sim(P \supset \sim x)$.

Post Russellian[81] predicate calculus **requires** that the domain **not** be empty, to avoid paradox's (and, e.g., to justify the fact that $(\exists x)Px$ follows syntactically from $(x)Px$). What is the meaning of this condition? That $x \neq F$; that x is **distinct** from F, the contradiction. But this is not an "imposed" arbitrary condition: It is the **way** x (the domain, or, more precisely, the **objective subdomain**) was constructed! Our two long-forgotten S1 and S2 **started** their adventure by **positing** a property that was **defined** as distinct from F: $\sim(x \supset F)$!

(2) This is one of the odd, sometimes disputed consequences of predicate logic: That $(x)(Px \supset Bx)$ follows from $\sim(\exists x)Px$. If $x \supset \sim P$, then $x \supset P$ is a **contradiction**. Small wonder it is, that it implies $x \supset B$. **F entails everything**.

a Jewish grave yard. All the tombstones had Hebrew inscriptions. Some of the graves were over a hundred and fifty years old. Gaya said: "It was restored; It was almost completely destroyed in the war." I pointed at one of the graves; "This one was the head of the Jewish congregation in Edam. He died in 1830. His name was Levy." "What else?" said Gaya. "I thought you'd be interested". "I am" I replied; "The last time I saw a place like this was two years ago, in Poland; wait a minute - it was **exactly** two years ago - almost to the date." Gaya looked interested: "You were in Poland?" We started walking away from the grave yard, resuming our walk on the perimeter of the village. On our left was Edam's first row of houses, and on our right, miles of green pastures with cows and sheep all the way to the horizon. I said: "Two years ago exactly, I went to Poland, to see where my father was born and raised." "Your father was born in Poland? How old was he when the war broke out?" She had a quick mind. "Ten years old" I replied; "He went with me; and so did three of his brothers, and five of my cousins." "Quite a delegation" said Gaya; "Did you find it interesting?" "Extremely interesting. And it seems more and more so as time goes by. We traced all the places they lived or stayed in; not only before the war, but also during it". We sat down on a bench that was facing outside of town, into the huge green meadow. Gaya was very interested in my story: "It must have been an overwhelming experience for **him**" she said. "It was" I replied; "I think he is still digesting it. And so am I". "Did he lose many relatives in the holocaust?" I was only half surprised that she used this term. "His father, and one sister out of a total of nine sisters and brothers". "Lucky guy, if you excuse my saying so." I agreed; "Yes, he says so himself". "Was his family orthodox?" "As orthodox as they come" I replied. "He lost this orthodoxy during the war; the **holocaust**, as you call it". "Was I wrong in using the term?" "No, no. It's just that it has become a word reserved for memorial ceremonies and documentary films. It's a **loaded** word". "I know what you mean" said Gaya, and continued the interrogation: "He stopped believing in God?" Good question. "I don't think so. I think he believes in God, although a different one from the God he knew as a child. But I know others that completely lost all faith".°

°**(3)** Let us turn to binary predicates (n-ary predicates are than a straightforward generalization). The transformation from predicate to propositional calculus maintains that $(x)(y)Pxy \Rightarrow x \supset (y \supset P)$ [or $y \supset (x \supset P)$]. Here the **objects** under discussion are **pairs**; **ordered** pairs, $<x,y>$. These pairs are also properties, and when a member in the subdomain, they are, as always, **objects**. An example is in order: Let P be the relation *"being the father of.."*, so Pab is the proposition "a is the father of b". a and b **together** are the **object** $<a,b>$. (Naturally, in this example, the domain consists of persons only). The traditional meaning of $(\exists x)(y)Pxy$ is "There exists an object, that is the father of every **object**". But it could just as well be understood as discussing **pairs**, not individuals: Every pair, **could** have (imply) (at least) the three following properties: (1) Its first term could (or not) be an object; (2) its second term could (or not) be an object; and (3) the first term could (or not) be the father of the second. Let us designate this three different properties with x, y, and P, respectively. Now everything is set for the transformation; First, in **English**: $(\exists x)(y)Pxy$ means, that there exists an object who is everybody's father; which is equivalent to saying that it is **false** that for every first

64

We were sitting and enjoying the beautiful, peaceful scenery. I said: "I think the best way to **describe** the holocaust is to say that it is the exact opposite of **this**." I made the familiar wide gesture, indicating 'everything around us'. "Then, it has a **place** in the world" said Gaya. "Well, if you say that **evil** is a necessary condition for the **good**, then it does" I replied, and added: "At least it served one purpose: It is an eternal exemplification of human evil; A lesson for humankind". "That it is" agreed Gaya; "It is an interesting exercise, although not quite legitimate in certain circles, to ask: 'Would it have been better if the holocaust did not occur?" "Would **what** have been better?" I asked. "I said the question is hardly legitimate" she said; "How old did you say your father was in 1939?" "He was ten" I replied. "So let me rephrase my question: Put yourself in your father's shoes, as a ten year old boy. And imagine that some prophet, or angel, or something of the sort, sits with you and explains to you the course of history from 1939 to, say, 2000. Then, he gives you the choice to **change** the course of history; for example, have Hitler killed in an accident before he invaded Poland. What would your decision be?" I took a deep breath, and gave it a try: "Let me see. The first thing that comes into my mind, is that **I**, the **me** of today, would not have existed if history were different. My mother came from Germany, from a

---

term, there exists a second term that is not his son. In other words, that it is **not** the case, that x's **being an object** implies that **P doesn't include y.** The transformation of this *wff* to P_1 expresses this precisely: $\sim[x \supset \sim(y \supset P)]$.

A similar exercise can be performed with $(y)(\exists x)Pxy$: "Everybody has a father". Or, the second term being an **object**, implies that there **exists** a first term while P is satisfied (implies that x does **not** imply $\sim P$). Again, this is precisely $y \supset [\sim x \supset \sim P]$.

In the standard model of predicate logic, three cases may be distinguished: **(1)** There is nothing **outside** the domain. In this case, the whole of predicate calculus is redundant: Every existential claim would have been true, whereas **everything** is **inside**. This is hardly surprising, in view of what I said several footnotes ago: That predicate logic was devised specifically to handle things which do **not** exist (predicates). **(2)** There is nothing **inside** the domain. This case was ruled out by Russell, for good reasons: It also makes predicate calculus trivial, and turns all predicates into tautologies. The **existence** of an objective subdomain (to define 'existence') must be presupposed. (A bit circular, is it not?). Language requires (the presupposition) of something it discusses. **(3)** There **are** things both **inside** and **outside** of the domain. This is the general, non-trivial case that predicate calculus was designed to handle. In this case, (x)Px does not make P a tautology, although it is true for every **object**. (x)Px is **informative**, whereas it makes a claim regarding the relation that prevails between two properties: P and x.

But is x **itself** an **object** or a **predicate**? I believe it is an object: "The whole (objective) world".

There are two ways by which a function Px may be turned into a proposition: Either by assigning an individual constant in place of the variable, i.e. Pa (in which case it may be transformed to a⊃P), **or** by quantification: (x)Px. If the quantification is viewed (as suggested here) merely as an implication involving the "existence predicate" x, it is, again, a case of assignment of a constant instead of the variable; Only this time, the constant is not the object a, but the object x: x⊃P.

totally different background from my father's. There is no chance in the world they would meet, if it were not for the war. **I** would have been someone **else**". "Self centered as usual" said Gaya with a smile; "The whole state of Israel would probably not have come into existence. The concept of 'Israeli' would not have existed. The world would have been a different place than it is today". Now I had her by the throat: "Isn't that exactly what I said? **I** would have been someone else!" For the first time since I met her, Gaya seemed lost for words. My education seemed to be progressing. She said carefully: "Yes. So from **your** point of view, the one you are holding **right now**, the holocaust seems a very important event; Not only did you, personally, not suffer from it, it gave you your **life!**" My Jewish instincts were screaming with protest: "In Israel they would have stoned you for these words!" She nodded in agreement: "I know, and rightly so. But don't get me wrong. Remember yesterday's evil duck? I did not deny that it was evil. Were I there by myself with the bread, I would have done what you did: Taken the side of the underling. But you, today, are in the position I was in, yesterday: There is no **reason** to feel sorry for the victims of the holocaust. You cannot do anything for them".

I said nothing. After a while she continued: "Let me try a different angle: Suppose an earthquake, or a terrible plague broke out in Europe in 1939. A natural disaster, that killed twenty five million people, including six million Jews. Would you feel as strongly about it as you do now?" I didn't hesitate; "No. The significance of the holocaust is not the **death** of so many people; not even their **suffering**. It is the fact that it was inflicted by human beings". "And if they were not human beings, but **Martians**?" I could vaguely see where she was leading. I replied: "I don't know; I've never met a Martian. Look: I consider myself a member of a **group**, a species: **Humans**. When a group of my **fellow** humans performs acts like the holocaust, I consider it a paradigm of **evil**. More than anything, evil is a question of **intention.** In a manner of speaking, the Nazis betrayed the human race". Gaya continued my sentence: "And in this betrayal, they provided a paradigmatic example of how humans **should never** behave. Do you believe something like the holocaust may happen again?" "Not as long as

---

°In his *introduction to the study of logic*[40] (p. 185) Bergman says: *"The conspicuous thing in the interpretation of **existence** by the universal quantifier in mathematical logic, is that this existence is **closely linked** to the predicate"*. I.e., that $(\exists x)Px$ claims the existence of **something that is P.** I prefer to view the situation in reverse: P participates in the **definition** of "existence". It is the **world** that we constantly describe, (or perhaps even **create**) using (our own, **known**) predicates. Mathematical logic automatically presupposes the **domain** to (logically) precede the **proposition**. Based on some apriori domain, we learn something about P by $(\exists x)Px$. I believe it makes much more sense to reverse this order: Every (true) proposition gives us more information about what is **really** interesting: about the world. There is no sense to describe predicates; Predicates were invented to describe reality.

the previous holocaust is not forgotten. This is why the Jews are so sensitive to attempts to deny it, or portray it as a mere unfortunate grand mistake". Gaya resumed her teaching position: "You are mixing the **importance**, or **significance** of the event with its **value**. No doubt you realize by now that **value** depends on point of view". "So does **importance**, or **significance**!" said I. "Naturally; But they are still distinct. From your father's point of view, when he was ten, it was both bad **and** important. But from **your** point of view, that of today, it is **important**, not bad. Do not forget: It gave you **your** life, the life you have and know today". Before I had a chance to phrase an answer, she continued: "Did you ever ask your father what he thinks his life would have been like if it were not for the holocaust?" "No, not in so many words. But I can probably portray it for you, after having seen where his family lived and what their lives were like. And I heard many stories". "Please try" she asked. "They would have stayed in *Chelm*, leading a very orthodox way of life, ten kids per family. When we were there, we entered the very apartment they grew up in. It hardly changed. It was under soviet influence until very recently. Believe me, nothing to write home about". "So the people that live in the same apartment today are a good example of what your father's life might have been, if it weren't for the holocaust?" "I guess" I said suspiciously. Gaya moved in for the kill: "Then, your father was in a position to **compare**: He probably leads a happy, modern life, judging from what you turned out to be, and the Polish people that lived in his old apartment supplied an excellent example of what **his** life would have been like, had he not fled Europe. Do you think he would rather have it the other way around?" Good point. What would he say to that? Probably express the wish to have the cake and eat it too: **Not** to have experienced the holocaust, but still go to Palestine, help put up a Jewish state, etc. etc. The main thing my father lost was his **childhood**, his youth. But in return, he received a brand new, extremely different life than he started. Is that a fair exchange? I shared this thought with Gaya. She couldn't agree more: "Precisely. It is a **rule of nature**: The worst, most horrifying predicaments **always** breed magnificent **changes**. The trick in life, **one** of the tricks in life, is to understand these connections. The Nazis were **bad**. As bad as bad can be. But they are dead by now, and the remainder of Nazis in the world are **so much weaker** due to the acts of their predecessors! Everything, when overdone, is self-refuting. Radical Nazism was the best, the **only**, cure for Nazism. Looking **back**, the holocaust may, and **should**, be viewed as **important**, not just bad. Its importance alone already loads it with value. The suffering paid off: You are here!"

It was a nice morning. Not as sunny and hot as yesterday, but very nice. We were sitting on the bench for a long time. I was getting ready to get up, when Gaya added a final remark: "And, incidentally, the reverse is just as true: Excessive **good** also breeds change; and for the **worse**". "How do you mean?" I inquired.

67

"Did you ever shoot heroin?" "Never went quite as far" I replied. "Well, any hard drug would do for the example. Drugs are paradigmatic in the **suffering** that emerges from extreme enjoyment." I could nothing but agree: It is **excess** that is bad. We got up and resumed our walk. I wondered what my father will say when he hears (or reads) the details of this conversation. We remained on the perimeter of the village, the green fields stretching on our right hand side. We had several short conversations with joggers and walkers that passed us, coming from the opposite directions: 'Have a nice day'; 'Have a nice day' (a friendly smile and a nod, sometimes accompanied by a mumble). Suddenly I saw the ugly dog again. Well, it wasn't **really** ugly; Not **nearly** as ugly as when I saw it last (and first). It was playing with the tennis ball again: Fetching and running, fetching and running. I felt as if I knew it well enough to permit myself to pat it. I approached the dog, but it preferred Gaya's pat. It ran up to her, wagging its tail. I told her about my first encounter with this dog, and the transformation it had undergone in my mind. Gaya burst out laughing: "**Ugly**? This dog is **ugly?** This is as **false**[43] as a statement can be! This is one of

---

[43] A statement is **false** if and only if I refuse to accept it as a belief. Iff a proposition is **True**, it is a **belief**. Its **meaning** is determined by other beliefs in the system, the ones that **imply** it (its species) and the ones that **are implied** by it (its genus's). How, than, is it possible to **understand** a false proposition P, in view of the fact that it refers to F; that it **is** a contradiction?

To understand the meaning of a false proposition P is to construct a **context**, a sort of "tentative" sub-system, where P **is** true, thus has meaning. This temporary subsystem, constructed (perhaps) solely for the purpose of understanding P, differs from the "regular" one in some relevant respects. Statements can only be understood "as true". If I am **unable** to construct a context in which P **can** be true, there is no hope for my understanding P. This maneuver enables an infinity of alternate "understandings" of the false proposition: "Snow is black" can, for instance, be interpreted as "snow is necessarily black", or "snow is sometimes black", or "snow is cold" (in case 'black' is synonymous with 'cold') etc. Under the first interpretation, the tentative, temporary subsystem includes a property 'black' that is implied by 'snow'; The second interpretation is based on a subsystem in which 'black' has no relations of implication (inclusion) with 'snow', and the third, of a subsystem in which 'cold' and 'black' are synonyms (equivalent, mutually including). Trying to understand a proposition "while" it is false, is futile.

The fact that I believe "snow is white" and (therefore) consider it **true**, does **not** mean that it is **necessarily** true. I can conceive an alternate belief system that rejects it, and accepts its negation as true. Only *wffs* with the contradiction as the antecedent are **necessarily** true, and **cannot** be false. There is no conceivable alternate system in which the proposition "snow is not snow" can be believed (or "If snow is white then snow is white" considered false): $S \supset \sim S$ is true iff S is a contradiction. Therefore, the proposition "Snow is not snow" can never be **understood** (except as F).

Necessary truths are always conditional, and supply no **information**. Understanding a proposition depends on its "contingency", (in the sense of "not necessary"); on the proposition's being interpretable as **either** true **or** false. this "freedom" the "contingent" proposition P "enjoys",

the most beautiful breeds of dogs that ever existed!" She said something to the dog's owner and they both laughed. I was annoyed; "What did you tell him?" "I told him you said his dog was ugly" replied Gaya. "How could you!" I protested. "It is nothing but amusing" she replied; "Don't worry. It is so absurd, it cannot be considered an insult. You cannot insult something **beautiful** by saying it is ugly. You can only insult by saying something that **could** be true". "This dog **cannot** be considered ugly?" I wondered. "Not in the language this man speaks" she answered. This reminded me: "I didn't know you spoke Dutch!" "Not a lot" she replied; "But don't forget I've been spending my springs here for decades. It rubs off on you. And it is not a difficult language, if you speak German". "And you do, naturally..." "Ja" she replied with a smile.

When we turned left, to return to the center of the village, we saw a shiny convertible *Porsche* parking on the curb. The tourist it must have belonged to was sunbathing, while enjoying the landscape. A few meters away, a local old man in raggy clothes was stretched in a similar position. I giggled to myself: "Like the story with the Mexican beach bum". "What story is that?" Gaya inquired. "Ah, forget it. You probably know some version of it, and it is really not that funny". Gaya insisted: "Come on, tell me". I told it as telegraphically as I could: "An American millionaire is sunbathing on the beach in Acapulco, next to a local beach bum. He says to him: 'Why don't you go get a job?' 'What for?' asks the bum. 'To make money!' 'What for?' 'To build yourself a business, and make more money'. 'What for?' 'So you can become rich, like me'. 'What for?' 'To enjoy life, go on vacations, lie in the sun...' 'And what am I doing right now?' asked the Mexican". Gaya laughed much louder than the story deserved. "What's so funny?' I inquired. "You people have this story upside down!" She proclaimed; "You must think the Mexican bum to have taught the American millionaire a lesson, right?" "What else?" I wondered. "He was a stupid Mexican" she explained. "The millionaire had a much better point then the Mexican, although he was a poor **speaker. His** way of achieving the stretched out position in the sun is so much better than that of the Mexican! For him, lying in the sun **meant something**. It was an achievement, a **prize** for his hard work, his persistence. The Mexican was just lying there - to him, it meant next to nothing. The Mexican could not even understand what the American meant, because he didn't take his lying in the sun as a **big deal**. Would **you** rather be the Mexican?"

---

provides its meaning: By accepting P as true, as a belief, (even temporarily), the meaningfulness of its negation is denied, and the meaning of P itself determined by its truth.

I am back in my room now. I developed a nice routine, a *rythmus*: Breakfast. Walk with Gaya. Then five pages above the line. Then lunch in my regular place. Then some reading, to get the philosophical juices flowing, and then five pages (or, more precisely, ten half-pages) of footnotes. I seem to have made some progress in the last few days: A discussion of **truth**, mostly *Davidson*. It is now again time to dive below.[44]

---

[44] So far, I have only **hinted** at the role of **morals**, or **values**, in determination of truth and meaning. Davidson, Rorty[82] and also Putnam[83], all emphasize, to one degree or another, this connection, a position broadly labeled "Pragmatism". I have tried to keep the logical discussion thus far relatively free from ethical considerations, but the time has come to bring them into the picture. I haven't yet made use of the fact that our radical translators, S1 and S2 (or, rather, radical **interpreters**, in Davidsonian jargon) have **desires**.

A speaker is not just a **belief** system. He is a **belief/desire** system. It **must** have at least one desire: To **speak**... He can (at least) choose between speaking and not speaking. If he chooses to speak, this means he considers speaking to be **better** than **not** speaking. Desires may be presented as propositions, starting with the words "I want" or "I wish" or "I prefer". A desire may be "fulfilled". Such fulfillment is simply an **abandoning** of the (fulfilled) desire: The belief "I want to eat" is **abandoned** once I have eaten.

Another way of saying the same thing, is to say that every speaker has a concept of "good", or "the preferred". This concept is a **property** (as is every concept), hereafter referred to as G. When I believe that a property A is a **good** property, I am holding the belief A⊃G. When I believe that B is bad, I hold B⊃~G. So far so good. The problems start when we try to determine whether G is an **object** or a **predicate**. On one hand, it is definitely a predicate: It does not **exist**. On the other hand, doesn't it? The definition of "existence" employed here is "being a member of the objective subdomain". Does not **every** (speaker's) subdomain include this notion? It is not the case with the predicate "red" (at least not for blind people), nor with any other predicate. But **good?!** I started this footnote with the announcement that being a **speaker** entails having a notion of preference, desire. Everybody has one. So it must be an object! A mystery.

Well, not quite. Western civilization made its choice: G is a predicate. The **good** is widely accepted as relative, as fluid, as vague. Over two thousand years of failed attempts to define the **good** had resulted in granting it the inferior ontological status of a predicate - of non-existent - not **in the world** - only in the (particular, subjective) mind. Still, everybody has one. In what follows, I shall argue for an "ontological upgrade" to the concept of **good**; from a predicate to an **object**. Furthermore, I shall claim that it should receive a status that is **preferred** to other objects; A preferred status similar to that of F (the contradiction), with which it all began. Every speaker has (an) F. Aristotle (with the help of Frege) added x. But beside F, and before x is (was) created by a community of speakers, there was already **G**.

The constitution of the objective subdomain was achieved by **sacrificing** (the objectivity of) **G**. A property may exist (be an object), **despite** the fact it was undesirable! Speakers may no longer (as was the case before they were thrown out of *Eden*) simply **deny** the undesirable. They are now **forced** by the community of speakers, for the sake of preservation of their creation (the objective) to accept the **bad** into their worlds. The few who tried to reject it, were declared insane (for denying the existence of "evidently" existent objects, or for affirming the existence of non-existent properties, namely, having delusions). The ones that managed to reconcile the objective world with their preferences, were **happy**. Others left society, or were committed, or simply ended up **un**happy.

June 21 - Solipsism

Today is the longest day of the year. Last night, after dinner, I felt like another walk. I needed time with myself; Between Gaya and the writing there was hardly any rest. I went to the west corner of Edam, by the big church, to watch the sunset. The church clock was striking ten. Ten at night? Ten in the evening? It didn't get dark here until eleven, and even then it wasn't **really** dark. It was **completely** quiet. Except for animal sounds, of course. Mainly birds, but also an occasional cow. The sun was just setting. I took a deep breath and thought about the Mexican. Well, I'm Ok. Much more **like** the American. I thought to myself: This is the feeling, or thought, that artists try to capture in their creation. Or **one** of the feelings. Are they really **different** from each other? (I mean the really **good** moments. The ones filled with **magic**). I think not. I believe they are all one and the same, just differing in **degree**. I also believe, that **everyone** (and **definitely** every speaker) knows it; had experienced it. Maybe this was the feeling Gaya's duck experienced in his breakfast the other day. For myself, I've had it quite a number of times. But in unprecedented frequency, here in Edam. You know what I believe? I believe this is the feeling, the property, the concept, the **object** (this word crept from below the line) of the **Good**. This is my **belief**, and it is therefore true, by definition. Don't ask me to substantiate this claim with a (rational[45]) argument, which in itself must be based on some other **premise**. No

---

[45] **Rationality**. What is rationality? and why now? Here is my meaning of the word, the relevance self-evident: To me, Being **rational** is what I thus far referred to as being a **speaker**. I don't know whether all humans are rational, or whether only humans are. But I do know what a speaker, a **rational** user of language, is: It is a logical system, equivalent to P_1, (hence consisting at least of the object F) **and also** equipped with a moral perception; a notion of preference, of **good**. The second characteristic can also be perceived as the worn down concept of **intentionality**[84]. I perceive **logic** and **morality** as the (only) two ingredients that make up a rational being. These two constituents, corresponding to **belief** and **desire**, are the "Yin and Yang" of rationality. The dichotomy between the two is no other than the age old dichotomy between **facts** and **values**, or **determinism** and **free will**.

Logic without an interest, a point of view, "objective logic", is empty. Just meaningless syntax. It has a kind of **truth**, but no **meaning**. An a-moral, objective logic reduces the world to nothing but a twofold reference: one **T** and one **F**. meaning does not even enter the picture; There is no one to **care**. On the other hand, morality without logic is **unintelligible**: There is no analysis, no distinction; Just a chaotic "good" floating around, in want of language to express it. Rational speakers **understand**, because they are equipped with **both** logic and morality. Combined, they are the necessary and sufficient condition for the formation of a belief system; a conceptual scheme.

The deepest source of **skepticism** is the disregard for morality's role in the determination of meaning and truth. Based on logic alone, there is no **certainty**: To arrive at true conclusions, true premises are required. And who would supply those? The first premises are always moral: They provide the context, the framework, the basic, 'primitive' concepts; the **irreducible** ones. It is a process that cannot be logically justified. It is **moral**. Without morality to determine (or, rather,

premise is more primordial, more **basic**, then this one. I **know** what is **good,** or what **Good** is, which are the same thing. It is **this**. Now, how can I convey to you this **this**? By creating a statement. A statement is a part of **language**. This was exactly Gaya's point with **art**. How can **I**, particularly, convey to my friends this **this**? What I basically want to do, is to give them a **description**. A description of the **Good**; not of **reality**. Reality is something Aristotle invented. The **Good** is something **I came with**. It comes from within me. And it is always **this** that actually gets described. Language does not describe the world. It describes, in an infinity of variations, the concept of **Good**. I felt a close, almost spooky intimate identification with **Plato**. The idea of the good. The idea of the good provides the light, by which everything else is seen, conceived. To **understand** something is to know how it is good; how it **can** be good; how it can **bring about** good. Or bad, of course.

Sitting there by the church, watching the red glare the sun left behind it, I realized that I am starting to understand **the** life (the world), instead of understanding **about** life. It is the difference between **knowing** and knowing **about**. The major difference between Gaya and me, is that she knows **the** things, while I talk **about** them, separating myself from them. I suddenly understood the difference between western thought and eastern thought. I should have devoted more time to eastern... No! I am regretting again. What I did was **right**: It got me **here**. I consciously pulled myself up from slipping back into my normal, **analytic** way of thinking. But still: Are there causal connections between (prior) events and actions, and between this wonderfully **good**[46] experience I am having now? Can it deliberately be brought about? Gaya would know.

---

constitute) the truth of the premises, logic is helpless. Without logic, morality has nothing to **judge**, accept or reject. Morality is **choice potential**, but alone it cannot recognize the **possibilities**. It has no language, no thought.

Morality is inherently **objective**. As *Moore*[85] pointed out, the notion of **good** is inherent, innate. It is the only thing, besides **contradiction**, that all speakers share. In a manner of speaking, only **it** may be considered a **completely** objective **reference**. Complete intersubjective understanding is achieved only in cases of agreement not only regarding the truth values of a set of propositions, but also regarding the **value** of the thing considered. The **Good** is the compass for **real** understanding. Maybe this is what Plato meant by his simile of the sun.[86]

[46] However, the common usage of the term *good* is not as an object, but as a predicate – a "non-existent" concept, residing only in the conceptual scheme of its beholder. Treated as a regular predicate, let us look at the proposition P⊃G. "Being P entails being good", or simply "P is good". Similiarly:

P is good $\Rightarrow$ **P⊃G**   P is not good (Not 'P is good') $\Rightarrow$ $\sim$**(P⊃G)**
P is bad $\Rightarrow$ **P⊃~G** P is not bad (Not 'P is bad') $\Rightarrow$ $\sim$**(P⊃~G)**

I thought about the book. I called it "the book", because I could neither call it "the thesis" nor "the diary". One would not be complete without the other. Like Yin and Yang. Writing is the only way I know, to **describe**. Writing and talking. Socrates was against writing. He did not leave a word behind him, and still had an enormous influence. Even more than he received credit for. But I'm sure he wouldn't mind. He wouldn't have it any other way. Just like Lao-tse, who shared his century. How far they were from each other, and yet how close! Like one person speaking in two very different languages. One person speaking two different languages. Expressing the **same** thing. The **only** thing. The only **objective** thing there is. **Intentionality**. Desire. Preference. Will. **Good**. Everything has been deteriorating ever since. Well, in some respect. In another, the age of *Pisces* served an important purpose. The divergence between the two **ways** of thinking, of apprehending reality, became an **abyss** over the last two thousand years, the last **age**. Neither, in itself, was able to provide a complete answer. The eastern and western way of thinking are **thesis** and **antithesis**. Only when combined, when **synthesized**, a new product shall emerge: Another **(metaphysical)** paradigm. A different way to understand what it is all about. Some have called it "new age", others "salvation". Sitting there in the twilight, I visualized a magnificently interesting future.

Nothing external invoked these thoughts. They could have "caught" me in my room, or back at home. The surroundings were inspiring, and I was already under a strong influence of Gaya, but it could just as well have happened two weeks from today, on another peaceful moment in my back yard. In fact, Everything I wrote so far, and everything I was going to write in the remaining ten days, could just as well be written as sheer fantasy. That is what writers (of fiction) do. Does it **really** make a difference to the few who are going to read this, that it **really** happened? Does this **really** make it more **interesting**? I think not. Maybe the contrary: I think a story that comes from inside its writer is a much more impressive achievement. The amateur Japanese painters **need** the scenery to invoke the feeling they want to record. Great masters don't even need that. Well, I never wrote anything before. I may still seek the help of my surroundings, the stories they provide, the feelings **they** invoke. Gaya would probably laugh at this; at my attempt to separate myself from the surroundings. She would say that it is **I** who brought the surroundings about, by picking this place, planning this trip, by **coming** here. I am writing these lines almost in a state of *automatic writing*, not knowing what the next sentence will be. I am just trying to relive, or reconstruct, yesterday's feeling. In a way, what happens to me now is exactly what I just said: I am not (now) **there**, by the church. I am here in my room, **remembering** yesterday by the church. Is there **really** a difference, even for **me**, whether I **actually** sat by the church or just imagining I did? For a second, I am not even so sure that I did. But I did. Or did not. What is the

73

difference. Do you think people will contemplate on the question whether I **really** did or not? What could **possibly** be their motivation in doing so? It would just be a reflex - an Aristotelian reflex.

The moment was over. It must have lasted fifteen, twenty minutes. I was just left with a feeling of **confidence**. Until now, I was still quite insecure about my writing. I was not sure I had something to say. And even if I did, I was not sure I will be understood. I was afraid to be too superficial for my professors and too boring for my friends. I felt those fears evaporating. Not that I was suddenly sure that I **did** have something to say, or that it is **not** boring. It was simply the realization, that I am doing exactly what I planned to do: To say all (and only) what I have to say. If it turns out not to be enough for anyone, it still is for me. I believe that what I am writing portrays my *worldview* as accurately as I am able. And this is all I came here to do. If my footnotes do not entitle me with a Masters degree, then, by the standards of **my own** world, I do not deserve it.

I had trouble falling asleep, and I woke a number of times during the night. I was dreaming like crazy. I was dreaming every night since I arrived here, which is very odd. Back at home I never remember having dreamed. As if my subconscious, or whatever, is extremely busy here. I dreamed about work, about home, about Gaya and mostly about logic and epistemology. I dreamed I got stuck in an airport, on my way to **Moscow** (yes, Moscow!) but have lost my ticket. This business with sleeping and dreaming is still beyond me. (This was S.H. Bergman's topic of philosophical interest during the last years of his life). Another thing I must ask Gaya about. My new Oracle.

I woke up to the sound of German outside my (permanently) open window. A group of German tourists were gathered outside, **just** by my window, one meter from my sleepy head. I was annoyed: How inconsiderate! Don't they realize that someone must be sleeping on the other side of the window they are sitting by? The phone rang. It was my father. Just to say Hello. Incidentally, he tells me, there is a problem that requires my attention But it can wait until I return. I ask him what it is. He tells me. We say goodbye, I hang up, and feel annoyed twice: Firstly at the person my father was telling me about (I'll spare you the details), and secondly at my father, who should not have brought it up in the first place, if it can really wait. I was annoyed three times before getting out of bed. Usually I don't get annoyed three times in a **month**. I get up, trying to make some noise, to attract the attention of the people outside my window. I sit at my computer, hooking up to my Email box in Israel. I get a message from Rivka, my associate, complaining I didn't answer her previous message. But I did! Annoyed again. I was tired and confused by the dream attack. It was late. I was afraid I won't make it to breakfast before ten. I took a quick shower and ran for breakfast. Gaya wasn't there. Dekker relayed a message from her: She had to go to Amsterdam early in the morning. I should have known, with a morning that started like this. Maybe better so. In fact, **definitely** better so. I didn't want Gaya to see me in this miserable mood. What a contrast to yesterday evening! I immediately thought of her words: Excessive good is harmful.[47]

I went on the morning walk alone. I went straight to the church, without even thinking where I was going. I sat on the same bench, and realized the bench, the church and the view had nothing to do with it. Everything was just as it was yesterday. Different, but still as beautiful. I could recognize this beauty despite of my slight depression. It cannot be the surroundings that are responsible for magic moments. It is **internal**. I realized I was thinking western again, separating inside from outside. But this time I didn't try to suppress this way of thinking. A man passed by and did not say hello. Neither did I. One cigarette later I got up and started walking back. Moments later, the church bells started ringing, continuously, as if they were out of order. They rang without pause, and sounded just like a fire alarm, or some sort of emergency bell. I became worried: What is the meaning of this? A **coincidence**? It sounds **just** like an alarm, warning me against great danger. I searched my mind for possible catastrophes. None. I searched my mind for something I **should** have done but didn't. Something I did **wrong**. Something I have neglected to **care** for. Nothing. I was approaching *De Fortuna*, and the alarm was still sounding. Suddenly I heard a noise behind the door of the house I was passing by, and a squirt of water shot out of the mail slot in the door and completely wet my pants. I was totally surprised. I looked at my wet pants, at the closed door, and realized that a kid had just shot me with a water gun. I burst out laughing, standing alone in the street, releasing all the tension that accumulated within me since I woke up. I reached *De Fortuna* just as the bells stopped ringing, and saw Gaya standing, smiling cheerfully.

We sat down and had coffee. I knew what I wanted to talk about. I said: "I have two questions for you". She smiled attentively. "Can magical moments be deliberately brought about?" I was prepared for an ordeal before she actually answers: 'What are magical moments?' or 'What is 'deliberately?' or something of the sort. Obviously she surprised me. Her surprises were not surprising any more; "But of course!" she said. "I know a cute story about a question like this. A Frenchman I once knew, Arnaud DesJardins, told me that he spent years in searching a particular Tibetan master. When he finally found him, the master was

---

[47] Many things are self-refuting – too much of them brings about their opposite. This claim has the feel of an oxymoron – a contradiction. I wonder how Plato would treat the notion of "too much good".

just leaving. DesJardins was extremely disappointed, and asked the master to give him a general advice, whereas it was impossible for him to stay, or for DeJardin to join him. The master agreed, despite the unorthodox request, especially in the east. He looked at DesJardins sincerely for a while, and then said: 'Take what I am about to tell you, seriously. You don't really need anything more than it'. He looked DeJardin in the eye, and said: **'Be happy!**[48]**'**. Then he left, and DeJardin never saw him again. When he told me the story, he said that these two words were the most meaningful and the most effective piece of advice he ever received. If he was a Zen-Buddhist, he would call it 'enlightenment'. And this DeJardin was no child - he studied with the most renowned masters in the east. He claimed to have understood the key to happiness, to "magical moments" as you called it. I tend to agree with him: All it takes, is a conscious decision to be happy. But for you, I'll throw in a condition: You must be *whole with yourself*". This sounded enigmatic. I inquired: "Whole with yourself? In what way?" "Ah, this you already know" said Gaya. "You must not **feel sorry**. You must not **regret**. If you made a mistake, correct it. If you don't, it will cloud your happiness, as much as you desire it. What is your second question?"

Apparently she didn't want to elaborate on the first one. I moved on: "Tell me about **dreams**". "Don't you have dreams?" she asked. "Of course I do. That is why I am asking". "So you know them. What do you want me to tell you?" Was she playing? "What they **are**. What is the significance of the phenomenon". "I am not avoiding your question" Gaya was reading my mind again; "But your question is like asking 'what are trees'. Trees are trees, and dreams are dreams. I can give you a detailed description of trees, and a similar detailed description of dreams. But this is not what you are looking for. What **exactly** don't you understand?" I tried a different angle: "To **understand** something involves knowing why, or how, it is good, or bad.." I remembered yesterday's conversation about the holocaust: "Or **important**, right?" "Yes?" she replied. "So what is their **function**. What are they good or bad for. Are they important?" Gaya seemed to prepare for a long answer. I leaned back in anticipation. "Dreams are experiences; feelings, thoughts. When you have a waking experience, and you choose to articulate it, you put it into form of language. More often than not, into **words**. This is how you can later give yourself and others an account of what you have experienced, of your **memory**. If you do not **pay attention**, or, rather, the things that you do not pay attention to, will not be remembered." She pointed out the window; "See the man walking there in the

---

[48] How to formalize "I am happy"? I would say as "I **am** good", or I⊃G. Of course, I must abandon this belief every time I am unhappy, or feel bad. This nicely exemplifies Socrates' most basic moral claim - the equation "I **am** good" ≡ "I **feel** good"[87].

street? He is carrying something. You don't know what he is carrying. If I ask you tomorrow what he was carrying, you would not know, or would not 'remember'. If you now pay more attention, you **will** be able to tell me, tomorrow or in a year, what he was carrying. It is up to you what you remember and what you don't. You were trained to pay attention to church bells, and ignore dreams. But there is no difference in **kind** between the two. Church bells ring only when there is a church around, and dreams occur only when you sleep. You are now in a period of extreme receptiveness. That is why you have so many dreams. You **pay attention** to them. You pay more attention to everything. No. Let me rephrase that. You pay more attention to **yourself**. There is no 'place' in which dreams **are** one thing or another. Dreams are part of you, as anything else is. Many people, especially of the western persuasion, do not pay attention to dreams. This is not **wrong**. For them, dreams **do not exist**. It is absurd to say 'I have dreams, but I do not remember them'. At most, it could be said 'I **could** have dreams, but I don't'. Scientists claim that they can determine that a sleeping person **has** a dream, although he later claims to have had none. It is like telling someone 'you have **pain**, but you do not **feel** it'. Having a dream, like having pain, or any other experience, is inherently subjective, it was not (yet?) added to the domain of **objective** phenomenon. If and when western science will **devise** a theory of dreams, that will conform with the rest of scientific theory, then your question will be answered by **it**. But for now it is outside this domain. Like Astrology, Tarot cards and a thousand other things[49]. Science does not provide a theory, so **you** are left with the decision what it **is**. No one can do it for you".

---

[49] **Ethics** are clearly **outside** the realm of science. It is not part of the objective (scientific) world, as Astrology and Tarot are not. Psychology, particularly versions of *psychoanalysis*, has tried to offer an objective account of phenomena that were, until Freud, considered purely subjective. I believe Ethics **can** be incorporated in a "scientific" theory. But there will be an **ontological** price to pay.

On the connection between Logic and Ethics, Carnap[88] wrote: "There is no place for ethics in logic. Let every one build his own logic, i.e., the structure of his **language**, as he pleases. But he is obliged to state clearly **what he intends to do**. It is not to ask: 'Are certain marks (in logic) **permitted**?' Because what is the point of **permitting**, if **no** ethics are involved?" Carnap is confusing consequent with antecedent: Is the irrelevance of ethics his **premise** or his **conclusion**? He continues: "One must therefore just ask: 'How shall we **want** to create a particular language? Shall we allow or refuse certain marks?... We are discussing here the **choice** of a certain language structure..." Carnap is **almost** there, although he explicitly denies it. Ethics provides the **basis** for language. It is impossible to adjudicate between languages, or logical systems, by using a **logical** criterion, whereas a **logical** criterion already presupposes the **logic** it belongs to. Allowing or refusing "certain marks" are nothing but the application of such an impossible criterion. The criterion which Carnap himself implicitly applies, is a teleological one: "...*what he **intends** to do*". One who proposes a new language, a new logic, must disclose his **motivation**. If we **like** this motivation, we shall embrace the proposed system. If the *telos* seems worthy, the proposal will be accepted. The consideration in picking a language, a logical system, is **moral, ethical**. If it is **good**, it is to be accepted. Two languages may be (internally) consistent, but the **good** one is the **right** one,

I could not complain. Gaya gave two detailed answers. Now she wanted something in return: "Tell me about your writing". "I thought you'd never ask" I said. "Really? and I wanted to be polite. Serves me right". "I am writing more or less about the things we talk about, only **technically**". I replied; "Philosophy of language, mostly. And logic. Some pseudo-formal logic. And ontology. and Ethics.." Gaya laughed; "You must be kidding. Didn't you leave anything out?" Again I was surprised by her reaction. "How can you say that! You are the one who taught me that everything is connected, that..." Gaya interrupted. "Sorry, sorry. You are right. It is a western reflex I acquired over the years. Please go on". "Well, it's not so absurd. Philosophy of language and logic go hand in hand. My thesis maintains, that the **reference** of language, what language **describes**, is not **ontological**, but **ethical**. I claim that ontology, what **exists**, is a convention, a human construction. On the other hand, **ethics** is primitive. The *Good* is there, *apriori*. Not the world. You know all this stuff. Many people do. I only try to articulate it for my fellow westerns".

"Nice project" Gaya said. "Ambitious. Many have failed." I agreed: "Yes, but times change. I see clear signs that western thought is ready for a change. A lot of relativism and pragmatism going round these days. French solipsism[50] is also

the one to employ. "Transcendental truth", which is not system-dependent, is a **moral** truth. Only the **good** is external to every system.

[50] It is now high time, half way into this book, to bring up the term which appears in the title: **Solipsism**. I share Christine Franklin Ladd's[89] view: ""I **am** a solipsist; It seems the only coherent epistemological persuasion. I always wondered why there were not more of us around". The way I understand the term *solipsism*, it applies to Hegel, Husserl, Heidegger, Sartre and Derrida (very partial list). Phenomenology[90] is intrinsically solipsist. Modern French thought is intrinsically solipsist (The only 'deviation' they make from pure solipsism is the notion of *"the other"*, the mysterious entity that is **posited** by the French solipsist behind his fellow's eyes.)

"Relativists do not, indeed, generally go quite all the way" Says Hilary Putnam[91] in *"Why is a Philosopher"*. Putnam claims relativism to be self-refuting. However, he implicitly presupposes a realist premise: The independent, shared objective reference. This is hardly surprising, as the term "relativism" is often used as an insult - as a title for a doctrine that is either **futile** or **incoherent** or both. The almost automatic condemnation of relativism is often coupled with the claim that the arguments leading to relativism remain valid all the way to **solipsism**. And as solipsism is evidently a ridiculous position, relativism is too. Maybe solipsism is what frightens Putnam's relativists who "do not go all the way". The problem with this reasoning, is that solipsism is so ridiculous, that not much attention has ever been devoted to understand it. In an important way, radical relativists (who more often than not happen to be French) are solipsists; Radical subjectivism (e.g., existentialism) is essentially solipsist. The last thing solipsism is, is **incoherent**. Nevertheless, it is often considered **uninteresting**, and sometimes immoral (or at least **a**-moral).

Solipsism is commonly understood as the denial of the **existence** of anything **outside** the subject. Its rejection is based on a **realist** understanding of the terms "existence" and "outside". When a

78

gaining ground. Do you want to read a small non-academic passage I wrote to demonstrate my view?" "Naturally" said Gaya. I went to my room to bring it. This time Gaya did her own reading. Here it is:

*"Picture A and B both **pointing** to object O, while A utters "this is good", and B utters "this is bad". This situation has **two** possible explanations: The first is based on the prevailing paradigm in the philosophy of language, identifying (at least in this simple case) the **meaning** of "this" with a **physical, objective reference**: A and B **share** the meaning of "this", but they **differ** in their understanding of **"good"** and **"bad"**. But there is a second explanation: What if they **do** share the meaning of "good" and "bad"? If they do, they must have **different references** for **"this"**! This second explanation represents a **challenging paradigm** in the philosophy of language, which does **not** assume **objective** reference - one that accepts **objectivity** only for evaluative, **moral***

---

solipsist says "I deny the existence of anything outside of me", he clearly understands those two terms very differently from a realist who counter claims "I affirm the existence of things outside of me". If the solipsist is sincere in his claim, **his** "existence" is something that he accepts of **himself**, but denies of anything or anyone else. On the other hand, "existence" for the realist is something that he accepts both of himself **and** of other things (including other speakers). The same holds for the second term, "outside". The solipsist (who is naturally also a phenomenologist) considers the whole world a **part** of him, **inside**, hence his claim there is nothing **outside**. The realist, however, does not consider the phenomena he experiences as a part of himself - he considers them **outside**. (Similar discrepancies prevail for the terms "I" and "anything" appearing in the disputed statement). The argument between the radical relativist (or solipsist) and the realist is a battle between paradigms - each employing its own vocabulary. The only hope of conducting a fruitful philosophical debate between two sides that speak different languages, is for one of the parties to agree to put himself in an inferior position by adopting his adversary's language, and try to present his case in a language that is ill-suited for the task. That is precisely what Putnam is doing in the abovementioned article. He is a relativist who wants to **communicate** with realists, to speak their language (i.e., accept their basic metaphysical premise). Putnam undertakes a courageous task - that of an **interpreter**. As such, he places himself in double jeopardy: of being accused by relativists for being a confused realist, and by realists for being a living example of the absurdity of relativism. A perfect example of such criticism from realist circles is provided by Michael Devitt in *Realism & Truth*[??]. Devitt devotes a whole chapter to the **Renegade Putnam**: Once a realist, who lost his (philosophical) senses and joined the fashionable anti-realist opposition. Devitt is not misled by Putnam's vocabulary: He perfectly understands Putnam's relativism concealed in his "version" of realism. But Putnam is on a mission of mediating, of opening a channel of communication between two alien points of view, and therefore deserves support, rather than criticism..

Putnam is in good company. Quite a few distinguished thinkers share his relativism. Richard Rorty[??] is a good example of a renunciation of the realist premise. He no longer presupposes objectivity in his thought. Nevertheless, Putnam interprets Rorty as having his own brand of objectivity: of ideas that (objectively) *"pay their way"*. In this interpretation, Putnam "blames" Rorty for holding an **objective** notion of truth after all. Putnam seems to sympathize with this view; but Rorty went "too far" in his relativism - to the extent of waiving the realist premise. Putnam gently pulls him back into the ranks of analytic philosophy, by recognizing the (supposedly inevitable) implied **objectivity** in Rorty's position.

*Concepts. There is no paradox in assuming A and B refer to **different** Concepts while saying "this". On the contrary: their **disagreement** regarding O's value, or desirability, is the best **proof** of this fact. A and B **speak different languages**, while moral judgments are the **yardstick**, the **criterion** for meaningful communication."*

"This is what you call 'not academic'?" asked Gaya when she finished. "Well, I had a version with two of my daughters and a tomato. One of them loves tomatoes, the other does not. Do you think that by 'tomato' they mean the same thing?" Gaya giggled: "**The** same thing? Who is to compare?" I took the page she was reading from, and before putting it in my pocket I noticed the paragraph that came next to the one I marked for her to read. I quickly read it, and returned it to her: "Look at the next paragraph. It is the best explanation of what I think I am doing. I must have written this a year ago".

*"All philosophers described **concepts**, existent in their minds. They each used **words** to describe their interconnecting concepts. They used **different** words, which is not surprising, as they spoke different languages (**different** in more ways than one). But how different were the **concepts** these words described? I would suspect they were much more **similar** than was ever suspected. Did Plato, when discussing the idea of the good, have a **different** concept in mind, than Spinoza had when discussing God? If **anything** is similar to anything, it is these two concepts (As well as Heidegger's 'Dasein', Hegel's spirit and others). This similarity is evident from two perspectives: In the **inter-relations** of concepts within each of the corresponding languages, and also from the strong convictions of the corresponding thinkers, expressed very explicitly, even in Wittgenstein's case. Every **new** philosophy must be able to reconcile all of history's "competing" philosophical theses, to **translate** them all into **its** language, showing them all to be **isomorphic**."*

Gaya seemed impressed. "Very nice. Was it a part of a paper?" "No." I replied. "I wouldn't dare turn in something like this. I would be expelled. I don't think anybody has read this before. Maybe my oldest daughter. Or my wife. They go through my stuff sometimes". "Include it in what you are writing now" said Gaya. "As it is. It has a nice rhythm, and it's short". So I did.

°Putnam identifies the problem of **representation** (or the lack of it..) with the problem of **intentionality**. The positivist reductionism does not cohere with the (personal, subjective) phenomenon of intentionality. Intentionality is not **observable**. It cannot be verified; It does not "fit" into the positivist worldview. Intentionality cannot be denied, therefore something must be wrong with positivism. The relativists, on the other hand, have no feud with intentionality; On the contrary: relativism is **based** on this intuitive notion. Relativism denies the **objectivity** of the object

I went for lunch to my regular place, and had my regular toast. I was paying attention. I watched the people walking in the streets. Two old ladies were walking down the street, arm in arm. One was old, the other **very** old. The very old one was speaking to the other. Not speaking, **shouting**. She must have been hard of hearing, or without control over the pitch of her voice. As they were passing by me, I had a short conversation with the less old one. She apologized for the yelling, and explained that the old lady, probably her mother, is a little crazy (or hard of hearing, or both), and look what she has to put up with. She said it good naturally, not as a complaint. I nodded and we both laughed. The whole conversation was in Dutch. Well, I didn't do much speaking. But I understood. Everything. At least everything relevant, everything **important**. I thought to myself, that one does not have to know the meaning of single words to speak a language. He must have an understanding of **situations**. **Human** situations. In this case, Dutch situations. I started to understand the people, Their **attitude**, not the particular sounds they happen to utter on a particular occasion. The same occasion fits infinitely many combinations of words, but there is only one situation, one thing to understand. If you got **that**, you got everything.

Two men came down the street. They seemed like workmen, returning from their lunch break. I looked in their eyes, although they didn't notice me. One of them was clearly drunk, although he walked and acted straight. But I saw the alcohol in his eyes. They were misty, a bit unfocused. He seemed in a good mood, looking around him in interest. He looked pretty much like me, constantly looking up and around at the beauty of Edam. But in his case it was different. Edam looked interesting to him because he was **drunk**, sedated, stoned. And then it hit me: That is what drugs do! They enhance the feeling, the one Gaya preaches for, that It **is** (all) **You!** The man in the street knew he was tipsy. He

---

of intentionality, not intentionality itself. If it was not for intentionality, the problem would not have arisen. The debate concentrates on the question "what **is** the subject's intentionality directed **towards?**" Aristotle's answer was "to the **objective** world", to **reality**, and (almost) everyone followed suit. The relativists, on the other hand, deny the need for an **external** object of intentionality. It is intentionality **itself** that is the subject of their investigations.

°Putnam makes **Quine**, on the other hand, much more relativistic than Quine seems to have intended. He interprets Quine's holism and his deflationary notion of truth as evidence for his (almost **French**!) relativism. Putnam does not attempt to uncover Quine's hidden "objectivity", as he does Rorty's. Instead, he feels protected enough to walk with Quine "all the way" to the wilderness, only to discover the horrifying **solipsism** awaiting at the end of the path. Quine, although a self-proclaimed devoted empiricist, is **too relativistic** even for Putnam. As an empiricist, Quine accepts the objectivity of reference; But as a holist, his deflationary **truth** renders **truth** system dependent, **relative**. Putnam, on the other hand, takes an opposite position, similar to that of Davidson: Insist on an objective, explanatory notion of truth, and still reject the objectivity of reference.

must have done it thousands of times before. He knew the feeling: The world looks slightly different. Among other things, more interesting. His drunkenness paints the world in a slightly more favorable color. By drinking, he knows he can change the world for a little while; Change it into something a little more enjoyable. The objective world is hard and cruel. There is nothing he can do about it. But there is! He takes a drink and changes the world. It always helps. The world **does** change. True, they say that it **actually** doesn't, but who cares when you're drunk! By drinking, the man takes charge of his own, **personal** world, and changes it to be more pleasant. Drinking enhances the eastern, solipsist attitude: It ignores **the real** world, and "artificially" creates a more friendly environment.

The man does not really need the drink to change the world into what it becomes when he drinks. But **he doesn't know that**. He's been told that there are no "private" worlds, just one big public one. And it is unchangeable, at least not significantly, definitely not by a hard working Dutch workman. But if one drinks, he is told, certain things happen **to him**. What **actually** (ha ha!) happens to him, that his inhibitions drop. He is not as much tied down by the dogmas he was raised under. He lets himself go; creates a nicer reality. In the case of heavy drinking or stronger drugs, a **much** nicer reality. What drugs do, is they "officially" transfer **control** over reality, from "nature" or "the outside", to its rightful **owner**: To oneself. This is why drugs were never a serious problem in the east, most of its drugs production intended for export. Because drugs do what for them comes naturally: They unite the person with his world. This is also why drugs and alcohol are so dangerous (excessive good!): At first, they do wonders: You feel as good as can be. But the addict does not **know** that it is him. He thinks it is the chemical. He **endows** the chemical with a wondrous **property**, the capacity to bring about a magnificent feeling. And science backs this story. In fact, the addict creates a world, in which there is one **good** chemical, the remainder a bad, vague bore. And this is the world he is stuck with. And it is **reality**, sheer reality: That is the world he created for himself; This is the man he is. Drugs **make it happen**; They enhance **subjectivity**, and thus present a major danger to the objective world. That is why the objective world defends itself against them. They are 'restricted materials', like explosives: They make an important contribution, in certain circumstances they are essential, but yet extremely dangerous, if not properly handled. At the same time, drug abuse is the ultimate manifestation of an objective-materialist *worldview*: It is the attribution of the extreme **good** (feeling) into a material **substance** (and, consequently, also the extreme **bad**).

June 22 - God

Gaya was right about my dreaming. I slept much better than last night, but again, I can clearly remember quite a few dreams. Like the night before, I woke up several times during the night. But this time I was prepared: Every time I woke, I tried to **pay attention** to the last dream. I had no problem falling back asleep, but I do remember the dreams. I will spare you the details; The interesting point being the radical change in my "sleeping behavior". Next bulletin tomorrow morning.

"What are the inter-relations between the notion of *good* and that of *will*?" I asked Gaya over breakfast. "Better to begin with *will* and the *bad*, rather than the *good*" said Gaya. "Why the *bad*?" I inquired. "Think of the very first **display** of will in a baby" she explained. "When is it manifested? When the baby is content? warm and fed?[51] It is only when something is **wrong**, when it is hungry,

---

[51] *"Imagine a Ping child who, in experiencing his pink and soft mother, thinks: "Pink goes together with soft." He cannot refer to the object Mommy in early Pinglish at all, and at his early age he has no need to identify the property of motherhood."* This passage is out of Ruth Manor's brilliant article *"Simulating Imagination".*[92] For me, this short article deserves special attention, whereas it is not only responsible for my interest in (the philosophy of) language, but also provided me with invaluable insight into the objectivist premise it employs.

Let me briefly describe the model that is the subject of the article, and after giving it a close examination, I shall turn to the motivations behind it and the conclusions that may be drawn from it. The **speakers** in this models are called *Pings*. They are pseudo human 'epistemic units', that have no **objective** perception: Their conceptual schemes contain no objects, just **predicates**. The Pings have a perception of **time**, manifested in their understanding of simultaneousness, or *coincidence*, in Manor's terminology. All the Pings can do, epistemically, is accumulate beliefs of *togetherness* of predicates, of properties they experience. The Pings have only one logical operator: Negation. The above passage exemplifies the way the Pings accumulate beliefs: The baby accumulated the belief {pink,soft}. Although the Pings experience an infinite variety of sense data, presentable as beliefs (each consisting of a group of predicates), they only have two mental **states**: A 'normal' *ping state*, and a 'nervous' *pong state*. The latter occurs when the Ping encounters a **contradiction**: A state of having two distinct beliefs such as {A,B} and {A,~B} (where A and B are predicates, and ~ is the operator of negation). The way a Ping in the nervous *pong state* **resolves** this contradiction, is by splitting the predicate A into two (distinct and contradictory) predicates, with the aid of a third, C: 'AC' and 'A~C'. By doing so, he substitutes {A,B} with {AC,B}, and {A,~B} with {A~C,~B}. The choice of C is such, that neither {A,C} nor {A,~C} are beliefs.

The article further describes the development of Pinglish (logic), including the operators conjunction and implication (Although this is redundant, because the Pings must be assumed to be in *apriori* possession of the full syntax of propositional calculus, as will be shown shortly), and of predicates that denote abstract (imperceptible) properties. Manor then proceeds to discuss **misunderstandings**: Different Pings may use the same name (of predicate) to denote distinctly different properties; Pings do **not** necessarily hold the same (or even similar) beliefs. However, they **cooperate**, in helping resolve each other's contradiction. In time, the Pings established the *Pingland Information Center* (PIC), a central data bank that is shared, **accessible** to all. Manor then proceeds

or cold, or if it is in pain. Only **then** the baby **exercises** its magnificent tool, its **will**: It 'decides', in a manner of speaking, to **do** something about its problem. It contracts its muscles, every nerve in its body aching with action, his vocal cords contract, the air is pressed out of its lunges - it **screams**". "What a mechanistic description!" I said, smiling. "I could have been a hell of a scientist, couldn't I?" agreed Gaya, smiling as well. I said: "This fits nicely with what you have said when I was feeding the ducks: That action is invoked by a moral problem, and when there is no **problem**, no action, no exercise of will, is required". "It does" she replied, and continued: "But let us go on with the story. The baby's mother speaks the language, although the baby does not. She **understands** that the baby is exercising its will **because** something is wrong in its world. Now, **she** has a moral problem. Not a big one; after all, it is **her** baby, her own flesh and blood. So even if she is doing something she really does not want to interrupt, like producing another baby, she will stop what she is doing, and take care of it. Well, not always; But we'll get back to this later. Now **she** acts, because something is wrong in **her** world: Her baby cries. Now the baby learned something: Crying **works**. It is a **sentence**, a means of communication, a momentary work of art: By exercising its will, the baby produced certain visible and audible phenomena, which, although very temporary and immediately evaporating, produce the desired consequence: The elimination of the source of the **bad**: It is fed, or whatever. This is the first sentence of every baby, and for it to emerge, something **bad** is required. Without it, it would have no language - the product of a **bad** feeling and **will**".

°

---

to describe the inner workings of PIC, as her focus is more on issues in information processing and AI, rather than Ping (or human) epistemology. But let us stop here, and examine the situation thus far.

°Initially, the Pings are very similar to our S1 and S2. They have the ability to perceive and store only **properties**, denoted by names: **predicates**. Manor does not explain how a Ping's **hearing** of the word *pleasant* or *mother* **differs** from regular sense data; In other words, when a Ping has an experience, how does it know that the experience is of a **term** in language, **denoting** something, rather than a 'raw' experience. But let us overlook this problem. Granting the Pings the ability to "put properties together" is nothing but saying that they are *apriori* equipped with the operator of **conjunction**. Conjunction (as we understand it) and **negation** are an (expressively) complete set of connectives. Hence, the Pings come *apriori* equipped with (at least) the full syntax of classic propositional calculus, equivalent to S1 and S2's P_1. This **supports** Manor's implicit affirmation of the fact that the Pings have **deductive** capabilities: *"..He compares notes with other Pings, tries to find out what follows (deductively) from..."* (p. 73). Therefore, the Pings have no need to 'develop' the logical operators - they have them 'pre-installed'.

The Pings states of 'nervousness' and 'non-nervousness' can be taken as equivalent to what I have termed "a moral perception": The Pings know what they want: They want to be **happy**, i.e., have no contradictions. Having contradictory beliefs is **bad**. The Pings turn out to be more and more similar to S1 and S2. (The experience 'unpleasant' that is used in Manor's presentation carries no moral

I wanted her to continue: "And if the mother does **not** respond to the baby's sentence?" I asked. "Well, if she **never** responds, the baby will not acquire language; he would probably not survive, anyway. But if she **sometimes** does not respond, the baby is confused. The same behavior on its part, **sometimes** produces the desired outcome, and sometimes not. The baby is slow in learning the language. The more inconsistent the mother in responding to its cries, the longer it takes the baby to master the language. Parents who ignore the crying of their baby **prolong** the period in which it cries. It is the paradigm of **misunderstanding**: The baby does not learn, what (of his) **actions** produces what result. Luckily enough, mothers usually love their babies, so babies learn the language. But the case is similar every time a language is taught: If the teacher acts inconsistently, if it **lies** to the student, the student will not learn. The teacher must **care** for the student, and must be sincere with it. **Love** is the most efficient tool in teaching a language. Love and care. But this is not news: That love has positive influence on **communication**".

°

---

value - it is just a simple property, or predicate, like all others). In the first example of a nervous *pong state* above, our ping split the concept A (originally *pink*) into two **species**: AC and A~C. Here the first serious problem arises: What happens to the (old) predicate A? It can be perceived as the **genus** of AC and A~C, but Manor does not address this relation. In her model, A must be **substituted** by the two new predicates, AC and A~C. To be consistent with the rest of the story, the predicate A must either be **forgotten**, or if it appears separately, in a different context (say, {A,D}), rendered **irrelevant** to AC and A~C. So, as far as we are now concerned, there is no more 'A'.

Manor does not elaborate on how the pings acquire **objective** perception: How do groupings of predicates **become** an **object**, rather than a mere grouping, and how they realize that they can be (objectively) **wrong**. It seems, that the Pings do not really need anyone to resolve their contradictions. Their method of doing so is completely self sufficient, and requires no outside help. If the Pings have the ability to manipulate abstract predicates, they can make up such an abstract predicate every time they encounter a contradiction: They can turn A into AC and A~C without even having (personally) experienced {A,C}. As the story goes, **personal** experience is not a requirement for adapting a belief, as the Pings constantly "compare notes" and rely on each other's testimony.

° I shall not go into the problems of *radical translation* that are evident in the Ping story, or into a detailed analysis of the case of inconsistent **naming**, as is the case with the Ping child and his sister, who understand the term *mother* differently. Those issues are not Manor's main concern in the article. But before turning to what is, a basic premise of Manor's whole discussion needs to be uncovered and explicitly stated: The premise of **objectivity**, of the **existence** of an objective reality the Pings all somehow **share**. This implicit premise is visible in several places throughout the article, and it is essential for what seems to be Manor's motivation. **(1)** *"..if a Ping describes his experience, he can list a finite set of predicates completely describing his mental representation, but the list describes only incompletely the experience itself"* (p. 72, bold type added by me). The experience **itself** is distinct from what the Ping **experienced**. This is a clear distinction between *phenomenon* and *nuomenon*, **(2)** In the next sentence, Manor claims the Pings to be aware that this **is** in fact the case, *"Because... they realized that no finite set of predicates could completely describe the experience."* **How** did the Pings arrive at such an outstanding conclusion, without

85

"When does the baby first learn about the objective world?" I was very interested. "Well, sometimes never. I don't think that Socrates, or Plato, or Jesus believed in it. But for most of us, it happens very early. I guess it happens on the first time the baby realizes that the distinction between 'good' and 'bad' is not "attached" to objects". I didn't get it. "Please explain". "Look: Until that day, the baby has no reason to believe there is anything out there but itself. The world **responds**: May be not **very** systematically, whereas sometimes its cries do not work, but generally, it finds itself able to solve its problems: It's wet, it cries, it gets changed. For the baby, there are undesirable 'things' and desirable ones. The dichotomy is clear. The mother represents the concept of 'eliminating bad feelings', something which is definitely **good**. Nothing in the baby's world can match this **goodness** of its mother. In time, the baby learns what works better than what: If the baby happens to have a mother that hates a particular sound it is able to emit, the baby will learn to use **this** sound when it wants something real bad. But listen to this: Suppose the mother really hates the sound, and decides to **punish** the poor baby, which still does not suspect, that there is an **objective** (and cruel!) world out there. She punishes the baby. The baby realizes, for the first time, that something **good** can (sometimes) be **bad!** What an unpleasant surprise! The baby is now forced to distinguish, in his developing conceptual scheme, between **good mother** and **bad mother**. The concept of 'bad mother' is the first member in the baby's objective world."

When we started on our daily walk, I said to Gaya: "I am writing about **God**".[52] "What do you have to say about her?" asked Gaya, smiling as usual. I didn't

---

Aristotle? **(3)** In describing *early Pinglish*, on the same page, Manor explicitly states that predicates **have an extension**. Here the presupposition of an objective reference, **distinct** from the properties that **describe** it, is almost explicit.

Manor would probably not deny having employed this premise, and would most probably be willing to make it explicit. Her motivation is not to describe the historic evolution of **human** language, but, as the title indicates, to make a point regarding artificial intelligence, and the role of **imagination** in epistemic systems. She advocates the possible employment of AI technology, with the purpose of acquiring insight into what thinking is; It is not the **particular** model that is important; It is the fact that imagination could be artificially simulated. And the Pings, whether objectivists or relativists, whether equipped with P_1 or any other logical system, clearly use **imagination** in solving their epistemic problems.

[52] Let us now return to our speakers, S1 and S2. They have already made quite some progress, each of them in possession of a **subdomain**, containing properties that are **objects**, and a variety of properties that are **not** objects, i.e., predicates. Having a subdomain, they each have the property x, designating what all **objects** have in common: **existence**. They have a subject-predicate based language, in which they converse. When they speak, they presuppose a shared, intersubjective meaning of the property **existence**. They also share the primordial **contradiction** and one special predicate that follows from their intentional character, G: the **Good**.

86

argue with her about God's gender. I spend my life with four females. "The discussion is **logical**" I replied. "I artificially built a concept, based on certain relations it has with all other concepts, and after having characterized it based on these generally applicable relations, I claim that it is no other than the concept **God**." "Can you elaborate? or is the logic involved too complicated?" "Not at all" I said. "It is quite simple." I told Gaya the contents of footnote 52, and after a moment of thought she said: "You know why you can hardly find the concept of **God**, at least the way you people understand it, in eastern thought?" I knew the fact, but not the reason. "Why?" "Because eastern philosophy has no "objective world" which is an agreed-upon subset of totality." She replied. I kept quiet, waiting for an explanation. It came. "Look: You make a distinction between 'everything' and 'everything that exists', right? You constantly speak of things that do **not** exist." "Go on" I said. "But eastern thought makes no such distinction. A 'thing' that does **not** exist is unintelligible: If you speak about it, how can it not exists? Everything exists. Things may be different - some material, some not. But this has nothing to do with **existence**. For the eastern philosopher, **everything** is included in what you call "the objective subdomain". For him, existence and God are the very same thing."

She was right, of course. I should have thought about it myself. In fact, this clearly belongs in the footnotes; But it is already here. Let it be. I said: "I once heard a cute story about a *Taoist* who spit in Buddha's face. He was brought before the chief Buddhist, or whatever he was, and was asked to explain his deed. He said: 'Show me where there is no Buddha, and I will spit there'". Gaya nodded in agreement: "Yes. I know the story. This is exactly what I mean. In the east, the 'super-predicate' you call 'Divinity' has many variations: 'The nature of Buddha', or *Tao*, 'The way'; It is not personified, or even **objectified**. It is viewed, as you rightly pointed out, as a **property** or a **process**. In ancient

---

Now let us approach S1, and ask him to create a **new** property, hereafter designated by the predicate **D**. What characterizes this new predicate, is that it **is implied**, entailed by **every other property** in his whole system (objects and predicates alike). Note, that this exactly is the relation prevailing between our well known **x** and the properties in the **subdomain**, that all imply it. But now, we want to create a property that is implied by **all** of S1's properties, not just those in the objective subdomain. If S1 already has such a property (which is, naturally, **unique**), we shall ask him to give it the name **D**, for the purpose of this discussion. Let us now closely examine D: **Everything** implies it. For every property P, P⊃D. It is the "mirror image" of F: F **implies** everything in the system: For every property P, F⊃P. Just like the property F is "always off", property D is "always on". In a manner of speaking, D can be perceived as the negation of F: D≡~F.

In natural languages, D is very often denoted by the name **God**. A concept that includes **everything**, is the primal **cause** and the primal **reason**, is **unchangeable**, and (very) well defined. D (God) includes, is **implied** by everything. If **anything**, then **God**.

Chinese literature, it is almost always described by what it is **not**, rather than by what it **is**. If your concept of God is as being the **negation** of something you call "contradiction", then I would say that for eastern philosophy, it is contradiction **itself** that is considered divine. This is why *Zen* stories, proverbs and poems sound like sheer contradictions: They **are**! They are **articulations** of what you call 'F'".

"All this sounds familiar" I said, "from a seminar I took last year. It was entitled 'Language for the Description of God', or 'LDG' in short[53]." Gaya was interested: "What about? Spinoza[54]?" she guessed. "Not at all" I replied; "It was not **about** anyone. Well, it was **about** God. It was a full year seminar. I only took it for one year, but it has been going on for three or four. The general idea was to get insight into the idea of God, and the language to intelligibly describe him, with the aid of the concept of contradiction. In fact, it was a somewhat chaotic venture: Taking two so obscure, even mysterious concepts as 'God' and 'contradiction', and trying to derive new insight by applying them to each other. At first, it seemed like gibberish. But slowly, some sense began to emerge out of the chaos. It was interesting. There were a variety of consequences, in different directions. For instance, that a **divine command**, as a opposed to a regular, human command, was that it is **inherently refusable**: A divine command is what **constitutes** human **freedom of choice**. Or a divine **declaration**: It changes reality in such a way, that it was never different in the first place - a kind of 'retroactive creation' - we called it 'decreation'. Or the question whether (the concept of) God was a **universal** or a **particular**." Gaya interrupted: "Which is

---

[53] The **'LDG'** seminar took place in TAU philosophy department by Ilay Alon and David Graves.[93] It focused around what was termed 'the Aleph rule': In LDG, a proposition is considered **true**, if it is **about** God, and if, when interpreted in NL (a **natural**, human language) seems like a contradiction. E.g., "God is merciful and God is not merciful" is a contradiction in NL, but a true proposition in LDG. Taking this proposition in its LDG interpretation, it means something like 'God is Aleph-merciful'. The major task was to **understand** the **meaning** of 'Aleph-merciful', or in general, 'Aleph-P', where P is a predicate.

[54] It is time to turn to **Spinoza**[94], with the aid of our two devoted speakers, S1 and S2. Let us see if we can make some sense of what he says, equipped with the newly formed super-predicate 'D'. This D, in **Spinoza's** conceptual scheme, was *Nature, or God*: the *Substance*. This substance **we** experience in two flavors, two *attributes* (although there could be more): Thought and Extension. Note: What is thought is not extension, and what is extension is not thought. Let us denote *extension* with E, and *thought* with T. Naturally, $T \supset \sim E$ and $E \supset \sim T$, while both T and E imply D: $T \supset D$, $E \supset D$. Both E and T are further 'divided' into *modes*: $T_{1}, T_{2},...$ and $E_{1}, E_{2},....$ The predicate that S1 and S2 call 'G' (Good), is Spinoza's *conatus*: His version of **intentionality**: *'The endeavor wherewith each thing endeavors to persist...".* S1 and S2's *wffs* that denote **objects** (things that *really* exist) are in Spinoza's language *adequate ideas*, and their **predicates**, things that do not (really) exist, are his *inadequate ideas.*

it?" I was glad to be the teacher, even for a moment: "Both. It is the genus of these two contradicting concepts, just as 'animal' is both a dog and a cat."

We were walking on Edam's main street (and canal). I already felt completely at home. I knew all the streets, quite a few shop owners greeted us as we walked by. In the last few days I have done quite a lot of walking, as Esti had commanded before she left. I kept looking for the smaller, more picturesque alleys, to find new points of view on (or of) the wonderful surroundings. Many points were inaccessible, and must have been privately owned. I wondered many times why there are never little boats on the canal, only yachts or large sailing boats. A boat ride on the canal could be a great tourist attraction. So much more could be seen from there! I posed the question to Gaya: "Is it forbidden to take boat trips on the canal? I mean small rowing boats, or pedal boats?" Gaya seemed mildly surprised: "Forbidden? Why ever? Look!" and pointed ahead, along the canal we were walking by. I couldn't believe it. She's done it again. Four or five small boats were making their way towards us. In a minute they were real close: Rowing boats. Two double seater canoes, and two regular rowing boats. They looked like two families of tourists; kids and all. They seemed to be enjoying. A lot. I raised my astonished eyes to Gaya, who seemed quite amused. I smiled and put both my hands on my head, in a gesture of "this is too much". People around us stopped walking and watched the strange scene. To them it must have looked as if Gaya played an extremely successful practical joke on me. Well, she did, didn't she?

She later denied having done **anything**, of course. She had a completely reasonable explanation: "I don't know why you're making such a big fuss over this stupid incident. If it wasn't so funny, I would be mad at you. What is the big deal? Up until now, there was no boating on the canals. Then you had a thought: Why in the world should it be prohibited? And really, particularly in **your** 'really', there was absolutely no reason. It was unquestionably **good** to have this nice way of sightseeing Edam. So you made it happen. I can even prove to you that this is no coincidence: I am positive, that as of now you will be seeing boats filled with kids and tourists all the time." I suspected she was right in her last

---

°But most interesting is Spinoza's conception of **truth**: *"A person who has a true idea knows at the same time that he has a true idea"*: If a speaker **knows** that an idea is true, the idea **is** true. This **knowing** does not come from outside: it is stipulated, **constituted** by the person. Spinoza's adequate idea only need to satisfy the requirement of **coherence**: Of adhering to the syntax of P_1 (or equivalent). Spinoza, as a perfect rationalist, claimed that understanding the prevailing logical rules provides the full picture of **reality**. The concept of **God** has, "folded" within it, a whole world of (adequate) ideas. Spinoza not only described the contents of his **particular** subdomain, as most thinkers did. He outlined the necessary logical **structure** of the world (or conceptual scheme), providing the rules by which **every** such scheme is constituted.

remark, but could not resist asking: "Tell me: Did **you** often see boating on these canals before?" For the first time in my six days of acquaintance with Gaya, she said: "Let us leave you with some mystery. You like it better this way", and said no more. The incident did not leave my mind: I was intensely looking at these canals since June 12th. Never have I seen a trace of boats - not with tourists, nor with locals. And **now** they appear.

Before we parted, Gaya said: "There was one thing I wanted to add about the difference between the traditional eastern and modern western attitudes towards the Divine: In the east, 'philosophy' and 'religion', and also 'theology', are one and the same. This is not the case in the west; at least not in the last several centuries. In the west, the **three** are clearly distinct." I didn't want to start an argument, as we were already standing at the door of *De Fortuna*, but still replied: "This is not true for the Jews. The **real** Jews. for them, like in the east, the three are one and the same[55]. But let us talk about it over dinner. Are you having dinner? Are you free?" Gaya smiled: "Are you asking me out?" I played along: "Will you have dinner with me?" Gaya replied formally: "will eight thirty be convenient?"

As I am writing this, I am thinking about my **heritage**. I never observed any of the commandments. But I absorbed a substantial amount of Judaism, of **tradition**. I used to always put down the emphasis my father laid on 'tradition', and even considered it a kind of hypocrisy: Going to the synagogue to pray to the same God whose commandments we do not observe. But this upbringing vested me with a deep religious consciousness. Never in my life have I had **doubts** as to the **existence** of a **good super-entity**, whom I conveniently agreed to refer to as **God**. (Even before I had any idea what **existence** is). I have lived with the concept all my life. (Incidentally, I never knew that God was a serious metaphysical subject matter before I took up philosophy). Frankly, I often refrained from advertising this belief: The world I grew up in made a strong point of completely denying the existence of God, treating it as a backward superstition, like believing in witches and fairies.

---

[55] I am a very small expert in Jewish philosophy, but a few words are in order in this context. Spinoza was strongly influenced by *Moses Maimonides*[95]. This 12th century great Jewish philosopher exemplifies the attempt to reconciliate (Aristotelian) philosophy with (Jewish) faith. Although (the existence of) God was for him not only a basic **premise**, but an eminent unquestionable truth, he still tried to **prove** the existence of God by employing Aristotelian principles. Maimonides is well aware of the possible conflict between philosophy and faith, and sees this conflict as particularly dangerous for the less educated, and to those who suffer from frail faith. His solution to this problem was to write in a deliberately complicated, sometimes cryptic style, so only learned scholars would understand. Maimonides maintained that knowledge of God should not be sought by formulating descriptions of him, but by the **denial** of (earthly) attributes; What is known as God's **negative attributes**. In the terminology employed in the preceding footnotes, Maimonides' approach was to describe D with statements such as $D \supset \sim P$, rather than $D \supset P$.

90

When I entered the dining room at eight thirty, Gaya was already there, reading an abbreviated translation of St. Thomas Aquinas' *Summa theologiae*.[56] When she noticed me, she closed the book and smiled: "This guy has **five** proofs that God exists. Apparently five is not enough!" I smiled back: "But he mixes his premises with his conclusions, does he not? As I recall, he made a great fuss out of proving what he considered unquestionable". "So what?" she asked. "Does this make him refute himself? Incoherent?" But I had still something to comment on her remark from this morning on east and west: "Aquinas is a good counter example of your claim from this morning. He must have been **Chinese**, because, for him, philosophy, theology and religion were inseparable." Gaya decided to be argumentative: "I said **modern** philosophy. There was a **breach**, sometime in the 16th or 17th century. But even before, the only reason the three went together was **fear**. Philosophy and theology accommodated themselves to the criteria set by the church. Theism and objectivism are inherently in dispute. Religion is so much more in peace with Plato than it is with Aristotle!" "What religion? Christianity?" I inquired. "Any monotheistic religion. Take St. Augustine[57], for instance." "I know next to nothing about him" I admitted. "You don't need to know much. Just that he was a Platonist. For **him**, Aquinas' problems did not exist, as he was not bound by Aristotelian objectivism. He had no serious conflict between philosophy and religion. He had other problems he strived to solve, like the problem of the nature of **time**. At no avail, needless to say. But let us not talk about Christian saints. Can you tell me about **your** God?" I was already used to Gaya's swift changes of subjects, and said: You mean God of the Jews?" "The one and only" she replied. "Well, where do you want me to start? You want the full or abbreviated version?" "I'll tell you what I want" said Gaya in a determinate tone. "I want you to tell me the abbreviated version, but in the **first person**." "You mean **as** God?" What an odd request! "Precisely" said Gaya; "Tell it as if it was **you**. Please." She said **please**. She never said **please** before. I hesitated for a moment, then started:

---

[56] Thomas Aquinas' "Summary of Theology"[96] deals with reason and revelation as means to knowledge of God. Like Maimonides, his philosophical roots were Aristotelian. But he developed a more elaborate metaphysics, in distinguishing **essence** from **existence**. He says: *"Every essence or quiddity can be understood without its act of **existing** being understood. I can understand what a man or phoenix is and yet not know whether or not it exists in the nature of things. Therefore, it is evident that the act of existing is other than essence or quiddity"*. This distinction (similar to Kant's who denied that existence is a predicate almost five hundred years later), does **not** apply to God. Decartes[97] uses one of Aquinas' proofs for the existence of God, based on this equivalence, which later became famous as the *ontological proof for the existence of God*.

[57] St. Augustine of Hippo[98] maintained that all human knowledge was of two **kinds** of things: Objects of sense, and things known independently from sense data (predicates?). He had a Platonic notion of **Good**, and explained the **bad** as nothing but the **lack** of good (~G)!

"There is a lot of stuff I don't remember; After all, It's been close to six thousand years since it all started. But I must have known in advance I will forget, so I wrote it all in a book; a kind of diary." Gaya was enthused: "Perfect. Go on". "It started like a game: I felt like **creating** something. So I started **splitting** myself into opposites: Heaven/earth, light/darkness, above/below. You know the game. I made quite a marvelous creation. In just six days. Then, one day, something got into me: I wanted to **participate**. You see, it is a bit of a **bore**, being so powerful, and yet just an observer. So I invented this **trick**: I **separated** myself from the rest of me. I was still **God**, but I **also** played the role of Adam. Not a very **complicated** trick; not for **God**, anyway." I started to get into it - even started to like it. Gaya was fascinated. "So I found myself thrown out of *Eden*, me and the wife. And some fig-leaves. I felt as if my eyes have just opened; I had absolutely no idea that **I** was God. I thought I remembered God as someone **else**; someone who's order I broke. Anyway, these were hard times. My first son killed my second son. Big tragedy."

"Hundreds of years went by. I don't really remember the details; I can look in my diary if you want them.." "No, no" said Gaya. "Please proceed". "The next thing I remember is being **Noah**. I believe that at the time, I **did** know that **I** was actually God. But I knew better than to tell anyone. Anyway, things were less than perfect. So I decided to 'wipe the board' and start anew. I kept what I wanted to preserve, in a big **ark**. And immigrated to Arrarat, to start a new civilization. I made new rules, and told everyone they were conveyed to me by **God**. I didn't tell anyone, not even my three boys, that this God was in fact (in) me."

"The next thing I remember is, again, centuries later. This time I was Abraham. I don't remember when I actually **realized** that I was the boss; I think it was a dream I had. I used to take dreams seriously back then. I took my wife and my nephew and moved to Kena'an. I did really well, but when I was already some hundred years old, my wife suddenly decided she wanted a son. Can you imagine? And she was ninety! She was really miserable, so I arranged it. As usual, I never revealed my true status to everyone. I told them all it was some external super power that worked the miracle. Like with Sodom: I heard terrible things were going on there. So I went to see for myself. **horrible** place. I destroyed it immediately. Earthquake." Gaya interrupted: "You went into the destruction business again?" "Yes" I replied. "But on a limited scale, not like the flood. I decided to handle things **locally**. There was no sense wiping **everything** out every time I didn't like something."

"Tell me about the sacrifice of your son" asked Gaya. "I was coming to that. It started quite innocently: Me and Isaac, and another two servants, went on a trip;

A kind of 'initiation' for Isaac. I meant to sit with him on the mountain for a couple of days, and tell him who he **really** is. I brought some fire wood, and the two servants kept wondering how come we didn't take food. We left them behind and climbed on the mountain, just Isaac and me. He was a smart kid. Real smart. He understood almost immediately. In fact, the story about sacrificing **him** was his own idea. He said it would be very impressive. He was right, of course. It worked wonderfully. As Isaac, I had a relatively enjoyable quiet life - no major events, no catastrophes. My only mistake as Isaac was that I had a hard time deciding which of my boys I should let in on the secret. I made the mistake my father didn't make: He told me on the mountain, when I was still a boy. But I dragged it too much, and told Jacob only when I was already tired of being Isaac. When I finally told him, the secret came out; someone must have been listening in to my conversation with him. Esau was very insulted. Nobody knows this, but I told him too. It was wrong, because it made them fierce enemies: The whole idea came to them as a surprise, they were already middle aged, and Esau, for some reason, couldn't bear the idea of two Gods."

"So who's story are you going to continue with now?" asked Gaya. She liked it a lot. "Jacob's, I guess. You asked about the God of the **Jews**, didn't you?" She nodded and I continued: "As I said, I found out relatively late. My father kept it a secret too long. He almost died without telling anyone. Had I not pulled the trick with the disguise, I would never have known[58]. He would have just told my brother. Anyway, he told both of us, and I left home. I didn't want to fight Esau. After all, he was my older brother. I didn't want to start my career with murder. I had big plans; I wanted to change the world, with this new incredible information. I started paying attention to everything, even dreams. I married two sisters and had a whole bunch of kids." The food was getting cold, so I paused and started eating. Moments later the whole game seemed foolish and boring.

---

[58] **Counter factual** propositions are implications, e.g., A⊃B, where A is a 'contrary to fact' proposition. In my terminology, A is **treated** like an object (a matter of fact, something that **actually** exists), although it is **not**. The variety of problems associated with counterfactuals all result from the unclear status of A. A is false, but **treated as** true for the purpose of the counterfactual proposition.

An example: 'Had I not disguised myself' (A) $\Rightarrow$ 'I would not have known' (B). The antecedent is clearly a predicate: The property of '(Jacob) not disguising'. It is a predicate and not an object because in the **world**, Jacob **did** disguise himself. The statement in question claims that this predicate **entails** another predicate: '(Jacob's) not knowing' (B). There is nothing wrong with this proposition, for every system in which A entails B (such as in mine). But supposing that in **my** system, ~(A⊃B); For example, if I believe that Esau would have told Jacob the secret **anyway**. In this case the implication is false. It is useless to ask which **is true**, whereas counterfactuals deal in predicates and not objects, hence, there is no **objective** truth. It is a categorical mistake to talk about what is **actually** the case when discussing **non-actual** things!

June 23 - Gender

°"Let us go watch the dogs" said Gaya after breakfast this morning. "What dogs?" I asked. "Just dogs" she replied; "local dogs". We went to the southern corner of the village - no more than a five minute walk. On a large grass yard, by the intersection of two main canals, about ten dogs were scattered: From a huge Great Dane, to a tiny pocket size dog with ribbons on its little head. It was a lovely sight. The dogs' owners were no less interesting to watch than their pets. They all came here for this sole purpose, to accompany their animals, and they were constantly busy with them: One kept pulling his dog out of places the dog wasn't supposed to go to (at least in its owner's opinion), like close to the canal, or across the bridge, or even becoming too friendly with other dogs. Another man, who came with three dogs, was constantly busy collecting their droppings in plastic bags, with which he came prepared. Our 'ugly' dog was there too, his owner busy with the tennis ball. The people were **working**, and the dogs were having fun (well, maybe except the dog who wasn't allowed to go anywhere). Gaya picked a bench that was relatively distant from the action. I asked her why, and she explained that she is following *Heisenberg*'s principle: She does not want the observer to affect the subject of observation. Very witty. I guess she knew that if she came closer, the dogs would gather round **her** (animals always did that to her), and **she** would become the subject of observation. Gaya was an obser**ver**, not an obser**vee**.

I thought *What is it like to be a dog*. Strange experience. I have two dogs at home (and a cat), so I know dogs. I always thought that dogs have a full mental life; That they **think**, and even make decisions. Watching the dogs there from a distance, this opinion became certainty. Their complicated behavior could not be explained any other way. I even detected **psychological** problems in the behavior of the dog with the hysteric owner. They **must** have consciousness. How **arrogant** on the part of so many philosophers, to deny animals a **soul**.
°

°After having written the last footnote, I returned and read the footnotes dealing in the distinction between objects and predicates, and I feel there is a point that requires clarification. There is no 'real' difference in **kind** between the two. The **only** difference between them is (the assumption of) the objectivity of objects, in the sense that they are **shared**. I explained that properties in the domain may either be "on" or "off". But in the case of objects, there is a constraint: **All** speakers are expected to change the state of **objects** simultaneously, otherwise objectivity is lost. Changing a belief regarding the state of an object must be **synchronized** between all speakers: All speakers must be aware of the **rules** according to which they are allowed to change their beliefs regarding (objective) **reality**. These **rules** are commonly known 'laws of nature', laws regarding the (publicly agreed) 'evolution' of the objective subdomain; Rules that are closely associated with the passage of **time** (which will be discussed in due course).

The dogs started to disperse, when two cars pulled by and parked. One of them had flowers and ribbons all over it. Out of it emerged a wedding couple, fully dressed; Vale and all. In addition to them there were three more men and a young women, and two cameras. They came to take pictures by the large willow that was bending over the water. The place was in fact a beautiful setting for a series of wedding pictures. We were still pure observers; However, a large tree was standing exactly between us and the action, so at any particular moment a certain part of the scene was blocked from view. I moved to the end of the bench, to get a better angle, but the field of vision wasn't better from there either. Gaya was amused to see me try to overcome the optical obstacle: "The tree bothers you? There are at least two things you can do about it." I turned to her: "One of them is probably to ask them to move to a place where I can see better, right?" Gaya laughed. "No. But you could **move** them, like have the photographer suddenly discover a better spot. Or, **you** could move. I will follow you." This reminded me of a story: "I have a friend, who had an extensive eastern education. He spent years in India, and was very close to a famous *Guru*. Anyway, he came to visit one day, and we sat in my upstairs room, the one I spend the most time in. This room is facing my back yard, which is quite a beautiful sight. However, the whole bottom part of the view is blocked, because the window starts only about one meter above floor level. I told him that I am contemplating knocking the wall down and replacing it with a glass window, so the field of vision will be completely clear. However, I added, it is not a simple project, because it is a thick concrete wall. He said: "Why knock the wall down? You can have a painter **draw** the missing part of the view on the wall!". It sounded like a very original idea, maybe even a good one. Anyway, I still haven't done anything about it: I haven't knocked it down, nor had it painted."

Gaya must have suspected the story was not yet complete, because she said nothing. I continued: "Listening to you talk about this tree, the significance of my friend's suggestion suddenly dawned on me; If he had your way with words, he would probably express himself so I would **understand**. What he meant, was 'Make the change **inside**!' like this photo session here: The experience I am now having, is **one with a tree in the middle**. So what? What is so important in seeing every detail of a photo session of a strange couple? The tree is **part** of **my** picture, and a pretty picture it is! If everything was always in clear view, there would be no **curiosity**, nothing would be **interesting** any more!" Gaya finally spoke: "Don't blame your friend for not expressing himself. For two reasons: First, you seem to **now** understand things much better, or, rather, very **differently** from the way you used to. You would not have understood even if he phrased it differently. You interpret things differently now. Besides, You are talking about **your** experience with your friend, not his with you; **He** had nothing to do with it in the first place." Gaya's second reason wasn't completely clear to me, but before I had the chance to say anything, the photo group **moved**. They took a few pictures behind the tree, and now they moved all the way to the right; Not only was the view clear, they also came much closer. I kept quiet, thinking of boats in the canals. Five minutes later I had enough, and said to Gaya: "Let's walk". Gaya smiled and said, while standing up: "First you wanted to see everything, and now that you see everything you want to go." She did not say it as a question, neither as a complaint. I replied: "Well, I'm not perfect. Blame the teacher."

We walked by the canal. We could see a man by the water, busy doing something with a bucket. As we approached, I saw that he was a painter, painting a nearby house. He was washing his brush from the paint. He did this by filling the bucket with water from the canal, and using it to wash the brush a few meters away from the bank. He went back and forth with the full bucket maybe five or six times, every time spilling the dirty water on the ground, not to contaminate the canal. I asked Gaya: "Why does he not wash the brush directly in the canal water? He could have done it in two minutes, instead of going back and forth like that!" "It is not done" said Gaya. "If everyone washed brushes in the canal waters, you know what would happen". I decided to follow up on the subject: "I see. But consider this guy. Say he is here **all alone**. There is no one in sight. This one instance of brush-washing will not make the slightest difference to the quality of the water. And by doing it he will save maybe ten, fifteen minutes of work. Why does he **still** do the right thing? What makes him so **moral**?"[59] "It is the **right** thing to do" Gaya replied, and continued: "And I don't mean from **his** point of view. I mean **yours**. Suppose **you** could decide what he does. What would you decide? No. wait a minute. Let me ask you another question first: What would **you** do, with a dirty brush in your hand, and no one in sight?" "Well," I said "In my **present** state of mind, and under your influence, I would use the bucket." "Here you have it!" said Gaya triumphantly. "You can understand why **you** would do it, and you are asking me why **he** does it? Why?"

---

[59] It will be a **crime** not at least to **mention** Kant[100] in this context. In a nutshell, Kant's deontological ethics maintains that: (1) It is **only** the (subjective) intentions that render a deed **moral**, not the (objective) consequences; (2) For the act to be purely moral, the intention behind it must be motivated **just** by morality itself, not the circumstances or particular context; (3) Moral rules (categorical imperatives) are inherently **general**: they apply generally, to any hypothetical person. Here is my interpretation to these three principles: (1) There **are** no 'objective' consequences. Objectivity is just a means, a **tool** to facilitate **language**. (2) 'Morality' is 'wanting the good'. It is the only ('real') motivation. Everything **else** is just **means** towards this end. (3) Human conceptual schemes, or **worlds**, are **coherent** (P_1 syntax!). For the quest for good to succeed, consistency is required. A person must be consistent with, abide by the rules of, **his world**, to be moral (and consequently happy).

We walked back, watching the small boats in the canal. I reflected on yesterday evening's surrealist conversation, and said to Gaya: "I am still thinking about **God**. What is God's gender? God **could** be a woman. But I suspect God is not a woman. Neither a man. "What do you mean?" She asked. "From a logical point of view, God is a 'super synthesis': Something, or someone, that, **within** it, **resolves** all the contradiction. It is another consequence from my LDG seminar[60]. God is neither a particular nor a universal, but their synthesis: something that is **both** (or either, which is the same). Similarly, God resolves the 'contradiction' between male and female; like he does for all **dichotomies**. God is a different gender, a gender that combines, or is made **of**, the contradictory **combination** between male and female". "But you are talking about every baby that was ever born!" said Gaya. "What is a newborn baby, but the result, or combination, of these two constituents?" Interesting. "Yes; We really refer to **babies** as **'it'**. Not 'her' or 'him'. A baby could be considered a third gender. But before long, the **it** becomes a 'he', or a 'she'." "How exactly does this happen?" asked Gaya. She is asking me? I tried to imitate her way of thinking. "Its parents **teach** it that it must have one, particular, fixed gender?" I tried. "Yes. And more! **they** make the decision for it. They don't ask it whether it wants to stop being **it** and start being 'she' or 'he', and they also **tell** it which it

---

[60] Here is a passage from the concluding section of my 'LDG paper':

*"...Is **God** a particular or universal? Let us apply our Aleph-rule to the conflicting propositions "God is a particular" and "God is a universal", and see what sense may be derived of it. I opened the discussion of universals and particulars with the claim that concepts could be **either** universal **or** particular. Now we are faced by the possibility of a concept that is a synthesis of the two contradicting concepts; A concept resolving the contradiction between 'universal' and 'particular': their **genus**. Let us name it **Divinity**. Divinity is the genus of 'universal' and 'particular', and is **neither** as it is **both** (just as 'animal' is neither 'dog' nor 'cat', but **both**). To conclude this discussion, let us examine the relations of **Divinity** to the concept **'God'**, the ultimate universal, and the concept **'Nature'**, the ultimate particular.*

*This relation, naturally, is one of **inclusion**: 'God' or 'Godly' was, until recently, at the **top** of my conceptual scheme: It was the synthesis of all my predicates. **Nothing included it**. Now, it is included in one new concept: in **Divinity** (as a **universal**). But examining **Divinity** from its second aspect, its **particular** aspect, takes **Nature** as the species of **Divinity**. The new top of my conceptual scheme is no longer **God** (a universal), neither is it **Nature** (a particular); It is **both**, and it is **neither**: It is the only concept in my (present) conceptual scheme that is outside the universal/particular dichotomy. Accepting one of these species automatically denies the existence of the other, hence the endless quarrel between Theism and Pantheism, between Spinoza and the Jews, realists and idealists. **Divinity** is **above** the universal/particular classification. It encompasses the idea, the abstract, the potential, as well as the material, the concrete, the actual. Naturally, the two realms are in contradiction - but there is no use in trying to fix **one** of them as "real", as a **permanent** concept, while permanently denying the other's existence, or **possibility**: It is just a question of **point of view**: When considered as a particular, **Divinity** is simply **Nature**. When considered a universal, it is **God.***

will be! Small wonder that homosexuality flourishes." "And why are there more male homosexuals the female ones?" "Are there?" she asked; "If there are, I guess it is because parents much more frequently try to **force** malehood on their boys, than femalehood on their girls. You said you have three daughters. **Why** do you think you have three daughters?" "Well, that is not hard to explain; Not even **your** way. I am a proclaimed feminist." "You mean you **wanted** daughters?" "Yes." "How odd!" she wondered. "Why ever?" "I'm not sure" I answered. "But I think the age of male domination is over. I think it is evident. I have been saying it for years, but no one believes me. I think for the next couple of millennia, society will be **matriarchal.** Not a *coupe* or anything like that. I believe that the male gender will voluntarily give women the lead. It will realize that this **dominance** is more of a burden than a privilege." Although Gaya seemed to me **above** petty male/female quarrels, she seemed very pleased: "How **Socratic**! It is a beautiful thought. I mean the 'voluntarily'. I tend to agree. I've heard astrologers say that about the age of Aquarius. You are **Pisces**, right?" "Does it show?" I asked. "Clearly" she replied. "Symbolic: You **Pisces** turn over the lead to us **Aquarius's.**" "**You** are Aquarius?" "Yes. Does it show?" "I have no idea." I replied. "But I have a funny story about that: Several months ago the papers were filled with a bizarre piece of news: Apparently a **thirteenth sign** of the zodiac was 'discovered' by astronomers: A hitherto undetected star system, that supposedly changes the structure of the zodiac: Every sign 'moves' a little bit, to make room for this thirteenth sign: the sign of the **snake** I think it was. Anyway, the papers were full of it for a few days. All the astrologers protested loudly, stating that it is absurd, and that astronomic discoveries have nothing to do with their trade. It was a topic of conversation for a week: Lots of TV interviews and debates between astronomers and astrologers. It was amusing. The fuss died out in a few days, and I didn't hear of it since. But within these few days, everybody was going around saying 'I used to be a lion, now I am a Scorpio'. **I**, myself, 'moved' from **Pisces** to **Aquarius!** What can you say about **that**?" It was a good story. All true. "Well, I'd say you were turning from a man to a woman..." she answered with a smile. "Really a bizarre story. I never heard of it. I suggest you look into it. It sounds as if you let this extremely strange occurrence pass without paying enough attention. You just remembered it now, for the first time since it happened?" "Yes." I said. "I'm not really into astrology. I am not **against** it or anything; I don't even doubt that it has significant **content**, but I am not into it. At most, I read an occasional horoscope" "Well, get interested" she concluded.[61]

---

[61] Astrology, as well as other phenomena that are considered 'super natural', cannot be ignored by philosophers. They **may** be ignored by various branches of science, but only because it is not their subject matter. Philosophy is supposed to be **general**. It cannot willingly leave significant phenomena unexplained.

After a couple of futile hours at the keyboard I was on my way out to stretch my bones when I spotted Gaya on a chair outside, reading a newspaper. I asked her whether she wanted to go to lunch with me, and she said she'd eaten, but she will gladly join me, if I want. I did, as I was stuck on my writing. As we were walking in the beautiful street, it occurred to me that in our long conversation about **art** as expressions in language, we casually touched on the concept 'beauty', but she did not explain, at least not explicitly, What **is** the **beautiful?**[62] It seemed like a terribly banal and worn down question, but with Gaya nothing was banal, nor worn down. I asked. She answered immediately, directly, without playing games: "The **beautiful** is to the **good**, what the **word** 'tree' is to **this tree** over here. A beautiful **piece**, be it visible, audible, extending or not, is a piece of **art**, which in turn is nothing but a **sentence**, an **expression**, of the **feeling** of **good** that its creator wanted to convey. Beautiful things are different descriptions of **the good**. They are simply descriptions in **different languages**. You speak many languages: music, Hebrew, philosophical jargon and many more. Each has **its** way of being beautiful, **its** way of describing the only thing worth describing: The idea of the good; or the **feeling**, if you can tell between the two. If something is beautiful, and it was **made** by someone, then you have to take it as the **word** denoting **Good** in this someone's **language.**

I was hypnotized by her clear, completely intelligible and extremely eloquent answer. "Did you **understand**?" she asked. "Loud and clear" I replied. "Just one question: And when I see a beautiful flower in the field? Something beautiful that is not a work of art, whereas nobody **made** it?" She answered without hesitation: "It is still expresses the **good**: The very **good** feeling you have when you look at something beautiful. Miserable people do not see beautiful things." "I understand". Again she was bright and clear. "It is not **I** that spoke more clearly than usual" she read my mind. "It is you. You are now opening up in incredible speed. I have never seen anything like it. And I have seen quite a lot. Let's make use of this moment - you now have great reception. Let's capitalize

---

[62] The *Beautiful* is traditionally considered to belong to aestheticians. I believe that it belongs in the philosophy of **language**. I believe that **beauty** is a property of *wffs*. Suppose S1 wrote a beautiful **poem**. This is a simple example, because it is made of **words**. But it can be made of musical notes or color on canvas. What is the **meaning** of the (beautiful) poem? What does it **denote**? I propose that by creating the beautiful *wff* (provided he intended it to beautiful, which is a fair assumption), S1 wished to denote the predicate G. The beautiful **denotes** the good. Plato was rather vague on this point.[101] He was a metaphysician, not a linguist. He understood that these two terms were somehow on "the same level", but he didn't read Frege, and didn't concern himself with **correspondence**. The reason for the infinitely many **varieties** of the *beautiful*, is the parallel variety of **languages**, or (Davidsonian) **idiolects**. Every idiolect has its own *wff* to denote it. The *Good* is (in) the **world**; The *beautiful* is its corresponding counterpart in **language**.

on it." She sounded almost like an American businessman moving to close a deal: "I want to clear up another point which must be bothering you, although you haven't asked me. You already realize that it is all **you**. You can almost feel yourself **doing** it. But you still have a feeling of **duality**: The **outside** and the **inside**. They seem to stand **across** from each other. You still think **about** things. You cannot get rid of the distinction between '**this bridge**' and '**this thought** about the bridge'. What you need to realize, is that **you can never have both at once**. Imagine you are sitting somewhere, say, inside a moving train, with the landscape passing outside. Now, say you are looking out, but are in deep thought; about your book, for example. Freeze this moment. Which is it? What is your experience? The landscape or the book? Which **are** you? The landscape? There is no landscape! If I asked you to describe the landscape, you wouldn't be able to. There **was** no landscape! What there was, as always, is just **you!** Your **thoughts**. Tell me what your thoughts were, or are, and I'll tell you what **reality** was, or is. When you are **observing** the view through the window, when you pay attention to the passing landscape, when you see the houses and the trees, when you **notice** them, you **cannot**, at the same time, think of your book! You cannot do both at once. Your **intentionality** has the nature of being able to focus only on **one** thing at time - there is only one **you**. You were trained to believe, that things go on existing even when you leave the room. Of course they do - they do not have to be **watched** to exist, but they **do** have to be **thought about** - what other meaning has the word 'exist'?"[63]

---

[63]   Gaya's way of thinking may be perceived as a version, or variation, of **Husserl's** *phenomenology*,[102] a **view**, or 'procedure', based on the examination of the contents of one's own consciousness. Phenomenology concentrates on **mental acts**, and consists, as described by Husserl's student, Heidegger[103], in step by step training in 'phenomenological *seeing*', while putting everything besides the present experience, particularly the infinity of beliefs regarding the 'objective world', into '**brackets**'.

Husserl studied with Franz Brentano[104] at the university of Vienna and was greatly influenced by him. Brentano maintained that what characterizes mental acts is the fact they always include '*an object intentionally within themselves*'. (Brentano's use of 'object' is of course different from my use of the term). In other words, **thought** is always **about something**. This 'something' may or may not be material. (It is unclear whether Brentano's 'object' was necessarily **shared** by all speakers). Like Gaya, the main thing Husserl wanted to eliminate, or at least 'suspend' in brackets, was what he called 'the natural attitude' (I suspect he meant 'natural **objectivist** attitude'). He refused to submit to the supposedly unquestionable notions of space and time. In his own words: *"I can shift my standpoint in space and time, look this way and that... I can provide for myself constantly new and more or less clear and meaningful perceptions and representations... in which I make intuitable to myself whatever can possibly exist really or supposedly in the steadfast order of space and time."*[105] He sounds as if he took lessons from Gaya.

Husserl tried to carry out what he termed a "phenomenological reduction" of the 'regular', objectivist point of view, to pure phenomenological experiences, as they are directly grasped in the mental act, without the imposition of organizing concepts or abstracting from them. In successfully performing this reduction, one discovers one's own *'transcendental ego'*, providing what he calls

She took a deep breath and continued: "Now look what's happening to you: You pay much more attention to your surroundings. You are less closed within yourself; You open up. You are in beautiful surroundings. You look **around you**. You **notice** the things around you; In other words, you **think about** what is around you. **That** is what you are - what you pay attention to, what you are focused on; In this case, the things **around** you, namely Edam. You did **so** right by picking a place that **you** considered beautiful! You needed a reason to pay attention to **outside**, to focus your attention on it. Most people who have gone the way you are, went the opposite direction: They almost completely **eliminated** their outside, and gained control over their world, that was almost completely private. I like your way more. It is more **social**. Others can benefit. I feel a strange resemblance to you. You remind me of when I was young."

I wanted to say "I'm not so young anymore", but didn't. I said nothing. I had multiple reasons to remain quiet, one of which her touching declaration of affection. Listening to her was another occurrence of the *magic moment* I had a few days ago by the church. Then I said: "Thank you".

'the Archimedean point': a pure consciousness, a distinct entity from the 'psychic self', the subject matter of psychology.

June 24 - Love

I made some real progress tonight; In my **dreaming** project, I mean. I slept much better, although, again, I had a multitude of dreams. I woke up around three at night, with a new variety of dreams still vivid in my head. Only this time I was fully aware of the **attention** they deserve. So I didn't just turn on my other side and make an effort to fall back asleep. Instead, I got up, drank a glass of water, and sat in bed, reflecting on the dreams; trying to reconstruct them, understand them. It was interesting. The dreams were interesting. After doing this for some ten or fifteen minutes, I involuntarily and effortlessly glided back into sleep. And woke up again this morning, feeling I've had a **good** night's sleep. I also remember the best part of the dreams. It seems that the original dream experience is not the **story** of the dream, but a variety of **feelings**, which got 'translated' into 'story format' upon awakening. Let me give an example: As I woke up at night, I tried to remember **who** my last dream was about. The person in question was someone close to me, in the context of work; my office. It was either Rivka, or one of two assistants I had years ago. I know it was someone I liked and depended on, but could not determine which it was. I only remembered my **attitude** towards this person, not the person herself. And then, sitting there in the dark, I realized that it **wasn't** one of those. It was **just** my attitude; no **person**. The 'attachment' of the person, the superimposition of categories like (identities of) people and (locations of) places, is not a part of the dream itself. It is something we do afterwards. We try to determine the **identity**[64] of the person, but there was none: The dream is pure attitudes, **feelings**. Almost as if we 'accumulate' a variety of feelings in our waking life, based on waking experiences, and then, at night, we just play with the feelings, without the **things** the feelings are 'supposed' to be **about**. Another bulletin tomorrow.

I got up relatively early, so I went on a short pre-breakfast walk alone. Today is Saturday (*Zaterdag*), and it is *Musikdaag* ('music day') in Edam. A kind of festival, or fair. People were putting up platforms and stands with a variety of goods for sale, especially artworks. It was a busy pre-market atmosphere - no customers yet. I walked between the stands, watching them work. I stopped by

---

[64]   **Identity**: What do we mean by 'They are identical', or 'A is identical to B'? Leibniz[103] maintained that identity between two things is their sharing **all** (their) properties: If every predicate that applies to A also applies to B, and vice versa, (including 'negative attributes, e.g. 'not red'). The problem that arises from this conception is: How, then, can they be **distinguished** for the purpose of making the **statement** regarding their identity? For identity to be **claimed**, the two terms must be distinguishable, thus already differing in **some** respect. Leibniz realized this, of course. He used this 'definition' of identity to make a different point altogether: To substantiate his claim that there is **no** identity! That the basic 'units' of being are completely isolated, and therefore **cannot** be compared.

one of the displays that was all ready, with an elderly couple behind it, sitting and having a sandwich. It was a display of clay sculptures, mostly people and animals. It was not completely realistic, more 'artistic', impressionist style. I found the sculptures very beautiful. I was observing them at length, thinking about Gaya's explanations, when I suddenly realized that the clay figures **were all sad**. There were many variations, but most of the figures manifested some sort of agony, or grief, or just sadness. At any rate, none of the figures seemed **happy**. When I realized this, I felt a bit repelled by the display. I told the couple behind the stand: "They are all very beautiful, but none of them is **happy**! They are all sad!" The couple was very surprised. They wanted to automatically deny it; They must have never thought of it like this. Before they said anything I continued: "Look! Show me one that is happy!". They were confused, maybe a bit annoyed at my criticism. The woman finally pointed to a huge (sad) elephant, with a tiny, hardly visible Indian kid sitting on it, playing an even tinier flute: "Here. **He** is happy." I looked closely at the skinny Indian sitting on the elephant. I did not see signs of happiness, but I cannot say he looked very sad either. I said: "Yes. He is happy." and left the stand.
°

I had a problem with Gaya's notion of **beautiful**. Some of those sculptures were real beautiful works of art, by any standard. Still, the emotions they 'contained' cannot be considered **good**; One of them is particularly vivid in my mind: A grouping of faces (of people), all clutched together into a kind of bundle, all bearing an expression of complete horror, eyes and mouths open with absolute fear. Very strong image. It reminded me immediately of holocaust pictures. Still, it was beautiful; very **artistic**. Is **this** a (lingual) expression of the **good**? It is an expression all right; I even agree that it is the expression of the feeling the artist wanted to **communicate** with his creation. But not of the **good**! I wanted to go back and find out whether the couple was **Jewish**; I bet they are. But I didn't. I told Gaya the story over breakfast. She asked whether I'll take her there after breakfast. I agreed, but added: "Works of art express **other** emotions besides *magic moments* or the artists feeling of elation. I would say the most part of art does precisely the opposite: It describes painful, sometimes **horrible** feelings!" Gaya replied: "I don't have to spell everything out for you explicitly. I am too

---

°I propose to understand **identity** as a property of (pairs of) *wffs*, not of what they denote. A *wff* is (itself) nothing but a property, but not every property is a *wff* (most are not). *Wffs* are a subset of (the totality of) a speaker's properties, and may be compared with each other. Example: Say A is a *wff*, denoting an object. (We may **think** about the object without using A, but we cannot **speak** about it without using the name A). If B also denotes the same property, then A is identical to B. We may, of course, also say they are **synonymous**, but than we would explicitly be making a statement about **language**, not the **world**. When we say that A is **identical** to B, we don't want to be understood as making a statement about language. We want to be understood as making a statement about the world. Especially for **objectivist** speakers, there is a **world** of a difference between the two.

explicit as at is. Part of the chewing you have to do yourself. You were writing about the **good**, and you were asking about the **beautiful**. Between **good** and **bad** there is a whole range of shades of gray, with a variety of undertones. Artists who want to communicate the very **good** that they know, create a beautiful piece that succeeds in conveying this feeling. But an artist who is in pain, and wants to communicate **it**, creates a piece like the one you saw this morning. If he is talented (is a very **competent** speaker), he will create something that (deliberately) invokes a **bad** feeling, an unpleasant emotion. People call these creations **beautiful** because they are **successful**: they succeed in conveying the negative feeling. But in my dictionary, it is not **beautiful**. It is **expressive**, saturated with emotion, displays talent, but not beautiful. Let me give you an extreme example: Think of a picture or sculpture of a big man whipping a small helpless child with a whip. The man has the most realistic evil expression; the child the most realistic and touching expression of horror. The artist was no doubt extremely talented. It is perfect craftsmanship, and the emotions seem to jump out of it and grab you. I think that a display of **bad** can never be considered beautiful. Although it is definitely **art**: Part of language."

It was a wonderful day again. It was still cool and cloudy before breakfast, but when I went again, with Gaya, the clouds were gone, and a real carnival atmosphere was already in the air. The musical events started with a 'bell concert': The bell tower of the smaller, older church in the center of Edam was playing tunes, that were on the border between classic and contemporary music. There were tourists everywhere. All the restaurants and cafes had all their chairs and tables outside, and we were walking amongst the crowd, feeling like the **hosts**. Funny feeling. I've been here almost two weeks, and felt completely at home; Not to speak about Gaya, who was at home everywhere. I was observing the infinitely diverse displays, enjoying all the things that I didn't really **need**. At another time, I would probably have bought some. At least some little things, particularly pretty ones, for my home, or for Esti, for the kids, for friends. But now there seemed no point. Buying things didn't really appeal to me. They were most pretty, and proper, where they were: On display, on the stands. I thought to myself: Good thing that most are **normal**, not like me; Otherwise all the peddlers here would have gone out of business.

°

°Speaking of Leibniz, a few more remarks are in order. He is considered the other great 17th century **rationalist**, besides Spinoza. (The two have in fact met once, not far from **here,** in Amsterdam, and had four days of philosophical discussions). Consider the following passage from the *Monadology*[104]: *"Now this **connection** or adaptation of all created things with each, and of each with all the rest, means that each simple substance has relations which express all the others, and that consequently it is a perpetual living mirror of the universe"*. Each of Leibniz's monades **mirrors** the universe from a **its own point of view**. I understand Leibniz as describing a community of **speakers**, each speaker (being) a monade. Each speaker (monade) has a **picture** of the universe,

I was particularly interested in two musical events that were scheduled for today: An afternoon appearance of a band called *Kweekbak*, I guess a Dutch version of 'quick buck', and an evening show of a group titled 'The bullshit blues band'. Blues is my favorite kind of music. I said to Gaya: "Maybe I **should** get something small for my daughters." She said: "Why not? otherwise you'll be deliberating about it the whole day." I decided not to buy anything, and **not** to deliberate about it the whole day. I don't need to necessarily **buy** them something, something they don't need, to show my affection. Buying presents is often the product of conditioning, sometimes of guilt. I thought of a question: "Tell me, what is the difference between **to love**, and between **to be loved**?" Gaya smiled. "Nice association. That's an easy one. **To love** you know, right?" "Tell me anyway" I replied. "**To love** is simply to **realize**, or **feel**, that what (or who) is loved is, **in fact**, a **part** of you. You know what I mean. You cannot conceive of a **conflict of interests** between you and your daughters. Can you?" "No," I replied. "Ok. And **to be** loved?" "That one is more difficult. I believe that the (passive) concept of 'being loved' is the product of western, objectivist perception. If you separate between what is **you** and what is **not**, than it is possible for what is **not**, to love **you**. I think that the feeling of 'being loved' is a kind of therapy, compensation for the (artificial) separation within oneself."[65]

---

of reality, from the point of view which the speaker **is**. The monades cannot communicate with each other; They are opaque, impenetrable. Each speaker is 'locked' within his own conceptual scheme. When two speakers (monades) converse, Everything that 'happens', happens **within** each speaker: Each has his own 'picture' of the conversation, his own interpretation, understanding, perception of it.

The question is, whether all monades perceive and describe **'the'** same thing, or not. Leibniz thought they did. He believed they **all** described **the** 'universe', the world which God created. This creation of God, he maintained, was the **best** of all **possible** worlds. Apparently, they **do** all describe the same world. But Leibniz's **reality** was not **material**. Hence, the joint, objective (best) world all the monades perceive (from different points of view), was an immaterial, objective and good reference. A small step to saying that all monades (speakers) describe the same moral reference: **The Good**.

Besides Leibniz's *Law of identity* discussed above, Leibniz also phrased the *Law of contradiction*, which is, of course, of special interest here. This law basically maintains that contradictions are **impossible**, and their negations **necessary**. Besides necessary truths (and their impossible negations) Leibniz recognized a second species of truths: **contingent** truths. This species was exclusively for **human** 'use', whereas for **God**, all truths are necessary truths. For God nothing is contingent, coincidental. Only the human limited epistemic structure has contingent truths (and their negations, **possibilities**, or 'unnecessary falsehoods'). I believe that Leibniz's contingent truths are beliefs that concern **objects**, properties that are members in the (human) objective subdomain, e.g., 'the earth revolves around the sun', while his necessary truths are those pertaining to predicates: 'red is a color'. (And compare Plato's two 'modes' of existence!)

[65] Plato addresses this issue in the *Symposium*[105]. **Socrates** is the last speaker in a series of speeches of praise to *Eros*, god of love. Socrates brings up the problem of the distinction between the (action, or state of mind) of **loving**, and the thing **loved**. There is a kind of contradiction in the

We sat by a table at one of the cafes. Gaya continued: "The feeling of being loved is not really a feeling. It is something you **think about**, not an emotion. You **know** that you are loved. You don't **feel** it." I claimed the contrary: "Sometimes I do! I can often **feel** the love of my daughters. Or of my wife." "No." She flatly disagreed. "What you then feel is **your** love for them, not theirs for you. Give me an example of **feeling** the love of someone whom you **do not** love (back). Don't even try. It's impossible. 'Being loved' is an ego thing; A kind of compensation for the cruelty of the objective outside; An island of care and compassion in a sea of hostility. I predict you will gradually grow out of the need to 'feel loved'. What you **will** feel, is a growing love **on your part**, as more and more external things will become internal, 'your own'. Being loved is nothing but a disguised version of narcissism. Look: Every love is 'self love': **Loving** someone, someone **else**, is also, in a way, loving oneself. The 'else' being part of you. But by **loving**, the **whole** loves the part. In 'being loved', the part supposedly loves the whole. It makes no sense. The sovereign should love its subject. The requirement from the subject to love the King is twisted, wrong. Besides, **loving** gives you a great feeling. It exposes you to **good**.[66] It identifies

---

concept of *Eros*. Does it symbolize **love** or the **thing** loved? The **lover** or the **loved**? These two stand **across** from each other, and as long as they are, they cannot be described as **one**. Socrates' point is, that it is the **love** that counts, that is important. Love is the purest *conatus*, pure intentionality: The **longing**: not for anything in particular: It starts with longing to beautiful things, but later the love becomes a love of the 'abstract' (and for Plato, the **real**) *beauty*. Here Plato's vagueness regarding the relation between **good** and **beauty** is particularly evident. If beauty is taken to **denote** the good, Socrates' *Platonic love* becomes simply **love of** (the) **good**. Socrates (or Plato, but I think Socrates) understands love as lov**ing**, a verb, a state, not a noun, and, like Gaya, turns the focus of attention from the **object** to the attitude, or state of mind.

[66] It is now time to examine another use (and a distinct meaning) of the word 'good': As in the sentence: "It is **good for him**". In **this** sense of 'good', it is meant as a predicate that is distinct and different from 'G'. Before elaborating on this new predicate, I'd like to draw your attention to a particular part of my (personal) conceptual scheme. A significant part of it is devoted to **other speakers**. 'Another speaker' is, naturally, not more than a **property** in my system, but it has many important and interesting relations with other properties. Consider, for example, the property of (being) Esti (my wife). I also have many other properties, E1, E2, E3 etc., that are not **my** beliefs, but Esti's beliefs; or, rather, they are **my** beliefs regarding **her** beliefs. E.g.: 'Esti believes that **liver** is tasty'. This is **not** the belief 'liver is tasty', a belief that I do **not** hold. I have many beliefs of the form 'Esti believes that Y', although I may not hold Y (or I may). My conceptual scheme may be conceived as consisting of 'clusters' of **my** beliefs regarding the beliefs of people I know (people who in themselves are nothing but my beliefs).

Now, each such cluster has within it beliefs regarding the **preferences** of the people in question. Esti likes liver, so, **for her**, 'liver is good'. Each 'cluster', corresponding to a speaker I know (Even if it is a hypothetical speaker, like 'The western man'), has an 'internal' notion of 'good'. Note: This is by no means a statement regarding what is (objectively) **good** (G), nor does it have any value or significance **outside** of my conceptual scheme. It is just how **I** perceive the preferences of the people in question; What **I** consider them to be attracted to or repelled by. In other words, I have a whole

you with good. Being loved gives you nothing. If it does anything, is make you feel guilty for not loving back. If you're half decent, that is."

We went to listen to the *Kweekbak* band. It was a twenty (!) piece amateur jazz band, with every conceivable instrument. They were standing on a special platform that was especially arranged on top of two large flat boats, on the main canal, in the center of Edam. As it turned out, it had nothing to do with 'quick buck'. They pronounced it like 'quake-duck'. It was the most pluralist musical orchestra I have ever seen. There was a fifteen year old drummer, extremely talented, beside middle aged men and women, two or three gays, and a black young woman. They were having a great time, playing and dancing on the platform, that was really small for them all. I had as much fun watching them enjoy themselves as I had from the music. We sat very close, and I could look into their eyes. After it was over, we went to my favorite cafe and I asked Gaya: "What is the difference between **writing** music and **playing** music? Both are **art**, are they not?" "Of course" she said. "That is the beauty of it. Look: Suppose a painter sees a sculpture he considers very beautiful. He is impressed. He paints a painting, which is later (maybe centuries later) seen by a composer. He translates his experience into musical notes. Than someone plays the music - his own interpretation of it. These are all different **forms** of art, but still art. Communication. The painter can do a much better job than the sculpture, from **your** point of view, or the composer may compose a wonderful piece that is 'destroyed' by a musician. But also the reverse can happen: A talented musician can turn a mediocre, or even poor musical creation into an enlightening performance. In **jazz** this is particularly noticeable, as it puts so much emphasis on improvisation."

°

---

group of properties, one for each person I know, g_1, g_2, g_3..., and naturally, $\sim g_1$, $\sim g_2$, $\sim g_3$... which are the different **'bad'**s. (Some things are 'good for Esti' or 'bad for Esti', just as some things are 'red' and some are 'not red'). g_1, g_2... are **not** a **super-predicate** like G (my **own** good) is.

I have been discussing G (the property "Good", What **I** consider good; What is good for **me**; What **I** want; The subject of **my** desire, my *conatus*) and D (the property "God", entailed by all other properties) as two separate properties. Now is the time to reveal the fact, that in my (personal) conceptual scheme, these two properties G and D are **identical**: $G \equiv D$. This super-property is very different from the multitude of **goods** g_1, g_2, g_3...

°When I speak to Esti, I use the word 'good' in the sense of g_1, not of G. I **never** mean G when I say 'good' to someone **else**. If I want to effectively communicate, I cannot use a word in a sense I know is completely private. I sometimes find myself in need to change g_1, e.g., if Esti no more likes liver (or if I was mistaken in thinking she did, which is the same thing), but when speaking to someone, the meaning of 'good' should be as close as possible to her 'actual' preferences.

But supposing I want to change Esti's mind regarding something. For example, to convince her to stop smoking. She thinks smoking is good, and if I adhere to her usage of 'good', how can I tell her

We watched the crowd. Two clowns were entertaining the kids on the street. Gaya observed them, concentrated on the scene. Then she said: "Did you ever think *what it is like to be a clown*?" "How do you mean?" I asked. "I mean from **inside**. Not what a clown **is like**, when **you**, or someone else, look at it. I mean **being** one. Were you ever?" I didn't have to search my mind for long. "No. Just once, when I was three or four years old. I don't remember the experience, but I have photos. It would never even **occur** to me to wear a clown's costume. I'm afraid the connotations I have from **being** a clown are negative. It is a kind of an **insult**, being a clown; being **ridiculous**." "I thought as much" said Gaya. "This is why I asked. But if you give it a second thought, you may discover that it may be quite a trip. First of all, no one should know who you **really** are; I mean, behind the clown costume. So you are not ridiculous; just a clown. The clown is never ridiculous; It is the **person** who **acts like** a clown that is the possible subject of ridicule. But when you see a (strange) clown, there is no one 'behind' the clown. Just the clown. Anyway, think about it: You are **inside**. Possibly even slightly drunk, or high, or whatever. In a good mood - good on the **funny** side. You are allowed to do the craziest things! You can bother people, you can sing, shout, dance, show your behind. You **become** laughter, as much as that is possible. Clowns are often said to be tragic people. I suspect this is true; They are not happy in their 'normal' appearance. That is why they are clowns. But, contrary to common opinion, **when** they are clowns, I believe they are very happy." I watched the clowns playing with the kids on the street. They did seem to have a lot of fun. I should try that sometime. There were hundreds of people on the little street we were sitting on. I said to Gaya: It is amazing. I haven't seen an **Israeli** for the whole period I am here. Not even today, with all this crowd. Usually they are everywhere - you find them in the most God-forsaken places." "You miss home?" she asked. "Not really. But I wouldn't mind exchanging a few Hebrew sentences. I tried to pick up Hebrew sounds in the crowd, but there were none." "So make it happen!" she said. Is she doing it again? I tried, but nothing happened. "It doesn't work" I said, thinking of Mary Poppins. "Only you can do these things." Gaya disagreed. "Sure you can. Close your eyes." I did. "Now, visualize an Israeli couple walking down the street. Do it yourself. There is no point in me talking you through this. Just **imagine** the whole experience. Have a short conversation with them. Not long; I haven't got all day. And keep your eyes closed." It was easy. I did like she said, and in two minutes sent the couple away. I opened my eyes and said: "Well?" "Well what?" Gaya asked,

---

that I think it is bad for her? I simply say "**I think that** it is not good', or 'It is my opinion that..', or even 'You should reconsider whether you want to keep 'smoking' as something 'good'. The crucial point is, that I am **not** trying to change her understanding regarding the meaning of 'good' and 'bad'. These are fixed forever (in **her** system!) What I am trying to do, is change the meaning of **'smoking'**! To change the relation it has with Esti's (private, super-predicate) 'good'. I say: 'Change **smoking** from 'good' to 'bad', **not**: 'Change 'good' to exclude smoking'!

smiling. "I still don't see anyone". "They left, didn't they?" she wondered. I meant to say something with 'really' in it, but then decided to take a different approach. "Did **you** see them?" Gaya pointed at a cup of coffee that was suddenly on the table. It wasn't there before. "I wasn't here. When you were busy with your Israelis I stepped in and bought a cup of coffee. I must have missed them." **Very** smart of her, to exit the scene at the crucial moment. She continued: "Come on. You had no significant **purpose** in wanting to speak with a fellow countryman. You just wanted a chat, and for that you didn't even have to get out of your chair. I admit, that if you wanted something more complicated, like to send a parcel home, or something like that, it would have required a slightly more significant **effort** on your part. And still, you would have achieved it, if it were important enough for you. But this one was really simple. You got **exactly** what you wanted. The memory you have of your encounter is yours. It is there, as long as you want to remember it. What are you after, **magic**? Magic is something that cannot be done. If it can be done, it is not magic. But I know of nothing, absolutely **nothing**, that cannot be done, if **really** wished."

While walking back, I told Gaya about an R&D project I had in mind. I have already told her before that I am in the software business. I said: "I have what you might call 'a technological dream'. I plan to design a machine that will function like a human speaker."[67] Gaya wanted to hear more before she offered

---

° In my system, G is a special predicate, unique in that it is defined as denoting the property that includes every other property in the system. It is the **only** predicate in my system that can **never** change via a 'belief change'. Everything else can happen in the system: objects can fall in and out of existence, predicates may 'flip-flop' into contradictions, but G (like F) never changes, due to its special method of constitution: It was **defined** as the 'universally implied', or 'universally entailed'. I already remarked, that G (I then still called it D) is the mirror image of F: 'The negation of contradiction'.

G and F are the **nucleus** of my conceptual scheme. They never change, they are eternal. the structure of the system depends on them. they are **built into the syntax**. The only thing I can safely assume regarding a fellow speaker (provided she **is** in fact a speaker, which is in principle impossible to verify, contrary to Turing's[106] conjecture), is that her system contains **an** F and **a** G. I **cannot** safely assume that she has an **x**, even if she utters the sound 'existence'. Heidegger uttered this sound, and definitely meant something very different than what other people I know mean by the term. If she is a Buddhist, she might not even have a term that I can recognize as her equivalent for my 'existence'.

Eastern philosophers often refer to F and G as 'Yin' and 'Yang', respectively. Together, they are everything. They are enough to produce an infinitely rich conceptual scheme (or 'world'). They are the only two **safe** concepts in communication. One can be **sure** he understands, only in two cases: When a speaker tells him that something is **good**, or when a speaker refers to a contradiction. The Zen-Buddhist way to enlightenment uses the latter: It makes repeated referrals to the contradiction, with the intention of directing the focus of attention towards F.

[67] The project in question is based on the claim which is the heart of this thesis: That **being a speaker**, or being **rational**, consists solely on the syntax of P_1, coupled with an *apriori* notion of

an opinion: "What do you mean 'function'? Just **speak**?" "Just?" I asked. "Don't you know that it is practically considered impossible? I hardly told anyone for fear of being laughed away! You know, artificial intelligence has become a complete disappointment in the last few decades. A machine that could conduct a human-type discourse, able to learn, to enhance its vocabulary, even **make up** vocabulary as we often do, is presently considered an impossibility." Gaya smiled. "By 'just' I didn't mean to imply that it is trivial or anything. But what is your **purpose**?" Frankly, although I thought of it a lot, I never asked myself for the **purpose**. "To prove a point, I guess. A point in the philosophy of language." "To **whom** do you want to prove the point? Evidently not to yourself. You seem to me quite convinced." I wanted to say 'to everybody', or 'to my professors', but I knew better. Instead, I tried a different approach: "It would be a major technological breakthrough. Science fiction." Gaya was still not convinced: "Is it a **good** purpose? Will it do **you**, or anybody else, any good? Look, I don't know that it is not, or that it won't. All I am saying is, that I feel you have the wrong reasons. I think moral considerations should be taken into account before you have a lot invested in it. World history supplies a perfect example: The nuclear bomb. And I'm not even saying that it was a **bad** invention. Just that it has moral implications, and that the scientists working on it lost a lot of sleep over the moral issue. They had a real serious problem, because the moral questions surfaced **after** it was practically clear that it was feasible. In your case, you have the privilege to make the moral considerations before you move a finger. It is much better."

She had a point. At least she took me seriously. **Too** seriously. I said: "Ok. Let's talk about it. Suppose I succeed. We will have machines with a notion of **Good**, with intentionality, and with **will**, directed, of course, towards this 'Good'. In principle, they will be completely human. In their **thinking**, I mean. They will have different sense organs than we have." Gaya understood very quickly: "'Helen Keller' type entities, right?" "Even with better sense organs than her's. I think computers can be supplied with a wider range of sense data than she had. She had next to nothing". Gaya reflected for a moment, and then said: "I'll have to think about it. I think that it is an important decision. If you succeed, you'll have a new race screaming for equal rights in no time. Society will have to protect itself. There will be problems. On the other hand, I sound awfully conservative. It is not like me to say things like that. To be afraid of the future." We were already at *De Fortuna*. She added a last sentence: "It is not **the future**

---

desirability, or 'preference' (mostly referred to here as 'G', or 'the good'): A **moral** perception. The aim of the project would be to empirically substantiate this claim, by writing a piece of software that will pass the Turing test: Employ human-like lingual behavior, in a manner indistinguishable from a 'real' human.

that I worry about. The future will take care of itself. It is **you**. I'm just trying to foresee possible dilemmas you might find yourself faced with; dilemmas that might adversely affect your **happiness**. I want you to be **happy**." She turned and went to her room, looking thoughtful.

I spent the rest of the day in my room, writing footnotes. I wanted to squeeze in as much writing as possible, since I was planning to go to the concert after dinner - 'The bullshit blues band'. Sounds promising. I read some Plato, some Leibniz, and some Berkeley (the Bishop)[68], switching from **language** to **language**. I find it so much easier to understand what they have all **meant**, ever since I realized that they were all describing **their** conceptual schemes, **their** notion of 'good', and not **the** nature (or structure, or content) of external **reality**. It is almost amusing to see how great minds from different places and different eras **seem** to agree only on one thing: on the nature of contradiction. (And even here, since they describe it using **other** terms, it sometimes appears as if they are discussing different things).

I didn't think I'll see Gaya again today, but while I was sitting outside my room in the sun reading Leibniz, she suddenly appeared. "You know," she said "Your speaking machine reminded me of a story I once read in a magazine. You like science fiction, you said?" "I used to. Before I discovered philosophy." "You want to hear it or am I disturbing you?" I had enough of Leibniz anyway. They say he was snobbish and arrogant. "No, no. Please tell me." She sat beside me in the sun, putting on her sunglasses. "Three machines land on earth. The story focuses on one of the three, but the story starts with the other two. One of them lands in a rehearsal room of some musical band, maybe a jazz band, and displays

---

[68] Just a silly, over-quoted quotation I couldn't resist including:[107]

> There was a young man who said: "God
> Must think it exceedingly odd,
> If he finds that this tree
> Continues to be
> When there's no one about in the Quad."

> Dear Sir: Your astonishment's odd:
> I'm **always** about in the Quad.
> That is why the tree
> Continues to **be**,
> Since observed by

> Yours faithfully,

> God.

amazing musical abilities. It can make any conceivable sound, of every possible instruments. It learns very quickly, by imitating the musicians. It plays with the group, improvises with them, in short - a regular musician. But it does nothing else - just plays music. The second machine finds its way to a **chess** club. Similarly, it learns the game, and quickly becomes a chess master. But, as I said, these two are only the appetizer. It is the third machine the story is about. It lands in the house of some guy, who is very depressed because his beloved wife had just died, and he is all alone in a cabin in the mountains. To make a long story short, just as the first two machines learned to play music or chess, this one learned to **speak**. The machine tells the guy that it came from another planet, and that it is not really a machine, but a living thing. The really interesting part of the story is its end: As it turns out, the machine is not a living thing, but just a machine. But it is very sophisticated, and just as the other two did a great job in imitating a musician or a chess player, so did this one imitate a human being, a **speaker**, including the claim that it is a living creature. It was just very well designed. What I liked about the story, what made me remember it, is the surprise in the last page: In the epilogue, the three machines return to wherever they came from, and are analyzed by the creatures that sent them. They were sent as probes, to find out about human civilization. They played back everything the machines went through, and failed to realize that the third machine had a **conversation**. They thought that **speech** was just like playing music or chess: A human **activity**, not something that has meaning, that is **about** something else. That's it. the whole story. Hope you liked it. Bye!"[69]

She left as abruptly as she arrived. Good story. I liked it. It reminded me of another SF story I once read, also about aliens investigating humanity. Only much more **frightening**, pessimistic: It was about a scientist who was investigating the phenomenon of **humor.** He analyzed thousands of jokes and comic situations, with the aid of advanced computers. He eventually realizes, that there is no other explanation as to the source of humor, other than as an artificially implanted notion, probably by extraterrestrial. When he explains his findings to his fellow scientists, he describes humor as a kind of **virus**, that was deliberately introduced into human society for the purpose of studying human psychology. But by discovering the truth, he and his fellow scientists (followed by the whole human race) develop an **immunity** to humor, just as a body can

---

[69] Evidently, it is my claim, that what happens in human discourse is no different than other social activities such as playing music, chess, or dancing the Tango. What is particular to the social behavior called 'discourse' (which is just a 'game', as Wittgenstein has so eloquently established), is the fact that **some** speakers (mostly with a western education) believe that it **describes** something **other** than the speakers themselves; That the expressions are **about** something, rather than just expressions (such as music, or dancing, or any other rule governed social activity besides language). The hypothesis of **shared meaning** is a product of the objectivist premise of a **shared reference**.

become immune to certain viruses, or certain bacteria become immune to antibiotics. As the scientist gives the lecture explaining all this, he says: Now that you know the truth, can anyone here remember any funny joke? **anything** funny? They cannot, of course. Humor is gone forever.[70]

---

[70] Philosophy has hardly touched the subject of **humor**. Another unsolved mystery. The reason it should be the business of philosophy, is that it is clearly related to intellectual capacities and to the concept of **understanding**, as in 'understanding the joke'. It is impossible to experience humor without understanding what is funny. Sometimes a joke is understood a long time after it was heard.

One of the very few thinkers who have addressed the issue at all was **Henry Bergson**[108]. He was a French Jewish philosopher who operated in the late 19th and early 20th century. He was awarded the Nobel prize, in **literature**. Bergson was a metaphysician, bordering on mysticism, and rejected the materialist and mechanistic accounts of reality. He was highly regarded by William James and had a strong influence on Heidegger and French Existentialism in general. Bergson's *Laughter* dealing in **humor**, was published in 1900.

June 25 - Humor

It is Sunday morning. The most **beautiful** Sunday, with a capital S. Gaya was not at breakfast, and I decided not to look for her and to walk by myself. I am glad I did, because it was a wonderful experience. I said in the beginning of this book that I am writing it for my friends, at least the top part, the one I am writing now. So I will take the liberty of giving you a few paragraphs of description; Just a description of my morning walk. There is no punch line. If you think you are not up to a banal description of nature, skip a few paragraphs. (I don't know how many yet, as I have not yet written it).

It was a late night yesterday for the whole small population of Edam, because of the 'Bullshit Blues Band', which played until one in the morning in the main village square. It felt as if everyone was still sleeping, although it was already close to ten in the morning. It was **completely** quiet; Except for birds, of course. I walked out of *De Fortuna* and headed towards the village square, where the concert took place last night (maybe I'll tell you about the concert later). I walked slowly, breathing the cool air, that hadn't had a chance to warm up yet by the beautiful morning sun. After less than ten minutes of walking I spotted a bench that was facing a wide canal and shaded by large oak trees. I set down, paying attention. I watched sparrows, doves and ducks. A sparrow was busy looking for food. It was very close to me; I sat completely motionless. I watched its eyes as it was closely examining the ground it was hopping on. I wondered how it decides what is edible and what is not. All the tiny crumbs on the ground looked the same to me. But still, the sparrow could tell. It never hesitated for a second before taking this bit and not that. Then it began to nibble at some short wild grass that was growing on the ground. It was funny - it didn't look like a **bird** at all, nibbling at the grass. More like a sheep or a goat. I remembered how I fed a few sparrows with a biscuit the other day, when I was having coffee at the cafe. The sparrows knew **very well** that they liked the biscuit. They were around me as soon as I took it in my hand. How can they tell? By its shape? Maybe its smell? I don't remember having read anything about this. Amazing.

° Bergson made the following observations about humor (He discusses **laughter**, but means comedy, or **humor** in general): (1) It is **human** - An exclusively human phenomenon; (2) It is alien to **emotion**: Where deep emotion is involved, there is no humor. Humor lies in the domain of **reason** , not feelings. (I would here substitute 'reason' with 'logic'). (3) It is **social**. It happens in **public**, when at least two people are involved. Bergson emphasizes that humor is often associated with the **mechanical**, or automatic, where conscious **choice** is in order. Bergson maintains that whereas social life is demanding, requires attention and **care** (a notion Heidegger will later develop as central in his thought), the **disregard** for this requirement prompts laughter, whenever this disregard is not grave enough to invoke humor's foe, emotions. Social life requires **flexibility**, and

A duck family was having a morning nap on the canal. A green necked male, its spouse, and the slightly smaller (teen-age?) gray ones. They were just **sitting** on the water, slightly drifting in the weak current. One had its head under its wing, sleeping. The other was cleaning its feathers, and the other two just sat still. I kept hearing flapping noises above me. I looked up and saw a dove fighting with a twig. The twig was still connected to the tree, and the dove was trying to disconnect it, break it, so it can be used as building material. She couldn't break the twig, and kept switching positions to get a better grip. It was difficult, because she had no place to maneuver, as there were branches all around her; there was no room to fly. That was the source of the flapping noises I heard: She was flapping her wings, trying to keep her balance on the thin branch she was standing on. She seemed to give up on the twig she was after, and turned around to look for another candidate. She approached several, but seemed not to like them. She turned around again, returning to the one she was originally after, and in one decisive pull, managed to break it. She seemed proud of herself. She improved the grip her beak had on the twig, which was unusually long. I wondered how she will manage to fly out of the bush without losing the long twig, but she did. I followed her flight to see where was the nest she was building. It was on the same tree, about ten meters higher.

°

---

the **lack** of it is funny. He takes laughter to be a sort of mild 'punishment' for not completely adhering to society's rules. In his words *"The comic appears just when society, or an individual, are freed from the care for their self preservation and start to view themselves as works of art"*. **Stiffness** is comic, and **laughter** is its penalty. Physical deformations are sometimes funny because they manifest a kind of 'stiffness'. Caricatures are funny because they enhance certain features, 'freezes' them, in a manner untypical to an inherently **changing** subject: A human being. Impersonating someone is nothing but mimicking the **automate** that characterizes his personality; Something that has become **fixed** in him, rigid, like an **object**, not a person. An extremely close resemblance between two people is humorous because it portrays people as if they were duplicable **things.**

° Bergson considers any form of **disguise** to be comic. Not only disguised people, but even displaced objects, such as plastic flowers in a real garden. He observes that category mistakes are funny, also in the opposite direction: By attributing human properties to still nature, such as lady that was invited by a famous astronomer to watch an eclipse, but arrived late. She said: "Would you please start over for me?" The conventions and ceremonies prevailing in society are therefore a fertile source for humor. A central motive in Bergson's conception of humor is the **automatization** where it does not belong; Undue rigidness. This principle is clearly manifested when too much attention is directed to a person's physical body, rather than to his personality: When a person is treated (or treats himself) as if it was **his body** that is actually **him**, the situation is funny. **Sitting**, for example, maintains Bergson, is much more comic than **standing**, because it is **physically** more convenient; Actors in tragedies hardly ever **sit**. Actors in comedies sit much more frequently (or lie down). *"**Comic** is every system of actions and events, that provides an illusion of **life** combined with a feeling of **mechanical** order."*

I heard duck voices. I saw two of them swimming towards the bend of the canal, out of my sight. Then the dove returned. This time she was searching on the ground, where the sparrow was a few minutes ago. She was a beautiful creature; Green, brown, gray and white. She had four parallel dark stripes painted diagonally on her neck, on both sides. Animals must have an aesthetic perception. There is no other explanation to the colorful beauty so many animals exhibit. Their courtship behavior practically proves that they do. The dove was examining a twig she found on the ground. It was much shorter than the one she got before, but otherwise looked the same. She weighed it in its beak for a few seconds, then dropped it. No good. Why? She searched the ground a few moments longer, then decided to go for a near by tree. Another dove spotted her and joined her on the tree. Now she has company. On the canal I saw why the two ducks swam towards the bend: They were welcoming a group of six or seven other ducks, that were on a Sunday morning swim. The two groups merged, forming a flock of ten or eleven all together. I kept watching them. They must have quite an enjoyable life here in the canals of Edam: No predators, plenty of food... Then I remembered the invalid duck from last week, and thought to myself that they must have their duck-problems.

A minute later the morning-swimmers were back on their way. They continued their journey, A big green-necked duck leading the way. The family of four resumed its morning nap. It looked exactly as if the group came for a Sunday morning visit, stayed a few minutes, and then went on, maybe to visit other families along their course. I thought of Gaya. She claims that it is **me** that is the source of... No, just **it is me**. It is **not I**, one thing, sitting and watching **it**, another thing. It is **I**, enjoying **myself** (or my world, which is the same thing). Well, let it be me; I am proud of my world. I was concentrating on the feeling of **oneness**, when I remembered a short piece of the video movie from my daughter's 12th birthday party. We had a *Tarot* card reader, a young woman, as part of the entertainment. She was reading cards for the guests. She also did Maya (the birthday girl), and the cameraman got it on the tape. I was not present when it happened, but I saw the video several times. She said to Maya: (I almost remember the exact words): *"This card means that you are in control of your* **reality***. You have the power of* **weaving** *for yourself any reality that you wish..."* I often wondered about her use of the word **reality**. I suddenly understood what this young woman was saying to Maya, as I never did before.
°

° A frequent manifestation of this mechanicality is the motive of **repetition**, so frequently used in comedies. Repetition is something **non-human**. When a person constantly repeats himself, he is like a machine. He is funny. Bergson's equation is: 'Put the mechanical into the **living**, and you get **humor**'. The source of **seriousness** in life is our **freedom of choice** - our capacity (and duty) to exercise care. The humor in life emerges whenever this freedom of choice is replaced by some

116

I got off the bench and resumed my walk. I am telling you all this because I feel it is important. It is a genuine description of my state of mind; The most direct, non-filtered account possible. The whole purpose of this book is to tell a few people what I think about some important issues, and what I am describing is inseparable from what I have to tell. The content feeling, the beauty around me, seemed to me a direct consequence from a new **attitude**. So, in a way, I am describing the **reward** for adopting such an attitude. I walked the quiet streets. In the distance I could hear the church choir, accompanied by an organ. Ten o'clock service. I decided to get closer to the church. The singing was beautiful. Behind me I heard a child screaming. It was a scream of joy and excitement. I looked back, and saw two bicycle riders, a husband and wife, each with a small child as a passenger: The woman with a little girl, the man with a little boy. The kids were screaming in excitement. They were American. The boy shouted: Faster! Faster! The bicycle ride must have been a new experience to them. They looked to me like a family of ducks in a morning swim. I sat on the church stairs, outside, listening to the music. For a moment I thought of going in, but it seemed too much of a commitment. They might be offended if I walk out in the middle. And the music was audible from here. I saw a Sunday painter stand nearby, painting the view. Maybe he picked this spot because of the singing; I wonder how he will show it in his painting...

---

mechanical principle. Bergson rejects Herbert Spencer's explanation for laughter: *"An effort that was suddenly faced with a void"*, or Kant's similar claim: *"Laughter comes from an expectation that suddenly evaporates"*. He claims that the reverse is also often comic: Small things that got 'inflated': An insignificant event that grew out of proportion. Laughter, maintains Bergson, is a 'diversion from life' (I would add '**real** life'). A human imitation of the lifeless. Bergson noticed that humor is often associated with the intersection of two seemingly unrelated series of events, especially common in situation comedies. Another aspect of the same principle is the construction of a comic phrase by introducing an **alien**, sometimes absurd idea into a well known figure of speech, which is also a kind of 'category mistake'. Bergson provides no explanation to this principle in terms of "the living vs. the mechanical'. *Don Qichote* is, for Bergson, a paradigmatic example: His severe categorical mix-up between objects (windmills) and people (fierce knights).

Towards the end of his short book, Bergson summarizes: Human conceptualization is **teleological**. We make our **distinctions** in accord with our **goals**, of what we **need**. Humor is a deviation from this tendency. In the third and final section he offers a brilliant account of **art** as a manifestation of personal originality and individuality, as completely **non** teleological. **Humor**, he maintains, lies on the border zone between art and science; between the 'real' (social!) world and the individual; It is a **diversion** from the moral to the scientific. It is a special case of an individual's failure to adjust to society.

Laughter is one of Bergson's early publications, but his metaphysical views and ideas are already clearly visible; Particularly the emphasis he puts on the flow of **life**, the **human**, on the constantly **changing** nature of human existence. Bergson operated before the dawn of the linguistic turn, and puts no emphasis on the relationship between 'language' and 'reality', which to **us** seems extremely relevant when considering humor as a social phenomenon. But his Idealism and (future) mysticism are already there. It is only a pity, that a book about **laughter** should be as **un-funny** as this one.

This is the place to return to if you skipped the last few paragraphs of emotional babble. When I returned to *De Fortuna* Gaya was having her morning coffee. I said: "It is a wonderful morning." "Good morning" she said; "Did you have a **nice** walk?" I didn't know if she was insinuating anything, so I said: "Wonderful. You want to go again?" "No." she replied; "You know, I was thinking: Yesterday I spoke to you about the clown. I later realized that I am quite ignorant about the subject of **humor**.[71] When I spoke about the clown, I was talking more about **having fun**, than about **being funny**. There is a difference; probably an important difference. But somehow it escaped me. I am quite familiar with the western way of thinking, but every once in a while my eastern upbringing surfaces. In the east, **humor** is not **nearly** as significant as in the west. Buddha is not laughing. It is just **smiling.**" I never knew that. "Really?" "I think so" she replied. "I'm no expert, as I just said; But I suspect humor is **very** western. Can you think of **humor** anywhere in history **before** Greek comedies?" Well, I am no expert either. Definitely not in history. "You mean to say that humor is the product of an objectivist perception? If so, it is a strong point in favor of objectivism!" Gaya agreed: "Indeed. But how many times do I have to tell you: there is no **quarrel** between the two paradigms. I am only preaching against the **exclusivity** of either! Don't be so fanatic!" I wasn't fanatic. I said: "I'm not. Maybe I'm behaving a little like someone recently converted: 'Holier than the Pope' so to speak". Gaya was back to humor: "Yes. This is what I mean. I am not **stating** it. I am suggesting it. Let me tell you why: First of all, I cannot

---

[71] I tend to agree with much that Bergson had to say about humor. I agree that it is **social**, that it involves **category mistakes**, often between the category 'living' and the category 'mechanical', which are (usually) mutually exclusive. I also agree that it is often a question of undue **rigidness**, and that it excludes (and is excluded by) strong **emotions**. What I find that is **missing** from Bergson's account is something that could hardly be expected to be found there, and which is the general **arena** of this thesis: The philosophy of language. More particularly, the connections between **language** and **humor**. This connection **must** be significant, because of Bergson's first three observations: That it is **human, social** and **logical**. What other philosophical topic qualifies here more than **language**?

Humor is a phenomenon of **language**. Where there is language, there must be humor. Where there is humor, there must be language. Language is the **place** where humor **occurs**, or, rather, **is perceived.** The latter claim is trivial: Without language, nothing **much** can happen, let alone said (or laughed about). But the first claim is stronger. It means, that humor, as a phenomenon, is a **necessary consequence** of language. The justification of this claim will be outlined in the next three footnotes. As speakers S1 and S2 have demonstrated, lingual communication (a bit redundant, whereas every communication is 'lingual') requires the constitution of an objective subdomain; An objective world, **about which** the speakers converse. It is a **condition** for meaningful communication (the 'meaning' in 'meaningful' is provided by that very objective subdomain). Moreover: Every particular conversation presupposes a **particular** subdomain for the specific conversation. E.g., when a **joke** is told, the necessary background information is provided as a part of the joke, to act as the **context** of the joke; supplying the **presuppositions** required to understand it.

think of humor before the Greek[72]: There is none in the bible, is there?" I searched my mind from when I was God, and came up with one example: "Yes there is. You know how **Isaac** received his name? It is a derivative of the Hebrew word 'to laugh'. Besides, the word would not have existed if there was

---

[72] The Greek were the first **pluralists**: The first to recognize that there are many possible 'right' contexts. This is what **sophism**[109] was preaching: We have **our** reality, **our** way of thinking, but others are possible; even **legitimate**. Greek culture was the first to recognize the possible coexistence of different cultures. Before that, it was just a question of 'defeating the barbarians', as the Bible so clearly manifests.

The constitution of a **conventional** shared context is required for meaningful communication. But the Greek were the first to recognize that this context is not *Physis*, but *Nomos*: It is constituted by **people**, not some divine force or rule of nature. That is when **comedy** emerged, mostly based on **mistakes** people made in interpreting, or understanding, this *Nomos* - 'the rules'. Breaking rules that are generally agreed and provide the basis for mutual understanding is absurd, funny. Provided, of course, nobody gets hurt. If someone ignores it to the extent of causing damage, society protects itself. But in case no such danger exists, it invokes **laughter**: At the one that is unaware of the (evident) rules; the evident **structure of** (social) **reality**. And sometimes not even **social** reality, just plain reality.

It is the essence of language to **denote**: To be **about** the (objects in the) domain, the shared context. Every time it seems that this is **not** the case, every time some speaker makes a **mistake** (often considered a 'category mistake'), and his words seem to 'refer wrongly', it prompts laughter. Even when no **words** are uttered. When a clown tries to hang his coat on thin air, his behavior is in the domain of language, in the broad sense of the word. It is as if the clown says: 'I want to hang this coat on **this** hanger', when there is no hanger! Or, 'I expect the coat to remain suspended in the air', when "the air" is not something that can support a coat. The clown manifests a significant **misunderstanding** as to the nature of things, the **real** structure of the **real** world. It is the very same reason why kids consider insane people **funny**. Humor always involves a misconception as to the **real** (evident, presupposed) state of affairs.

Humor is found in **situations**. Situations are always a <u>lingual interpretation of some state of affairs</u>. A **wrong** interpretation, when it is **harmless**, invokes laughter; Maybe a laugh of **relief**, for no damage was caused as a result of the unfortunate instance of **misinterpreting reality.** A 'correct' picture of the world is essential for survival; Particularly essential for **society**. Failure to comply, to properly understand reality, is either **punishable**, or **funny**. In this I share Bergson's view, that laughter (particularly ridicule) is a sort of 'mild punishment' for not properly grasping reality, not completely adhering to the publicly agreed upon nature of things (or laws, or public **context**).

In a manner of speaking, **humor** is the thin film separating **epistemology** from **ontology**. If epistemology is taken as the (grasping of the) **picture** of ontology (what there **is**), Every instance perceived as doing it the **wrong** way is funny. The bigger the deviation from (what is considered) the **right** interpretation, the bigger the laugh; Unless there is **damage**. Humor emerges only when no damage is apparent (to the **laugher**, of course). In a way, it is a **substitute** for the **anger** society should feel when one of its members fails to adhere to its requirements regarding the (real) nature of objectivity. That is why mistakes in the (proper) employment of language itself are considered so funny. When a language is not well spoken (e.g. by a tourist or an immigrant) it is an endless source of laughter, because the incompetent speaker seems as if he has a completely confused objective subdomain: As if he has his **world** upside down: A strange, incoherent subdomain.

no laughing. It is absurd to say that before Aristophanes people didn't laugh." Gaya wasn't convinced: "Wait, wait. Don't jump to conclusions. Don't be so **dogmatic**. **What** was funny about Isaac?" Now I was the teacher. "That his mother should have a baby at ninety years of age." Gaya seemed to have taken it personally. She couldn't be **that** old; "What's so funny about that? I'm **serious**: **Why** is it funny? **What exactly** is funny about it?" Now I saw what she was doing. She was examining the first recorded case of **humor** in human history... Or was it in **western** history? I replied: "Let's see. It is **well known** that women of ninety have no kids." Gaya pursued: "You mean like a **law of nature**? We're talking about **God** here!" She had a point. I played along. "Sarah's having a baby at ninety was a **freak**. Even if God himself made all the rules, they were still rules. God's possible **deviation** from the rule, even if his own, seemed to her **funny**. This suggests the humor is somehow associated with **breaking a rule**." Gaya nodded in agreement. "Fine. But, of course, not **every** instance of rule breaking is funny. What makes **this** instance of breaking a rule **funny**? Besides, **who** broke the rule, and **who** laughed?" Maybe she was on the right track. "Let me see: **He** (if you don't mind me using the masculine) made the rule, **he** broke the rule, and **she** laughed. What do you make of that?" Gaya was thinking. I could **see** her thinking. I was fully aware of the significance of the event: This is the process by which she reaches her **conclusions**, her **truths**. Then she said: "No. I think this is a dead end. Breaking rules *per se* is not funny. Neither is breaking **one's own** rules. Maybe along the lines of 'laws of nature', like you said before. Ignoring a 'natural necessity', an inevitability. God's law can be perceived by Sarah as such. Suppose it has to do with ignoring an inevitable consequence, a necessity: Sarah was **doomed** in her childlessness. It was too late. If it just **happened**, it wouldn't be funny. It would be a miracle, but nothing **funny** about it. What was funny to her, is the absurd **belief** that it was at all possible." She was gaining confidence, and seemed to be thinking aloud: "Sarah, Abraham and God had a **shared context**. A certain agreed upon **structure** of reality, and the rules prevailing therein. All of a sudden one expresses a belief (even if it is God. He is extremely personified anyway): Reality **could**, or can, be different. Absurd. And funny. What do you think?" I tried to rephrase her idea: "You mean that the funny element is **breaking out of an agreed context**?" Gaya continued: "And there must be a kind of **blindness**, unawareness (to this context) which is involved: Someone is not **aware** of some fact regarding the **real** context on which the conversation is based... Wait, I think I got it. Look: Every conversation requires some agreed set of presuppositions. Right?" She didn't wait for an answer. "This set is clear. Obvious. It is the context the whole **conversation** is based on in the first place. The conversers are **aware** of this fact. Then someone, either one of them, or someone **else**, says or does something which implies his **unawareness** to some important aspect of the context in question. This unawareness is **funny**." She turned to me: "Can you think of a counter example?" I tried. I found it hard to recall any jokes. Anything funny. Maybe I developed **immunity**. Then I said: "Why are clowns funny?" Gaya had an answer: "Because they are **stupid**. They don't understand the evident: That they cannot pick up the ball if they keep kicking it. **Cartoons** are funny for the same reason: You know that cartoon figures only fall when they **realize** that they are standing on thin air. Falling is perceived as **epistemic** rather than 'natural', which is a funny disregard for the way things **really** are." I tried another direction: "Some cases of ignorance or unawareness can be **tragic** rather than **comic!**" Gaya nodded. "Good point. When does something stop being funny and becomes sad? When is it **overdone**? Sometimes it is not funny **in the first place**. I guess it depends on the **consequences**. If it is a hypothetical story, no one gets hurt. Even **death** or **torture** may be funny: Look at jokes taking place in **hell**. If a real person gets a creamy cake in his face, it **is** funny, because no **real** harm was done. You are right. Not getting the context may be a grave business sometimes. **But when it is not**, the reaction is laughter! 'Breaking the rules' is serious business. Society objects to it. So every instance of breaking the rules which does **not** have serious consequences, is funny! This is why extreme **fear**, if it proves **unjustified**, is followed by a burst of laughter! It is relieving, to find out that the proper context was missed, and **still** no harm was done. It's like 'getting off the hook'. Ignoring the rules without paying the price invokes laughter." I was already quite convinced that laughter is in fact associated with ignoring or disregarding some important and obvious assumption. I said: "This explains why **category mistakes** are funny: Taking things out of their proper context. I remember the funniest **impression act** I ever saw: Two guys impersonating **vegetables**.[73] It was hilarious. The **ultimate** category mix-up. It also explains **wit**: The ambiguous use of words so they have a second 'hidden' meaning, **not** in the regular context of the discussion. Paraphrases are like that: The adoption of some quotation in a different sense than originally intended. Incidentally, why do **children** laugh more than adults?" Gaya offered an explanation: "Because they are just **forming** a shared world, putting together their version of **the** world. Things keep jumping in and out of it. Also, what is funny **changes**: What used to be funny fifty years ago may not be funny today:

---

[73] Impersonation of vegetables is a good example of a category mix-up. Here the humor is particularly effective, because it comes in two layers: First, the very **idea** of impersonating a vegetable is funny, because it is usually **people** (and sometimes animals) who are impersonated, in the **real** 'impersonation context'. If everybody starts impersonating fruits and vegetables as well as people, this (funny) aspect would disappear, whereas 'impersonating vegetables' will join the objective, public context (of impersonations). Secondly, there is the impersonation itself, as is the case of mimicking anything (or anyone): The impersonator is **not** the one he impersonates; he is somebody **else**. Still, it **seems** it is someone else: It is as if he is saying: "I am him!" When he clearly (really) is **not**. Therefore, the more he **resembles** the subject of impersonation, the funnier the situation.

Either because the **world** changed, or because the joke became so well known, it became a part of it; or rather, of **language**. It is **always** just in language: It is a **product** of language, of the notion of 'shared context' which language **requires.** That's why funny costumes are funny: They are displaced - 'do not belong' so to speak. Also, what is funny to one may not be funny to the other. They might have different notions about what the agreed context actually is. But if two people are close, know each other well, they are bound to laugh in the same places.

Gaya had enough: "It's not **so** important, is it? You don't think we are **guinea pigs** of some extraterrestrial, do you?" "No" I replied. "But I have a personal interest: I seem to be losing my sense of humor. I used to be a great joke teller. Now I can hardly remember anything funny. I'm afraid I'm losing it." Gaya laughed: "It is a well known fact: Solipsists don't have a sense of humor!"[74] Then she smiled and said in a reassuring tone: "Don't worry. If I am right, there is a perfectly logical explanation. You are now in the process of **destroying objectivity**. You reject **any** shared context. You are fighting the materialistic conventions, trying to prove them for what they are. For you **now**, nothing is inside the context. Nothing is **self evident**. Nothing is a **ground rule**. Except **God** and **contradiction**, maybe" she said with a smile. "Maybe I should think of a joke about contradiction. No, seriously. To find something funny, you must take **some** context for granted, without questioning its **reality.** But you can still **understand** jokes, right? If you are **provided** with a particular artificial story, just for the sake of the joke, you still find it funny, don't you?" I agreed: "Yes. It's just that lately I haven't had many situations containing artificial contexts. I was too obsessed with finding out **the truth**." Gaya knew exactly what I was talking about. "Yes. You are much too serious. Time to change that. I think it will change anyway. You cannot float in your metaphysics for the rest of your life. You are bound to resume your **human** activities some time soon.

I wasn't **completely** satisfied. Not as I was when she taught me other things. But she said herself that she was not an expert. Maybe there will be a sequel. It was almost noon, and I said to Gaya: "I have to get on with my work. I am reading **Bergson**." "Oh, another Frenchman!" she proclaimed; "I like him. He deserves more credit than he got. He had some **really** interesting things to say about

---

[74] Solipsists don't laugh. They find nothing funny. For them, there **is** no objective subdomain: There is only **the** world, one world: Their own. Even if the figures appearing in it are acting strangely, it is, for them, just one of their own oddities. Nothing to laugh about. Nobody is mixing the language with the world. Only when the solipsists joins the (language) game, takes himself as a **player** in the game, not just as audience, he is able to laugh. To speak, he must use **language**, hence **some** objective subdomain; **some** context to speak about. And with this in place, there is already plenty to laugh about.

time."[75] "I'm more interested in what he had to say about humor" I replied. "It is your fault. You brought it up." She persisted: "And now I am bringing up **time**. Just pay attention, if you read him anyway. He **always** says something about time. I believe this is his biggest contribution. If you want, we can talk about it tonight. Or tomorrow". I knew that it was inevitable. I **was** going to hear what she has to say about **time**. Not that I wasn't interested.

I decided to take another solitary walk after dinner. Maybe because the morning walk was so nice. Besides, I wanted to watch the sunset again. So I went to the church. It was getting cool, and there was a breeze. I had my coat, but I was still cold. I got to the church and sat on the bench. I was blinded by the sun, that was still about two inches above the horizon. I forgot my sunglasses. I was cold. This was no magical moment. I thought of Gaya: What would she have said? I knew her very well already. We haven't spoken **that** much, but in an hour or two a day for ten days you get to know someone. And besides, she was on my mind most of the day, which also makes a difference. She wasn't there, but I still received her advice: "So why are you sitting there if you don't like it? Go do something more pleasant!" I obeyed. I started to walk the streets aimlessly, without knowing when I'll make the next turn. I did right (needless to say), because walking was much better. First, I wasn't cold any more. In the inside streets there was no wind. Besides, it was interesting. I was nodding hello to several couples of locals whom I passed; The locals have this habit of waving to their neighbors and friends who are sitting at home, behind the large glass windows. The people inside are hardly visible from outside, because for some reason they like sitting in the dark; Sometimes with the television on, sometimes with a small reading lamp. Either they save electricity or they like privacy. (But then, why have the large glass windows?) I was walking close to the windows, peeking into every house. I let myself do that, because, after all, this is **my** world; remember? I don't think they minded. I was just as much a sight for them as they were for me. Maybe **that's** the reason for the large windows: Maybe they are curious: Maybe they want to know who is walking in their street? The houses were all **very** tidy.

---

[75] The concept of **time** is central in Bergson's philosophy. He distinguished between **objective** time, a scientific concept, and a **subjective** perception of time, *duree*, which is a *substratum*, a domain **within which** humans live and act. Time is the subject of Bergson's first publication, *Time and free will*[110]. The scientific notion of time is **measurable**. It is an abstract, theoretical notion, posited by the intellect. It does not **exist**. Reality, on the other hand, is **made out of *duree***; a flux of shifting experiences that **never** repeat, never re-occur. It is purely subjective, and cannot be shared. It is closely related to his notion of **freedom**, which is also completely subjective, personal, private.

Free action, for Bergson, is the manifestation of **creation**. A person's carrying out what he authentically **wants** is a pure act of divine creation, a product of the *elan vital*, the life force, that characterizes everything **alive**. Bergson regards Zeno's paradoxes as products of attempts to conceptualize where conceptualization is not in order, but an **intuitive**, unintellectual perception[111].

Everything in place; Many ornaments. Behind one of the windows I passed sat a middle aged women and practiced first-step piano pieces. Two cyclists passed me. They were riding their bikes at high speed. I knew the people: A couple of locals who ate at *De Fortuna* occasionally. Probably on their way to visit some friends. It's really convenient, this bicycle business: Gets you anywhere in two minutes, without the hassle of a car. Nice walk. Good thing I didn't insist on the sunset. Serves me right, trying to duplicate a magical moment. Can't be done.

June 26 - Time

I went to bed with Bergson last night, to find out what he said about **time**. At some point I switched to *Heidegger*[76] whom I find even more enlightening on the subject. Before I fell asleep last night I zapped through the TV cable channels, and landed on one of the 'Karate Kid' movies (I think it was the second or the third). I was watching it for a few minutes, when I suddenly understood something about the eastern mind. A standard motive in most 'Ninja movies' is that the (good) master always tries to avoid a fight. He knows (as well as the audience) that he can easily defeat the bad guys, but the master's fighting skills are inseparable from his philosophy, his values, and he never fights unless it is absolutely necessary; Unless it is immoral **not** to fight. The master is often willing to be humiliated and laughed at, but still won't fight, until his life (and more often, some other innocent life) is seriously threatened. I always had great sympathy for this attitude, but always understood it as a basic **moral value**, a manifestation of the absolute morality of the hero of the story.

Watching the movie, (with Gaya, as always, in my mind) I suddenly realized that the Karate master had (and in general, **has**) her point of view. He knows that **it his him**. He takes the bad guys as just an unpleasant aspect of **himself**; They are

---

[76] As the name of his great book indicates,[103] Heidegger considered **time** a concept of major importance: On the same level as **being** itself. For him, the time coordinate was something **completely** different from **space**, which (for him, like Bergson) was just an artificial product of conceptualization. Like Bergson, he considered time (the subjective kind) to be an irreducible, primitive concept.

I already mentioned, that Heidegger understood the essence of being as **care**: *Sorge*. This care has three moments, or 'directions': (1) **'Towardness'** (*Sich vorweg*, or *'Zu'*), representing the human *telos*, its intentionality towards the **future**; (2) **'Withinness'** (*Schon sein* or *'Auf'*), representing the human circumstances, its awareness of the **past**; (3) **'Byness'** (*Sein bei* or *'Bei'*), representing the human context, its surroundings of the **present**. In those three respects we **care**, 'exceed our limits', extend **out** of ourselves (*'extatic modes'*). Time is the **mode** in which we live: The three extatic directions 'build', so to speak, the temporal domain of past, present and future. The things we know, or are, or care for, are of three 'kinds': 'Pastly' things (like **memories**), 'presently' things (which we understand as **occurring**) and 'futurely' things (which are our plans, wishes and fears).

The human situation consists of the 'projection' of these modes of 'care', to constantly 'reconstruct' our 'regular' past, present and future: a different, 'inferior' kind of time: time of **things**, not of *Dasein*. Heidegger distinguishes, in each of these 'directions', a 'right' way and a 'wrong' way of being: (1) Actively caring for the future, making plans, **vs.** just waiting for it; (2) Living the **moment** (another Heideggerian concept, meaning the moment of authentic exercise of free will) **vs.** passing the time, or 'killing time'; (3) Redescribing one's past, taking interest in one's own history, **vs.** forgetting it. The minute I was born and the minute in which I will die are **not** one event that is already over and another that did not yet arrive. They are both here, in us: They mark our **borders**, our 'two ends' (to use a spatial metaphor).

his experience, not an **external evil**. He does not want to fight (himself), create destruction and death (within himself). He does not mind being humiliated (as it is **by himself**). He cannot be insulted (by himself). He knows that he cannot lose the fight (unless he happens to have enough of this world, which happens to most of us sooner or later). There is no question of 'who will win': It his **him** who wins <u>and</u> **him** who loses anyway. The important thing is who plays the villain and who plays the hero. The master, playing the part of the hero, acts like one; and as such, he cannot lose, because he acted like a hero. He has no fear; just compassion for the poor adversary. When the master has no more choice, because he is faced with one of those unpleasant moments in one's life when a choice between two evils is in order, he **chooses**: He decides that the least evil would be to save the life of the innocent victim, while sacrificing the life of the villain. So he fights, and has no doubt whatsoever regarding the outcome, whereas he made the **right** decision. The complete confidence he has, is in itself a determining factor in the fight. He is cool, calm, focused, and he wins. It could not be otherwise, whereas the villain, as well as the victim and the whole surroundings anyway depend on the master for their existence: They are **his** experiences, his representations, his **reality**. I lay in bed, looking at the little Chinese guy (or was it Korean?), and could almost feel the quiet confidence he had, of not **being able** to lose, after he was compelled by the circumstances to engage in the crucial fight.

How could anything be **wrong**, if you are doing the **right** thing? The only source of wrong is the immoral action (or lack of it). When you **do** something wrong, it has a tendency to complicate: You have to cover up, from others, but especially from yourself: You start doing and thinking things designed to **justify** your wrong action. If you are lucky, your conscience bothers you; You feel **bad** for what you did. If you are lucky enough to have the chance, you try to make amends; You try to somehow **pay** for what you did. Not so much to improve on the situation of the damaged party, as to free **yourself** from the heavy burden of having been **bad**. Socrates was laughed at (and misunderstood to the present day) when he said that punishing a criminal is **only**, and completely, to the benefit of the criminal; That the **worst** punishment that could be inflicted on the criminal, is **not** to punish him. Sounds absurd, but how true! God did not punish Cain for the murder of his brother. He did **precisely** the opposite: He **marked** him, and warned the small population of the world (including animals) **not to touch him**. The worst punishment, by far, that could be inflicted on Cain, was **to let him live**. And the longer his life, the longer the punishment. Had God killed him right after the murder, Cain would not have been punished for his terrible act at all! God achieved a dual goal in keeping him alive: He gave him a (long) life sentence (in the role of the first and greatest villain in the world), while supplying humanity with a (literally) living example of **crime**.

126

It is summertime in Edam. No more clouds, just a friendly warm sun. I am dreaming regularly, but decided not to bore you with my dreaming bulletins. If something **startling** happens, I will let you know. I am starting to miss home, although I have not (nearly) had enough of Gaya. I still have almost a week. I met her at breakfast, and told her about my Ninja revelation. She laughed but said nothing. I asked: "Let me see if your theory about humor works: What was **funny**?" Gaya laughed again: "I hope this was a rhetorical question. Did you do your homework?" She was starting to act like a high school teacher; I wasn't sure I liked it. I said: "I tried, but failed". Gaya softened up. She said: "You know, you can **ignore** me if you want. I am not forcing myself. It is an age-old question, who is to blame for the student's failure: The teacher or the pupil. Even Plato failed to solve this question." I wondered at her explicit confession of being my **teacher**. I said: "Is it true what they say in the east, that it is the *Guru* who finds the pupil, and not the other way around?" She answered like a shrink: "What do **you** think?" She was smiling, so the question was, of course, rhetorical: No doubt **she** found me. I said: "Following your teachings, I would say that I **summoned** you. So in a way, it is the pupil who is the **cause** of the encounter. Besides, the question is wrongly phrased in the first place: There is no sense in asking 'who finds whom?', **objectively**. I have **my** point of view, **the** point of view of **the** pupil; I was emphasizing the **the** deliberately; "And from this point of view, which is the only one, **I** found **you**." Gaya did not praise me for my deep understanding. instead, she focused on my way of speaking: "You keep using the phrase 'point of view'. You make it seem as if it is just a question of your **angle**, of the **place** from which you observe. It may be misleading. You may be understood as saying that different people have different points of view of **the** reality." I was aware of that. I said: "I know; But the alternative is unintelligible. It is next to impossible to explain, to understand. This is why solipsists were always laughed at by most. How can I speak to someone, and explain to him that he does not **independently** exist? It is so self-refuting! By engaging in the conversation, I already **accept** the very thing I deny: Objectivity!" Gaya nodded in agreement. "It **is** a major problem: *On what we cannot speak, we must remain silent.*[77] But there is a trick. When trying to

---

°Heidegger rejected the common conception of time, by which **we**, our consciousness, **move** along the time axis. He maintained, that such a conception renders everything inexistent: The past already passed, the future is not yet here; Neither **are**. And the present, before we have a chance to say anything about it, falls out of existence. Heidegger took **being** as fixed, 'stationary', so to speak. it is the **world**, the 'story', that moves: We keep rewriting our **past**, as well as the future. It is the framework by which we grasp ourselves.

[77] **Ineffability** has nothing to do with mysticism, contrary to common opinion. Something is ineffable if it undermines the very presupposition of effability; the pre-condition to the employment of language. Language **requires** an objectivist premise: A **something** that **is** discussed. Discourse is

convey this idea to someone, instead of claiming that **I** am alone, I claim that **he** is alone. I adopt **his** language, if I can, and **join him** in what you call '**his** point of view'. After having done that, after 'joining his world', I show him how everybody **else**, particularly **myself**, are dependent on **him**. I make **him** the center. This cannot be done in **writing**, because I have to gain his confidence as someone who speaks his language, who understands him and is understood by him. This is why Socrates didn't write a single line. You are in for a great disappointment, if you think you can transfer all this to a hard document. You will not be understood. Nobody was." With this I strongly disagreed: "You are **wrong**. I am not writing this for the general public. I am writing it for my **friends**, including close relatives. These are people who not only speak my language, but already have the required confidence in my sanity and motivation." She retreated: "In this case I agree. All the others also had a close circle that understood; In different languages, in different eras." I carried on my attack: "And I also disagree **in general**. Who was the last philosopher who offered a complete system, in writing, that was phrased in non-technical jargon? After Plato, I mean. Kant, Hegel, Heidegger, all had **systems**. I don't think they understood **less** than I do. But they were all academics. Their environment was academic. Their **ordinary** language was professional jargon. The ones that spoke the same jargon, understood. **My** ordinary language is much more **ordinary** than any of them. That is why I am writing two texts at once. I think my ideas are **grounded** in logical considerations, and my footnotes provide the **credibility**, so I won't be considered another mystic lunatic. But the stuff I am writing for my friends could be understood by anyone. Maybe the logicians will say I have a point in the footnotes, and this will draw attention to the ordinary language text, make it worth the effort of trying to understand it."

We started to talk about **time**[78] as soon as we embarked on our walk. I said: "I found more in Heidegger than in Bergson." "Tell me" she said. "They manage to

---

social, it involves more than one conceptual scheme. So some premise of shared context is required. It doesn't make this premise some kind of 'eminent truth', but it still is a condition to engage in the language game. Arguing for Solipsism does not cohere with the presuppositions required for **arguing**. That is why solipsism is impossible to defend, and the reason Wittgenstein[112] kept quiet about it.

[78] One of the few recent attempts to address the issue of **time** is what is known as *McTaggart's* paradox.[113] He (also) distinguished between two separate 'time-series': **(1)** Series 'A', characterized by the concepts 'past', 'present', 'future', 'now', 'tomorrow' etc. This is the subjective, intuitive notion of time. **(2)** Series 'B' is characterized by the concepts 'earlier than', 'later than', 'simultaneous with'. The paradox is based on the following two claims: (1) Series A is more **basic** than series B; (2) The use of series A in science leads to contradiction and infinite regress. Moreover, although series A is clearly more basic, series B is **irreducible** to series A. McTaggart's conclusion: Time is an illusion.

explain 'time' in general. Particularly its importance, its primitiveness. But I couldn't find an explanation for the simple, day-to-day phenomenon of 'passing time'. For example: We met in the dining room about half an hour ago. Let me rephrase it into subjectivist language: **I** met you in the dining room half an hour ago. I am **now** in the present. I have memories from half an hour ago, and memories from a minute ago, and I have various beliefs regarding the connections between the two. How is this distinction created? Both Heidegger and Bergson have two separate notions of time: Objective, scientific time, which they consider a convenient fiction, and **real**, human, subjective time, where human authentic **will** is manifested. The second kind is still vague to me, and it does not explain to me how the 'regular', objective time-difference between **now** and half an hour ago was constituted." Gaya listened carefully, and then replied: "Let us see. You are **used** to the passage of time. I mean, your *worldview* has a whole bunch of rules that are constantly in operation. For example, you consider it completely impossible that the time now would be the same time as it was when we had breakfast." I asked her to continue. "Had you **not** assumed that, your whole *worldview* would collapse. You **want** time to pass, because it keeps your beloved world intact. You **could** stop it, of course. If it is **not** beloved. You could jump off a bridge. But, for some reason, it is beloved. It is your world, it has 'rules of operation', and you don't want to lose it. That is why thirty five minutes have passed since you met me at breakfast. It's your **choice**. Your **will** that this **should** be the case. Now, suppose you don't want to **stop** it, just make time pass **quicker**, or **slower**. When would you want that?"

^o

So far so good. McTaggart had not said anything that Bergson and Heidegger didn't know. What is interesting, is some claims made by distinguished thinkers (including Quine), that series A is the one that is reducible to B. In other words, that A is **not really** more basic than B, contrary to our basic intuitions. This is not the place to elaborate on the details of the proposed reduction; But the problem centers on defining the **present** in terms of series B. There is no escape from admitting the **subjectivity** of the present, be it conceived as simultaneous with a **mental act** or a reflexive **utterance** of some speaker.

Here is my view regarding the McTaggart paradox: I believe McTaggart's analysis to be valid, although not **paradoxical**. Why should either series be reducible to the other? Because both are denoted by the same English word? Because they seem related? 'Time A' and 'time B' are as different in nature as is **pain** from **gravity** (although gravity can cause pain, if one falls). It is a clear case of a category mistake. One is a very subjective concept, like 'love', 'fear' or (the sensation of) **red**, and the other a scientific concept, like 'atom', 'force' or 'wave length'.

^o An **objective subdomain** shared by (at least two) speakers is composed, basically, of just two **kinds** of things (properties that are **objects**): Of **rules** (mostly 'laws of nature') and of **past events**. The first kind (rules) is none of our concern here in the discussion of time, and will therefore be ignored (although I hope to address it later on). I wish to concentrate on what constitutes the **bulk** of any shared context, any objective subdomain. It has already been established and reiterated, that language **requires** such an objective subdomain, a shared, fixed **context**. A group of things that

She got right down to business. Either she had a great analytic mind, (In case she was doing this for the first time), or she knew the answers, and just systematically led me to them. I cooperated: "When I am having a really pleasant time, I want it to pass slowly. Like when I sat by the church." Gaya took another step: "And? What happened? You don't wear a watch, but you sat there as long as you **wanted**, right? When you got up, it wasn't because time was up. It was because you didn't **want** to sit there any more, right?" I agreed. she continued: "Now, let us suppose that you had a meeting, and you didn't have all the time you **needed,** to enjoy what you were doing. Suppose you were meeting **me** at, say, ten thirty, and you only had ten minutes to sit there by the church, if you didn't want to be late. What would the situation be then?" I thought for a moment, and replied: "First of all, I wouldn't know. I don't wear a watch. I took it off several months ago, because it somehow felt wrong to be governed by a little instrument on my wrist. Come to think of it, I haven't been late once since I did this. Just because I don't wear a watch, I take wider margins. I always have an extra fifteen minutes. So it is very unlikely that the situation you described would happen. If I had a meeting with you, I would not have gone to watch the sunset. Maybe it is a kind of **care**: If I want to be both spontaneous **and** responsible, I don't put myself in such situations of conflict. Still, it could happen. But I'm starting to see your point: You say I **could** stretch time, even if I was in a hurry; Only there would be a price to pay; A **moral** price: I would be late." Gaya continued: "Not so fast. First let us examine the other case: You want time to pass more quickly; to 'shrink', so to speak. What do you do then?" I laughed: "I go to sleep". Gaya lightened up by this answer: "Wise move. But let us say you are sitting in an airport, and your flight is delayed. You cannot go to sleep. You are not tired enough to sleep on a bench. You'd like time to **fly**, but it doesn't. Why?" I identified with the situation. It happened to me more than once. I said: "Now the concept of **boredom** enters the picture. If I wasn't a person who gets bored, I wouldn't want time to pass quicker. But sometimes it is the mirror image of the preceding case: When I am **suffering**, I want it to end quickly." Gaya seemed puzzled: "Let me see: You mean your suffering is somehow

---

cannot change, so that everyone would be able to speak about them without them changing meaning in the middle of the conversation. The fixed, unchanging beliefs that are shared by everyone are the facts of the past. These facts are **constituted** as unchangeable, for the benefit of effective communication. It is **agreed** that the past cannot change, because 'the past' is a general name for everything in the objective subdomain that cannot change any more. A speaker (such as Dummett[114]) that will have the nerve to claim that the past may be changed (not our view, or interpretation of it. **The** events themselves) will not be taken seriously, because such a claim undermines an extremely important constitutive premise: that there **is** a certain subset of things that will not change any more. It provides the speakers with a clear, solid base to construct their (shared) world on. "The past" is the **hard** facts of reality, the unquestionable, undebateable part. There may of course be debates regarding **what** the events of the past were, but it is agreed that what **is** in the past, remains like it is forever.

externally regulated to last for a specific period? Give me an example." I searched my mind, then found one: "The dentist. He has a clock on the wall, and I know it usually takes twenty minutes. And it hurts." "Fine. What is **bad** about this pain?" Again a moral question entered the discussion. First **responsibility** and now **bad**. What didn't I like about pain? What is **really** the problem with pain? Particularly with the dentists, where the pain does not **signal** a problem, but marks its **solution**! I had no answer. "I don't know." Gaya said: "I don't want to divert the discussion to **pain**, although it is an interesting topic. Let us remain with the dentist. You could easily 'shrink' the time, solve your problem: You could simply leave the chair. There would be consequences to pay, naturally, due to the specific structure of your world, in which evading **this** pain will cause **more** pain in the future.[79] But you could still solve the particular problem and shrink the time."

Gaya went on: "So you can **stretch** time, sit by the church for as long as you want, and you can also **shrink** it, by just leaving the dentist's chair. What you seem **not** to be able to do, is to control the little arms on the face of the clock. But these arms are certainly not **time**. No one claims that they are. It is an instrument, designed to help people do various things. Do things simultaneously. Coordinate their appointments. Like 'we shall meet at the oak tree when the sun is highest in the sky'. You have no reason to want to affect the movement of the little arms. On the contrary: You do **not** wish to mess up everybody's appointments. It is your subjective feeling that you want to affect, and you clearly **can**! I think that Bergson's and Heidegger's distinction between the two 'kinds' of time was a bit misleading to you. In **your** vocabulary, It is **private** time and **social** time. Social time is part of the objective world; A concept that is an important tool in communication. It is **posited** for this purpose, just as you posit 'the law of gravity' almost a century after Einstein. Forget about this

---

[79] And what, then, is the **future**? It is everything that is left, besides the past. The present can be safely disregarded, because it is so insignificantly 'thin', practically inaccessible. The **future** is the contents of the objective subdomain, for which it is **agreed** (amongst speakers) that it **may** change. The future is the 'space' in which the lingual conventions **allow** us to exercise our freedom, to make our choices. I may say: "I **will** write a book", or "a book **will** be written", although no speaker knows the book I am talking about. My use of the future tense explains to the community of speakers that **although** they do not have a corresponding object, they may safely add it to **their** subdomain, because it is something that is **allowed** to happen: A change in the world which is **permitted**. The **tenses** language contains are required to make the distinction between the **factual** (things the community of speakers **forces** into every speaker's subdomain), hence not subject to human will, and the **possible**: subject to will and intention. It is here important not to mix this notion of 'possible' with usage such as 'It is possible that Plato had a beard'. This second kind of possibility is not subject to anybody's will. No one can retroactively grow a beard on Plato's face. This second usage of 'possible' is not **ontic**, but **epistemic**. These two meanings of 'possible' are clearly distinct.

concept. It is clear and well defined. What you find mysterious is the *Duree*, Bergson's concept I suggested you read about. It is a **feeling**, a subjective feeling; One that cannot be shared. Some of your **moments** are good, some are bad. They are not **long** moments, neither are they **short** moments. They are just moments. They become 'long' or 'short' only when something **interferes;** if something is **wrong**: Either if you didn't have **enough**, or you had **too much**. In order to understand *Duree*, you must first understand how it is that you have too much, or not enough. These are situations to **avoid**."

We were making real progress. We sat down on a bench facing a thousand cows. I wanted more: "You mean that the pain by the dentists is also a question of responsibility, just as the case with our ten-thirty meeting? That I have a moral obligation to do something, so I **voluntarily** endure the twenty minutes by the dentists, or shorten my pleasure of watching the sun set?" "Yes" she said. "To preserve **both** your *worldview* and your morality. Your **moments** are as long or as short as you **want** them to be. It is better to say that they 'have no length'. The standard *meter* in Paris that is the standard for measuring lengths **has no length**. It is absurd to say that it is one meter long, because it **defines** what 'one meter long' means. *Duree* cannot be measured in units of time. It is just a **moment**. Every isolated conscious experience you have is exactly one **moment** long. You may also say that it lasted ten minutes, but this would only be a way to **communicate** with someone, because you cannot share your *Duree* with someone else. You need to relate to concepts that you **share** with him." "But **you are now** talking about it! about *Duree*, about a **moment**." "But you **realize** that it is just **your** moment we are talking about, not **an objective** moment. The word 'moment' is a really interesting word: It survived the objectivist plague: It is completely undefined (regarding its **length**, at least), yet widely used. Incidentally, you were right to bring up **boredom**. Another sad side-effect of objectivism: You sit at the airport, having a **moment**. Why do you want to do something else? **Who said** that you need to do something else? Only if you are in a **strange** world, in someone **else**'s world, you can feel bored. If you realize that you are **at home**, in your own world, boredom is impossible." After a moment's pause, she added: "Unless you have a dirty conscious. Then you want to **forget**. You want to do something distracting. Sometimes this is what boredom is all about. I can almost **guarantee** that you have seen the last of **boredom**."°

° I meant no disrespect for **Dummett** (whom I greatly admire) in saying that he had the nerve to claim that the past can be changed. On the contrary: His anti realism (regarding many things, **including** the past) is a view I strongly sympathize with. Dummett addresses this issue in two brilliant articles: *Bringing about the past*[115] and *Can an effect precede its cause*[116]. His point being, that there is no **logical** constraint on affecting changes to past events. In fact, it has been done. It is done all the time. This is what **historians** do. It is usually disguised as 'opinion' or 'interpretation'

I was **very** content. I felt it was a really significant lesson. And she prepared it in advance, no doubt. She specifically ordered me to read; gave me a home assignment. I decided to **stretch** this long moment as much as **morality** would permit. I said: "Tell me more about **moments**." She willingly continued: "Heidegger thought that a **moment** was when **freedom** is carried out; When **care** is exercised. What Kirkegaard meant by 'moment' is: 'A burst of **eternity** into the flow of time'. I have a slightly different conception; a different **articulation**, because I definitely mean the same thing. I prefer to think of a **moment** as the **gap** between two conscious choices, two **decisions**. In mean 'decision' in a moral sense. Some people are like automatons: They hardly ever decide. They are like **objects**, manipulated by circumstance. They have very 'long', blurred gaps between the few conscious decisions they do make. A **moment** is a **gap**, a *Duree*. A decision is a **point**, an instance. A decision marks the end of one **moment** and the beginning of the next. When you **decided** to sit on the bench by the church the other evening, it was a conscious moral decision. It marked the beginning of the **moment** you called 'magic'. Then, at some point, you made another decision, another choice: You decided to leave. This marked the **end** of this moment. Even if you lit a cigarette in the middle, it didn't break your **moment**, because it was not a conscious, moral decision. But if you consciously thought of lighting a cigarette, weighing the moral implications, You would have had **two** moments there on the bench: The decision to light (or not to) marking the end of one and the beginning of the other. What the wise always preach for, is for **all**, or at least most of one's decisions to be moral, conscious ones, not automatic: Ones that mark the borders of **moments**. A young private in a battle field may have ten separate moments in one **minute**. A chairman of a large corporation, on the other hand, may have (meaningless, practically unconscious) moments that last days, or weeks. You should read more *Existentialists*.[80] They have a good understanding of **time**, although they are poor **speakers**."

I decided to follow up on another topic that came up before: "And how about **sleep**? It apparently serves as a sort of 'time machine': I **decide** to go to sleep,

---

or 'analysis', but in the cases they manage to **convince the public**, to the extent of affecting the literature and encyclopedias, They did precisely what Dummett claims can be done: They changed the past; They changed the contents of the community's objective subdomain. (The same thing happens with **rules** or **laws of nature**: Scientific 'revolutions' change these laws 'retroactively', affecting a change in everybody's objective world. More about rules later).

[80] The way I understand the term 'Existentialism', the view presented here is clearly existentialist. The terms **Care**, **Duree**, **Authenticity**, and many others are all part of existentialist jargon. It is a great pity that their writing is often so obscure. But then again, how clear can they be, when they undermine the basic premise of **objectivity**.

thus marking the beginning of a moment, and the next thing I know, I **decide** to get up (in the morning)." Gaya smiled: "Or **not** to. Yes. I agree. Every **sleep** is such a gap, a moment. Unless you wake up in the middle, and squeeze in another decision." I thought of the other night, waking up several times, paying attention to my dreams. I said: "But **why** do I need to go to sleep? Why do I **decide** to go to sleep?" Gaya replied: "There are two answers. First, your *worldview* has the concept of 'sleep' as something which fits in the picture: Living things need **rest**. So you comply by the rules of your own world. But there is another, maybe 'deeper' explanation: Sleeping is a sort of 'trick': You keep your world 'running' without personally supervising it. It is tiring, exercising **care** all the time; Keeping your world in motion. The development of the ingenious concept of **objective** time, the use of mechanical **motion** to measure this objective abstract entity, enables a person to take a break. **Not** to be there, and yet enable his world to go on spinning. You 'set it', and it can run by itself, for short periods. Sometimes for longer periods, as in cases of a long coma. Only then, there is the danger of waking up to something quite alien, of course."

She was patiently waiting for my next question. She must have decided to let this go on for as long as I **chose**. She had this way of **explaining** and **demonstrating** at the same time. Naturally, I thought of **dreams** again. Dreams **happen** during a **moment** of sleep. What is their significance? I asked. Gaya smiled. "Am I having a *Deja vu* or have we been through **dreams** already?" I smiled back: "That was before you so nicely explained **sleep**. Besides, now that you brought it up, you might also explain the phenomenon of *Deja vu*."[81] Gaya sighed: "What

---

[81] The phenomenon of **Deja vu** is similar to that of **dreams** in the relative disregard it receives from philosophical circles. At most, it is left to the attention of psychology and cognitive science. It is an inherently subjective feeling, unmeasureable, hence not a convenient subject matter of science. So it is forgotten in the twilight zone between science and non-science. The failure of the prevailing metaphysical paradigm to explain these phenomena (and many others) acts as evidence for the need to replace **realism** with a better explanation.

I believe **Deja vu** is a case of an **unconceptualized memory**. Memories must be conceptualized; To be remembered, an experience must have a **place** in the network of beliefs that is my *worldview*. The memory cannot just 'hang' there by itself. It has relations with other concepts (beliefs and properties). Even extraordinary events have a context to which they belong; their 'environment' in my conceptual scheme. When something happens which fits **completely** with my system (e.g., the sun rises) there is no reason for me to remember it: It "was there" to begin with. When it is, in a sense "new" (e.g., the streets of Edam), new concepts are formed, having their particular place in the total network. The big church in Edam is a new concept, with relations to old concepts ('church', 'big' etc.) and to other new concepts (the street it is on). Still, some parts of my system I call 'beliefs', and others 'memories'. They are both properties, but 'beliefs' belong to the genus 'generalized', while 'memories' to 'particular'. The distinction is clearer when we view 'memories' as something that may be forgotten, and 'beliefs' as something that are not. Memories are the 'end-nodes' of the system: They do not include any other property. The particular memory of a tree I noticed on my walk, is **included** by many other concepts, but includes none. If I lose it (forget it),

will happen when you run out of questions?" I replied without hesitation: "I will start **answering** them, like you." She had nothing to say to that, so she complied: "Describe to me the feeling of *Deja vu*." I said: "What's there to describe? A situation seems **familiar**, although it is not a memory." "Nicely put" she started; "You feel you've 'been there before', right?" She didn't wait for an answer; "What is this **'there'**? **Where** have you been before? In the **situation**, right? It is a sort of **reoccurrence of a situation**. Now, what is a **situation**?" This time she expected me to reply. "A feeling? The state of my world?" I tried. She had a forgiving smile: "A **moment**. We just discussed that. It is a similar **moment**. But in what **way** can moments be **similar**? When you have the feeling of *Deja vu*, you are suddenly forced to **pay attention**. Even if you were not particularly conscious, the feeling **makes you** conscious. It is as if you are telling yourself: 'Pay attention! You've seen this before! Right?" I had to agree, but asked her to say more. She continued: "It is, of course, **wrong** to ignore it. It is significant. I believe it is simply a **point of decision**, one in which it is **right** for you to decide something. A kind of reflex, reminding you that you neglected to pay attention, to care for something that is somehow associated with the scene you are experiencing.$^{\circ}$

I was thinking about this morning's conversation the whole day. Everything seemed to support Gaya's story. For example, the fact that children have a different subjective feeling of time: For them, a month is a much **longer** period

---

No **other** concepts will be lost. 'Particular' concepts (memories) do not support **other** concepts in the system. They are just **supported** by others. If I lose a memory, my *worldview* remains intact. If I happen to lose a generalized concept, a **belief**, my *worldview* will be damaged, because all concepts included in it will be lost as well.

$^{\circ}$But some experiences are not even conceptualized: I am not **conscious** of having the experience. I am walking in the streets of Edam, I hear a dog bark behind me, but I do not conceptualize it. The experience of the particular bark does not get **connected** to any other concept in my system. It is possible, that it will be conceptualized an hour later: If someone will say to me: Remember the dog that barked behind you? The bark will immediately become conceptualized: It will become a **memory**, a member in my conceptual scheme. The mystery lies in the status of the bark in the interim period: The hour that passed between the experience and the question (and consequent conceptualization). I have no clear explanation to this mystery, although I suspect that it has to do with the fact that the 'one hour' is **itself** just a part of the system, as outlined in the discussion about **time**.

Nevertheless, if we assume the possibility of 'detached' concepts in the system (like the bark, before it was conceptualized), properties that, although included in the system have no relations with any others (except, of course, F and G), then we would have absolutely no **access** to them. Their 'isolation' will make them impossible to reach. In other words, **nothing would bring them up**, as they are not **associated** with anything. A further speculation may lead us to assume, that we may, **by accident**, come across this 'isolated concept' again. We would not **remember** it, whereas it has no relation with any other concept; But it is still **there**; Hence the odd feeling of Déjà vu: "I **know** it, but it connects with nothing".

135

than for an adult. Children have **more moments**. They are not restrained by as many **external** rules, laws and constraints. They spontaneously choose and decide, sometimes once a minute. Having more moments results in a subjective feeling of a 'long time'. Routine, on the other hand, in which not many decisions are required, makes time **fly**. This is also the reason, why the first few days in a new place, in new circumstances, always seem like a longer period than the last days in the same place: My first week in Edam seemed like eternity, while this, last week simply flies by: In the first days I constantly **decided**: Eat here, eat there; Walk here, walk there; I tried a variety of alternatives, checked out nice locations. I don't do this anymore. I already know the place; I am in a **routine**, making much less decisions, have less **moments.** So time seems to pass much more quickly. Some people feel that their life 'simply flew by', and before they noticed, it is almost over. Those people simply refrained from choosing, from making (real, authentic, free) decisions; They had very few **moments**. For me, the last two years of my life seem like three life-spans.

After dinner I went to watch the sunset again. I've become addicted to sunsets. This time I didn't go to the spot by the church; I knew better than trying to duplicate a magic moment. I went to create a new one. I exercised **care**: dressed warm and took my sun glasses. I went around the village, on the pathway on the perimeter. I spotted an appropriate bench, on the west side (obviously), that was facing a huge meadow, stretching for a hundred and eighty degrees, on both directions. I had about twenty minutes before the sun would touch the horizon (about two inches). This time of day is rightfully called 'the magic hour', as nature is getting ready to go to sleep. It was a success. I enjoyed it a lot. The panoramic flat view was astonishing. It was completely still and yet there was life everywhere: a large variety of birds, ducks, geese, frogs, cows, sheep, and millions of insects, who were very careful not to bother me. The soft red light of the setting sun painted everything in magnificent colors, and the scenery had an accented three dimensional effect, probably because of the special lighting. I was completely alone. You might think that many people would be attracted to a scene like this. But most everyone takes it for granted, or has 'more serious' business to attend to. I didn't. I thought that if Disney world offered an attraction like this, a kind of **virtual reality**[82] ride that gave a perfect **illusion** of what I was experiencing, people would come from all over the world for it. I know I would. Sunsets and beautiful views are like air and water: It is all around, so hardly

---

[82] Virtual reality is bound to significantly affect the prevailing metaphysical paradigm (namely, **realism**). 'Cyber space' is quickly becoming **reality**, and soon people will argue if a certain virtual reality experience or phenomenon was **really** there (in the VR space) or not. The obvious meaning of the frequent term **really**, or '**really** really' will evaporate, while exposing the contextual nature of **every** such 'really'.

anyone recognizes their **value**. Virtual reality is considered a technology that will change the world, while all it does is **imitate** it. Why go for the **virtual** when you could go for **reality**? A lady and a dog were approaching. I watched them get closer, their long shadows reaching me long before they did. The dog was running forward. It ran **to me**, wagging its tail. It stood on its hind legs, putting both its paws on my thigh. I smiled and stroke him gently. It was wagging its tail, looking really happy. Something of Gaya must be rubbing off me. I stayed on the bench until the sun was gone. Then I **decided** to end the **moment** and start a new one. I started walking again, and completed a full circle around the little village. Although I was already through with today's writing, I decided to convert my raw, unconceptualized impressions into **memories**, and turned my computer on again, to connect my mental representations with the rest of my conceptual scheme. I didn't want to **forget** them, or to let them get lost in my crowded *worldview*, **disconnected** from the rest of me. Good night.

June 27 - Law

I couldn't fall asleep last night. Strange. After a **moment** of insomnia (that lasted about half an hour) I took a sleeping pill, half a *Xanax*, something I rarely do. I still had trouble falling asleep. It seemed as if I didn't, when I realized that it was after two in the morning, and that I must have been asleep, because a strange dream was still vivid in my mind. I tried to reconstruct it, and managed to remember the most part. Then I decided to make a hard copy. I got up in the dark, took a writing pad, and scribbled the whole thing on paper, writing 'blindly', as it was almost pitch dark. I finished and fell back asleep. Some time later I woke again, with another, completely different dream in my head. I lay in bed, thinking about it, but decided not to write again. My next moment of consciousness was already in the morning.

I lay in bed, thinking of **dreams** and *Deja vu*. There are similarities. Naturally, I could remember the first dream much better than the second, which was almost completely lost. The only thing that remained from it was its **location**: An old, half wrecked building, that was some kind of television studio. I thought: Had I **not** made an effort to remember; had I just ignored it, as I usually do, I would probably not have remembered either dream. Had I not consciously tried to remember the place (and later written it **here**), it would most probably have been lost forever. **Or would it**? Suppose I didn't pay attention. Suppose I only had it in my mind for a moment when I woke in the middle of the night, and made no effort to remember it in the morning. **And**, suppose that years later I happened to come to a place which looked just like the place in the dream. Would I then have the feeling of *Deja vu*? I believe there is a good chance that I would.

I had no idea what Gaya had in store for me today. After yesterday, I started to suspect that she was following some kind of preplanned *syllabus*. I decided to pay close attention to the evolution of the next topic of conversation, see if it is just coincidence, or if she ingeniously diverts the conversation to a topic she was aiming at. She wasn't at breakfast, and I asked Mr. Dekker if she had already eaten. He said that she had not, and that she will be down in a few minutes. He seemed tired; He was working double shifts, because his brother has been on vacation for the last two weeks, and was due back only by the end of the month. I had a coffee, thinking about home. Never in my life have I been away from my family for so long. The girls were already calling me on the phone every single day for the last few days. It was hard for them too. Not that I had regrets or anything; I could hop on the next plane and be home in a few hours. But I wasn't finished. I made quite a distance, but the journey was not yet over. As I was thinking that, Gaya arrived; her smile preceding her person. "What a lovely morning!" she said. It was, but lovely mornings have become a **routine** here.

"You are almost late" I smiled back; "It is almost ten o'clock". "So what?" she wondered. "They wouldn't serve us breakfast at ten fifteen?" Now it was my turn to wonder: "Maybe they would, but breakfast hours are until ten o'clock. Why put them in the dilemma? And if all the guests showed up after ten?" Gaya smiled again. "A rule without exceptions is not a rule. If it wouldn't occur to Eve to eat the apple, God's directive would not have been a directive; It would just have been a **forecast**."[83] I sensed an interesting topic, and pursued it before she brought up whatever she had prepared, **if** she had prepared anything. "You mean that it is in the **nature** of the concept of 'rule' that it has, or **may** have, exceptions?" Gaya nodded, pouring the coffee. "Precisely. I bet you cannot give me even a single example of a rule that does not." I tried: "The law of gravity". Gaya wondered: "You consider it a **rule**?" I wasn't sure what she had in mind: "You mean there is a distinction between **rule** and **law**?" She replied: "There must be, otherwise there would not be two distinct words. But never mind this distinction. We could talk about it later, if you want. I'll take **gravity** as a rule. You think there are no exceptions? Maybe we understand the term differently. How would you define the rule you are talking about?" I phrased it carefully: "Two material objects attract each other in proportion to their masses". I neglected the part about the squared distance. I didn't think it mattered. Gaya said: "Would you consider my cup of coffee and your cup of coffee as objects?" She got me again. I didn't even try to argue, or think up another example. Instead, I asked for **her** interpretation of 'rule'. She started: "Rules[84] **always**

---

[83] This observation about the nature of a 'Divine commandment' was revealed to me in the abovementioned LDG seminar. It appears that the nature of a **command** is such, that it **must** be possible to disobey. This is not only the case with Divine commands, but with commands in general. This is contrary to some views[117] about the speech act 'command', taking it as something that cannot be disobeyed. This first Biblical command, which produced the first **rule** in human history, simultaneously introduced the notion of **freedom**. There is no sense in 'freedom', where there is no **limitation**. The 'freedom to choose' must **presuppose** a distinction between courses of action that are distinguished by some applicable **rule**.

[84] Contemporary philosophy distinguishes two basic **kinds** of rules: **Regulative** rules and **Constitutive** rules. Regulative rules are conceived as regulating some (human) activity which exists prior to the introduction of the regulative rule system, and has some external **reason**, or **purpose**, independently of the rules regulating it. E.g., traffic laws are a paradigmatic example of a system of regulative rules, whereas **driving** is an activity which is independent of traffic laws, who only facilitate efficient (safe and swift) driving. Constitutive rules, on the other hand, constitute the **framework** of the activity which they also regulate. A system of constitutive rules also constitutes the **purpose** of the activity; It is **internally** defined: The activity is **defined** by the system of constitutive rules. E.g., the rules of **games**, such as chess, are a paradigmatic example of a set of constitutive rules, whereas the game has no meaning outside of the framework provided by the rules; It has no **purpose** outside the purpose specified by them.

This distinction has a particular application in the philosophy of language, in what is known as **Pragmatics**. *Speech act theory*, developed by Austin[118] and Searle[119] maintains that language is a **rule governed system**, consisting of 'linguistic institutions' such as 'assertion', 'question',

have to do with the **future**. Rules always specify how things **will** be. Of course, we often speak of rules in past contexts, but even then, the **way** we speak about them, is by temporarily assuming a point of view that is **prior** to the event in question. When we say that the apple fell on Newton's head as a result of the 'rule' of gravity, we mean that the falling was **inevitable**, even before the event. The rule 'pre-described' a future event. Here lies the difference between 'rule' and 'law'. You were right to assume that they are of the same nature, but language distinguishes between the cases where human **will** is involved, and between the cases it is not." I was confused. What she said seemed to explicitly contradict her conception of the unlimited range of human will. I said: "Wait a minute: What do you mean by 'human will is not involved?" Gaya smiled: "I mean that it is **agreed** amongst humans, what you call **speakers**, that they **cannot** be broken. Just like changing the past: It **is considered** impossible, just as laws of nature are considered universal, unbreakable. Although they get **changed** by scientists, every now and then. Language distinguishes between two kinds of rules: The ones that (it is agreed, constituted by language) are 'the way things are', beyond our influence; Those are laws of nature. The other kind are understood as humanly constituted. In fact, many of those are also called **laws**, like laws of the state. This distinction is **conventional**, or, rather, **lingual**. It is the distinction between the Greek *Physis* and *Nomos*. In the Homeric period there was no such distinction. It happens, although rarely, that a **rule** (*Nomos*) becomes a **law** (*Physis*)." I was surprised to hear this: "Really? Give me an example." She didn't have one ready, but in a moment's thought she replied: "It was once considered **impossible**, because of the structure of reality, to kill a person from a mile away. Nowadays it is just **forbidden**. As civilization progresses, the number of 'laws of nature' constantly decreases. Last time I looked, it was reduced to just four kinds of sub-atomic 'forces', that supposedly explain everything. But it must have changed again since then. It is the ideal of science: To identify a single principle, or very few principles, that are 'basic', that explain everything. Science's traditional goal is to uncover the 'real' basic laws of nature. But I believe that science today already realizes the futility of this goal. It is simply based on a false assumption. But let us not discuss the philosophy of science. Much too much has been said about it already. I think you are more interested in rules that were made **by** people **for** people. It was my claim that every such rule must, in principle, have exceptions. If it had not, there would be no need for the rule. Let me think of an example of such a rule: 'People

---

'promise' etc. Each of these institutions is in itself a set of rules, specifying the proper usage of the corresponding speech act. I shall not go into the details and problems of speech act theory; Needless to say, I disagree with the notion of language **as a** rule governed system, although under a particular interpretation it **could** be conceived as such as I will show at the end of this footnote. A comprehensive account **against** speech act theory and pragmatics in general can be found in Stephen Schiffer's *Remnants of Meaning*[??].

must breath at least ten times an hour'. Absurd, is it not?" I was not impressed with this example: "Wait, there is an ambiguity here: When you say that rules **have** exceptions, do you mean they **can** be broken or that they **may** be broken? I agree that there is absolutely no point in constituting a rule which **cannot** be broken, like your example. I thought that by 'exception' you meant that the rule **may** be broken; That there are **always** possible circumstances in which it **should** be broken!" Gaya seemed very happy with my complaint: "Now you arrived at the crux of the matter. Did you hear what you said? 'A rule that (under certain circumstances) **should** be broken. This 'should' - is it an 'external', transcendental 'should', or is the breach permitted by the rule **itself**? If it is the rule itself that specifies the exception, then it is no exception, just part of the rule. What I mean is this: Every rule that was ever constituted, or will ever be, has a circumstance in which it is **right** to disobey it. This **right**, or **should**, is not part of the rule. It is part of a **higher** rule, a 'transcendental' moral rule, which has the authority to override any socially constituted rule." I was in a disobedient mood. I said: "Rules **always** deal in moral issues; In what is good, bad, right or

---

° The focus of my discussion will be, rather, on the accepted distinction between **regulative** rules and **constitutive** rules in general. I claim that this distinction is the product of a particular implicit premise: The premise of objectivism, or **realism**. My claim is based on another basic premise, explicitly stated repeatedly throughout this thesis, that **every** human activity has a **purpose**, and that it is always 'external', in the sense applicable to regulative rule systems. People never do **anything** which is **not** for this purpose: The purpose of attaining **good** for themselves (and/or their surroundings, which amounts to the same thing, whether they realize it or not). Let us examine a system that allegedly does **not** comply with this claim: The game of chess. It is claimed, that it has no (external) purpose: That its purpose is to 'capture the opponent's king', a goal defined by the rules of the game. If this were the case, playing chess would not be a human activity. Engaging in a game of chess is no different (with respect to its **purpose**) from taking a fun ride in a new convertible car. I am at home with my wife. I say to her: What would you rather do - have a nice game of chess or go for a nice ride in the new car? If she chooses chess, we play by the rules of chess. If she picks the ride, we drive by the rules of traffic. There is **absolutely** no difference. 'Driving' is not some transcendental, God-given activity, that was always there. It is man-made; It is **good** for something. Chess, on the other hand, is not just a time-passer: For some people it is a way to make a living, for others a means to enhance their intellect. If people do it, it is good for **something** - at least for the ones who do it, and often for others as well.

What, then, is the source of the mistake? Why the consensus over the distinction between 'regulative' and 'constitutive'? It is because **realism** takes **reality** for granted. Realists assume, that there is one "super-context" which is **the real** context. The context of the game of chess, the one the rules constitute, is considered 'unreal': The king is not real, the fight is not real, the victory is not real. **Traffic**, on the other hand, is a **real** context: It is **there**, regardless of the rules. Wrong! without the rules, it wouldn't be **driving**! Can you imagine driving with **no** rules at all? I will spare you the description. It's not that there would be more accidents. The rules of driving include the rule 'put the key in the ignition'. It is not in the book, because there is no point in putting it there, but it is a rule as any other. If anyone would park his car in the middle of the road, there would be no traffic to **regulate**. Driving is a context like any other, not a "super context", a **'real'** context, as opposed to the 'unreal' context of chess. Regulative rules are taken to regulate activities that 'are already there'. There is no such thing, 'are already there'. It is man-made. It was **constituted** at one time or

wrong. There is no question about that. There is no **point** in making a rule that is morally neutral. So the whole **body** of rules of some society at a given point in time, the punishable ones as well as the ones dealing in manners and customs, can be viewed as this society's **moral code**. There **is** no supreme, 'divine' moral code which stands 'above' this society's moral code..." As I was speaking, Gaya's smile was becoming wider, and I saw my mistake. I started over, trying to correct: "Wait. I think I see what you mean. **The** moral considerations for social laws change constantly, together with the changing world. Nothing is **immune** from change. When you said that, in principle, every rule has an exception, you meant that the rule **itself** is subject to change. No rule, nor any other part of reality is inevitable, essential. Except for the **private** notion of **Good**, of course." Gaya completed my short speech: "Which, itself, provides the **motivation** for these constant changes."

She **couldn't** have planned this in advance. I paid close attention: This whole thing started with her (almost) being late for breakfast. She read my mind, as usual: "It depends **why** I am late for breakfast. If I was saving someone's life, I amend my rule: It is **allowed** to be late for breakfast, **if** it is for the purpose of saving someone's life. I didn't have a 'ready made' rule for this case. I never saved someone's life before breakfast. But **when** this happens, the rules change. **My** rules change. If the painter who was washing his brush in the bucket was in a great hurry, for what **he** considered a good reason, he would be **allowed** to wash his brush in the canal." This invoked another question: "But it is conceivable that

---

another, and at that moment it already required a set of (constitutive) rules to govern it, otherwise it couldn't be a **social** activity. Wherever more than one person is involved, rules are required to define both the 'wide' context and also particular details associated with the activity.

If we agree to posit one superior "super context" above all other contexts, like "**this** is **the** reality", then the distinction starts to make sense. **Then** we might say: 'Every set of rules that is designed to govern an activity that is included in this "super context" shall be hereafter called "regulative". And every set of rules **defining a sub-context**, an inferior, "unreal" context within the wider "real" context, shall hereafter be called "constitutive".' I don't think there is anything **wrong** with this terminology, as long as we understand what we are talking about. The situation could also be perceived in reverse: The distinction between 'regulative' and 'constitutive' **helps define** a particular context that humanity chooses to **prefer**. By making the distinction, the **real reality** is defined.

The world can go on **without chess**. Nevertheless, it can also go on **without driving**. The need people have to get from one place to another **seems** more basic to the 'nature' of humanity than the need for a recreational game. I don't think Bobby Fischer or Kasparov would agree. Chess is as much a part of reality as traffic. Large parts of the world have no traffic. Some of them may, however, have chess. In fact, chess was probably around **before** traffic (as we know it) was. People have the tendency to take a part of their *worldview* **for granted**, positing it as the real reality, while taking another as contingent, unessential; The **real** part acting as the base, the unquestionable 'substratum' for all the rest. The problem is, that different people have different substrata.

142

his reason was **not** good enough: Suppose he was in a **great** hurry to finish his beer?" She replied: "Who are you to decide for **him** what's important? If it is not **really** important, **he** will know. And if he contaminated the canal for no good reason, **he** will have to live with it. He probably knows this, because we saw him use the bucket. When we see someone that is breaking what **we** consider the rules to be, we should not hastily judge him. This does not mean that society should not have punishable rules. Society very conveniently provides its members with clear circumstances, so the moral dilemmas are more intelligible. It provides a basic scale, a list of priorities: What is more important than what, what crimes are severe, and what are just slight vices. The law of the state changes, when many of its members have an 'internal' priority which is significantly different from it; Like the case with the prohibition on alcoholic drinks, or homosexuality."°

° Let us now turn to the implications of the above claim to the philosophy of language, particularly speech act theory. It takes language to consist of a set of **constitutive rules**. This implies that speech has no purpose **outside** of these rules! I shall disregard the question in what **language** these rules are supposedly formulated. Can we seriously consider the claim that language serves no purpose outside the purpose specified by the rules of language? Why do people communicate? So they can communicate? There must be an **external** purpose! If we assume that is nothing but a set of rules, then they must be **regulative**! they serve the speakers of the language so that they communicate effectively. Hence, an essential **presupposition** is in order: An agreed, shared, objective **purpose** which language **serves**. Without this presupposition, the whole account of language as a rule governed system loses its meaning. What could this purpose be? The **same** purpose for all speakers! As I consider myself **a** speaker, **my** purpose in engaging in the language game must therefore be the same purpose as other speakers' purpose. I **know my** purpose: I want to feel **good**. This is my personal **sole** purpose in doing **anything**. How is it possible that this should be a universal purpose?

Well, it is not; Not under the **realist** premise employed by most (all?) pragmaticians. If realism is presupposed, **Good** becomes **relative**, not universal, not **absolute**. The only way language **could** be perceived as a rule governed system, is to abandon realism. In doing so, an **objective** notion of absolute, universal **Good** becomes possible, coherent. And it can act as **the** purpose of the activity (discourse) that language is designed to **regulate** (not constitute!). So here you have it: **(1)** If realism is presupposed, language cannot be a rule governed system; and **(2)** If language is assumed to be a rule governed system, then realism is incoherent (which it is for many other unrelated reasons). This is speech act theory's modest contribution for the substitution of the metaphysical paradigm of **realism** with another metaphysical *worldview*: That of an **objective moral reference**.

What does speech act theory **become** under this new set of hypotheses? As I said, language may still be viewed as a rule governed system, only this time the system is **regulative**, not constitutive. It regulates the speakers' shared objective goal: providing each other with descriptions: Descriptions of the objective moral reference: **the Good**. Each speaker has (is) a belief system. The 'topic' these systems are 'about' is not the **world**, but the **Good**, each speaker with his own 'version' of it. When speakers engage in the language game, they **exchange beliefs**. Discourse is a mutual 'trade' of beliefs: Speaker S1 **exports** his beliefs to S2, and **imports** S2's beliefs (the ones he decides to accept). Speech act theory is thus **reduced** to just **two** basic speech acts: 'Export', also known as **assertion**, in which S1 <u>offers</u> a belief to S2, and (a request for) 'import', also known as **question**, in which S1 <u>requests</u> to offer a belief. A conversation between two speakers is thus perceived as an **erotetic dialogue**[120], a dialectical 'ping-pong' of beliefs. This explains the significance of the

There was one more thing that needed clarification: "You said that rules always concern the **future**. Please elaborate." Gaya replied: "Reality is composed of two main 'blocks': The past and the future. The past provides the shared context, everyone's joint, social circumstances. The future, on the other hand, is where people are 'allowed' to express their will, carry out their intentions. But society does not tolerate chaos. It has to regulate the future as well, so people don't

---

phenomenon of **lying**: When a speaker exports a proposition he **does not hold**, he breaks the basic rule of the language game: To export (genuine) beliefs.

But let us disregard lying now, and assume the speakers play by the rules. Let us investigate two paradigmatic examples of conversations. First, let us consider a case where S1 tells S2 about some experience he had. Here S1 is the principal 'exporter'. He provides most of the information. The 'data flow' is uni-directional: S1 supplies S2 with 'facts' concerning his experience. At some point in the flow of information (beliefs) from S1 to S2, S2 encounters an **incoherence** in S1's story. It seems to S2 that S1 uttered a belief which contradicts another belief, previously exported (and previously accepted by S2). S2 does not tolerate contradictions in his system (whereas he is equipped with the syntax of P_1), and therefore stops S1's sequence of beliefs, and injects a **question**. He must have **misunderstood** (we ruled out **lying**). This question is a **request** for a specific belief S2 is interested in. This **request** S2 made, is in itself **also** an instance of **export**: S2 exports the belief 'I did not understand...'. S1 supplies the requested belief, clarifies the situation (there should be no problem, whereas S1's system is also necessarily coherent; the problem was in **language**, not in his belief system), and can proceed with his story.

The second paradigmatic example is that of an **argument**. S1 and S2 are in **disagreement** regarding (the truth value of) some proposition B. The dialectic process goes something like this: S1 exports 'B'. S2 takes B to refer to a belief he clearly does **not** hold (Again, lying is here disregarded). S2 protests: He claims that B is impossible. He substantiates his claim by the following proposition: C⊃~B. If S1 takes this proposition to be true (holds it as a belief), the argument is over. (Provided, of course, he also holds C). **However**, S1 may **deny** the truth of C, **or** of (C⊃~B). Let us assume he denies C (the case is similar if he denies C⊃~B). He then claims: ~C! and substantiates it with D⊃~C. If S2 accepts both D and (D⊃~C), the argument is over. This dialectical process continues until one of the parties is convinced, or until time is up and the argument ends unresolved. (Truthful) discourse has the effect of **convergence** of S1 and S2's belief systems. Every conversation brings their systems a bit closer together (in terms of their logical structure) – a little more isomorphic..

Let us return to the claim I made in footnote 20: People often say "I understand you, but I don't **agree** with you". It is my claim that disagreement consists as **proof** of (a case of) misunderstanding. It is impossible to **understand and disagree**. When S1 and S2 disagree regarding the truth of B, this means that by 'B' they mean different things. When my little daughter says 'there is a witch in my closet' I cannot say 'there is no witch in your closet', and still mean **the same as she** by 'witch' and 'closet'.

This observation is particularly significant in day to day situations. People are often in disagreement, and yet claim to fully understand each other's claims. This conception is counter productive, because what they **should** do, is find where the misunderstanding **lies**: Which is the 'crucial premise', the one they do not share, and focus on **it**. This is what a dialectical dialogue is all about. None of the parties is 'objectively wrong'.

144

wake up to a different strange world every morning. So society has **very** basic rules, such as 'the sun **will rise** in the east every morning', and rules on the periphery, such as 'no vehicles **will park** in this street.' The punishment for breaking the first rule may be getting committed in an asylum, while the punishment for the second is just a fine. Even table manners are like that: 'Guests in restaurants **will use** a fork and knife', the violation of which resulting in getting punished by other guests in the restaurant, or its manager. Rules are intrinsically **social**. They support **objectivity**, makes the objective world intelligible." I still had another question: "How does this fit with **Kant**'s[85] conception of 'rule'?" "oh, dear Kant" she said. "We almost forgot him. Kant

---

[85] I was greatly influenced by Kant's *Fundamental Principles*[121]. The first sentence of the first chapter will always remain in my mind: *"Nothing in the world, nor **outside** the world, could be considered infinitely good, but the **good will** alone "*. This sentence comes as close to the **definition** of 'Good' as I have ever seen. Kant pointed to the close, inseparable association between the concept of 'Good' and the concept of 'will'. Nevertheless, this statement implies, that there is such a thing as 'bad will', while the position I portrayed thus far, is that the meaning of (the) 'Good' is 'what one **wants**'. At first sight, there seems to be a clear contradiction between those two positions. But only at first sight; What **is** 'bad will?' It is not to **want** the **bad** for oneself. It is to want some**thing** which is (wrongly) **thought** to bring about (the) Good, but does **not**. A person with a bad will is making a **mistake** in identifying the (some)**thing** as good.

Kant perceives the **will** to be subject, subordinate, to **reason**. Reason has **control** over will. It can **direct** the will so it becomes **good**. The will is **blind**. It can be good or bad (in Kant's terminology), but it needs reason to **determine** which is which. The will is the capacity to **act**, to carry out, always for the purpose of attaining the good for its owner. Failure of **reason** to direct this force **properly** will result in will's **failure** to attain this good (or to **be** good, in Kant's terminology). Therefore, Kant appeals to **reason**, and supplies it with information to do the job (of directing) successfully. For this purpose he posits an entity: (the) **law**, (in his jargon - the categorical imperative). This entity 'exists' in the mind (conceptual scheme) of any creature that has **reason**. It is up to reason to **recognize** it, and direct the **will** to adhere (**cohere** seems more appropriate) with it. It is the **duty** of **will** to **cohere** with the **law**. The requirement is one of **coherence**. The problem remains, of course, to identify this entity, the 'law' (what Gaya called 'rule'), and find out its content: **What** does it prescribe?

Kant uses the German word *Achtung* to describe the proper attitude towards this **law**. It can be translated as 'observing' or 'obeying', but I prefer the Heideggerian term **care**: '**Caring** for the law'. What **is** this important entity? My *worldview*, or belief system (or conceptual scheme) implies certain **rules** of behavior, even for circumstances I never experienced. E.g., in **my** world, racism is **bad**. This belief has a (potential) consequence, even if I never made the inference: That I **should** not object to my daughter marrying a husband that has black skin. What Kant prescribes, is **coherence**: 'Act in coherence with your beliefs'. If I am against racism, and **still** object to my daughter marrying a black person, my *worldview* is incoherent. It's as simple as that. Kant makes no claim regarding the question whether **in fact** racism is bad. His advice concerning the **generality** of the applicable rule is but a convenient way to make himself understood, and his advice relatively easy to follow. A person with a completely coherent set of beliefs (factual and normative alike - they are inseparable anyway) such as Kant himself, can never be immoral. He (apriori) wants the **good** for himself, and by the requirement of coherence, he **automatically** wants the good for everyone, and acts accordingly.

145

didn't speak about **society**, neither about **language**. I suspect he was a genuine solipsist, like me. When Kant said 'rule', he **only** referred to the **private** one, the one by which an individual acts. Kant was preaching for **consistency** as the means to happiness. He said: 'Act in accordance with your beliefs, otherwise you will be confused and unhappy'. He even prescribed **how** to do it. He said: 'Make your rules **general**, applicable to everybody' (including yourself). That is why I suspect he was a solipsist: Because he didn't think it at all **possible** to apply a rule differently to **oneself** than to someone **else**. The 'else' for him was just a part of **his** illusion. You know that he considered the *worldviews* people have as illusions, a creation of the mind. He denied his solipsism, of course. He was an extremely wise man. He would not have gotten half of the attention if he admitted his Idealism".[86]

---

[86] Kant perceives the human being (or, rather, a **rational** being) as a **legislator**, and human society as composed of sovereign **legislators**. Each person, in a way, **makes the rules** (creates his own *worldview*). When I first read Kant's expression, 'kingdom of ends', I had the visual image of many 'Leibnizian monades', a multitude of isolated 'bubbles', each enclosed within its own universe, of which it is the sovereign, the maker of the rules. It is **absurd** for a legislator to break her own rules. It is of course possible, that **others** will disobey, but what of it? Rules were **made** to disobey (see *Eve*). But the legislator **herself?!** the legislator may, of course, change the rules from time to time. It is only natural that this would happen in time. Things change; worlds change; *worldviews* change. But at any point in time, there is **one** world, one set of prevailing rules. Not adhering (cohering) with one's own rules inevitably results in unhappiness.

I already stated my belief that Kant was an Idealist. He insisted on the 'existence' of *the thing in itself*, but in *Fundamental principles* as well as in the second critique, the nature of the thing in itself is revealed (although not explicitly): It is the **legislators** themselves. Kant was greatly influenced by Leibniz, and I believe that he shared his view regarding 'the structure of reality': What there 'really' **is** behind everything, the mysterious, inaccessible thing in itself, is nothing but the (community of) speakers themselves. Kant persisted we cannot, in principle, **know** anything about it. Still, I am sure that Kant considered **himself**, particularly his **reason**, to be no other than **the** thing in itself.

Moral dilemmas are notoriously difficult to solve, theoretically, because when considered, they are viewed from **outside**: Speakers S1 and S2 are discussing a (real or hypothetical) dilemma of **speaker S3**. This cannot be done. No wonder ethical problems are as obscure nowadays as they were in ancient Greece. In order to assess the dilemma S3 is in, S3's whole *worldview* (his world!) must be taken into consideration. S3 cannot be judged by S1's standards. It is senseless; Or, rather, another inevitable consequence of metaphysical realism. If there is just one 'real' world in which we all roam, the **good** will remain relative and **ethics** an eternal mystery. Somewhere in the Jewish canon it says: 'Judge not thy friend before you have taken his place' or something similar. A moral dilemma is intrinsically private, whereas it hinges on the particular structure of the belief system in question. This does not mean that **advice** is impossible, particularly if there is reason to believe that there is some similarity between the beliefs of the two speakers. But if they happen to be in disagreement regarding a moral issue, it certainly proves a **difference** between the two systems.

In footnote 84 I discussed regulative rules vs. constitutive rules, and concluded with the claim that the distinction is 'artificial', and leans on a realist worldview. I further maintained that all rules are in essence regulative, whereas they all regulate one shared, superior purpose: The 'quest' for the

146

It was too late (and too hot) to go for a walk. It was already after eleven. And I had to call my office. Before we parted, I said to Gaya: "So, the **law**, including manners, customs and habits of a particular society, is simply **What most people believe to be <u>good</u>**. What **I** take the objective law to **be**, is a kind of 'average', of what I **believe** the 'standard' person's beliefs regarding the **good** to be. Every **law** which I happen to disagree with, is a manifestation of the **difference** between my beliefs regarding the good, and what I take to be the **common** belief about it. But this 'common' belief is **also** in **me**! How does this discrepancy come about? How is it possible for me to have 'two opinions' regarding what is right: One is 'mine' in one sense, the other 'mine' in another?" She answered, in a serious tone: "It is a manifestation of a discrepancy **within yourself**. I suggest you follow Kant's advice, and try to find out what is wrong with **your personal** view, not what is wrong with **'the'** law. The law is always right, not because of its contents, but because of what it **is**: The law[87]".

I spent most of the day with Kant. He was not as **lively** as Gaya (and he wasn't smiling either), but other than that, he was just as impressive. Amazing man. He reminded me of my mother. She is the only person I know that completely behaves in accord with his principles. I always took her complete disregard for her own personal interest as naive, a product of a strict moral upbringing. I could never understand why she volunteered to do something unpleasant just because it was **more** unpleasant to somebody **else**. She always said: "But I don't **mind** doing it; He **does** mind; It's completely **logical** that I should be the one to do it!" I sometimes even got **angry** at her for this attitude. It seemed to me that people

---

good. While discussing Kant, it is time to review this conclusion in the context of 'speakers as legislators'. Kant perceives reason to **constitute** its own rules; He sees a rational creature as **self constitutive**. It may be claimed, that this Kantian legislation renders the **purpose** of the legislation **internal**: That the rule system created by a rational creature is constitutive, not regulative.

[87] Kant himself answered this hypothetical polemic, by claiming that the categorical imperative is **objective**. Whereas the **practical rule** employed by a particular person in particular circumstances is **subjective**, there is only **one**, objective categorical imperative. The concept of **duty** is the same for everyone. This conception differs from mine, whereas I see the **Good** as what is objective, but still, the **purpose** is external: It is **not** speaker-dependent. And as such, the rule system **legislated** by the speaker remains **regulative**.

Kant also offered a second 'version' of the categorical imperative. He suggested to act in a manner that renders **humanity** (both in oneself and in any other human) an **end**, and never just as **means**. In other words, never to treat (other) people just as **things**, but as a **purpose**. For some reason, Kant limited the scope of this prescription to **humans**, to exclude, for instance, animals. I prefer to understand him in a broader sense; To treat the **whole** surroundings as the ends, and never just as means. You may breed **cows** for their meat, and treat them as means (for food), but as long as they are in your care, **care** for their well being as an **end** in itself. Treat them as living things; as an end **in itself**. This idea of a person **as** an end is known in some ancient cultures as *Love thy neighbor.*

were taking advantage of her good nature. Only in reading Kant I realized that she did the right thing, although I doubt she had the theory to back it. She constantly exercised (exercises) **care**: Care for **her** world. It never mattered to her that people didn't understand the **reasons** for her ways. I doubt there even **were** logical reasons, although she insisted it was 'logical'. Logic was only a rationalization of something that came naturally. It must have simply **worked** for her. And it took me forty years to understand. Well, better late than never.

June 28 - Extension

The ducks here are amazing. They can walk, they can fly, they can swim, and they can even dive, for incredibly long periods of time. And they eat practically everything. I was sitting with Gaya on a bench in the shade, watching them. Several of them were gathered in the canal, a few meters away from us. One of the ducks constantly tried to scratch its neck; It dove in the water and then scratched; dove and scratched. Finally it jumped out of the water, and Gaya said to me, in a soft, almost inaudible voice: "Watch". She made a clicking noise with her tongue and tapped the bench gently. She was holding a white tissue in one hand, pretending she wanted to feed it to the duck. The duck approached, and when it came within range, she moved her other hand gently, and touched the duck's neck, at the point he was scratching. In no more than two seconds she found it. A large black beetle. By that time the duck realized she had no food for it, but at the same time it must also have realized she removed the cause of the itch. It rubbed its neck against her, and left, to rejoin its friends in the water. I was very impressed. I said to her: "You are amazing. How do you do it?" She smiled and said: "I speak their language." I didn't know how literally she meant it. I asked: "What do you mean?" and she willingly explained: "Look: If you went, say, to some remote and backward place in China, and met some people that spoke a completely different language and lived a completely different life from yours; You would **still** be able to communicate with them, Right?" She didn't wait for an answer; "You would be able to take care of one of them if he was wounded; You would be able to be their guest, be nice to them, and recognize it if they would be nice to you, although they are very different. Unfortunately, animals don't get a similar treatment from most people. You can imagine **yourself** as one of the Chinese people, but you cannot imagine yourself as a duck, or as a dog. All it takes, is a bit of **compassion**, of 'identification' with whoever, or **what**ever you want to communicate with. I was never a duck, or at least I don't **remember** having been one, but it is not too difficult to understand their world, if you pay a little attention. They have a relatively simple world; Much simpler than the world of the 'simplest' Chinese farmer. I think it is, in principle, far more easy to communicate with animals than with humans; There is no **sophistication** that stands in the way of communication. There is no **suspicion**, unless there is explicit reason for suspicion. Sometimes it is more difficult; When the animal had some bad experience with humans. Then it takes time; You have to let the animal recognize you personally, distinguish between **you**, personally, and humans in general. But it is always possible, to some degree. Look at the dog over there;" She pointed at a dog that was avoiding its owner, a teenage girl, standing near by. She was trying to tie him to the leash she was holding in her hand, but every time she tried to come close, the dog retreated. "She has no **communication** with her dog. She does not respect its 'doghood'. She thinks of it as human, judges it in human categories. I already told you, that I always try to take the 'point of view' of whoever I speak with; try to share **his** world, understand what **he**, or in this case **it**, considers as **good**. I bet that for the dog over there, the leash is **bad**. Why should it **agree** to be tied to it? It may be **forced** to, but this will only reinforce its **opinion** that the leash is bad. I take animals not only to **feel**, but also to **think** and **understand**[88]. It is my prerogative, whereas it is **my** world. I respect the differences. Most animals have different **senses** than we have. I cannot smell like a dog. So I take it into account; I realize that there are things in a dog's or a duck's world that I have no access to. But one thing I know: They can tell **good** from **bad**. And this is enough for **communication**. **Quite** enough".

On the ground beneath us I spotted a gray seashell. It was completely whole, and had a nice shape. I picked it up and asked Gaya: "What is this?" She looked at it, and answered, in a puzzled tone: "A sea shell. What of it?" I explained: "In the language we now use, the name of this thing is a sea shell. But what **is** it? I have the concept of **this** sea shell in my mind (or in 'my world', if you want), and **you** also have something in **your** mind that you refer to as 'this sea shell'. My question is, what makes it shared, the **same** sea shell, **besides** the name we both use. I don't mean 'sea shell' in general, as a **universal**. I mean as a **particular**. We can talk about things in general, and I think I have a pretty good picture how this is achieved **although** we are communicating out of completely separate worlds. But there is something that escapes me when we discuss **particular** objects. Things that are **substantial**, that have **substance**."[89] Gaya still wasn't

---

[88] Kant didn't think so. But then again, Plato didn't consider **slaves** as completely **human** either. Some peoples only 'joined' the human race in recent centuries, not to speak of **women**. Things change.

[89] The first modern account of the nature of **substance** was offered by British Empiricism. John Locke[122] was the first in this line of empiricists. (Locke wrote his *Essay concerning human understanding* in **Holland**, to where he fled for political reasons). Locke maintained that human knowledge is ultimately derived from sense experience, which he considered primary. He rejected the idea of **innateness**, and claimed that the human mind comes into the world as *Tabula rasa*. Locke may be viewed as the first modern **realist**, implicitly accepting the realist metaphysical premise (practically reigning the western *worldview* until this day).

In his treatment of the concept (*idea* in his terminology) of **substance**, Locke distinguished between its **primary** and **secondary** qualities; the former being intrinsic, inseparable from the object, and the latter 'produced' in the mind of the observer **by** the primary ones. Locke considered primary qualities **real**, *'whether anyone's senses perceive them or no'*. Locke was partly aware of the problems in the concept of **substance**: *"...not imagining how these simple ideas* (color, taste etc.) *can subsist by themselves, we accustom ourselves to suppose some **substratum** wherein they do subsist, and from which they do result, which therefore we call **substance**"*. As a consistent empiricist, Locke **should have** rejected the notion of **substance** (as his successor, *Berkeley*, indeed

150

sure she understood my problem: "But I think we've been through this, unless I'm having a *Deja vu* again. We said that the physical world, the **past** physical world, is the common **ground**, the **creation** of the speaking community, which enables all speakers to safely refer to the **same** things without them changing all the time. The past is full of **objects**. Physical objects that are (agreed to be) **unchangeable**. We **have** discussed this, have we not?" I didn't give up: "You still don't understand my question. Let me try another direction. I realize that **reality** is a posited shared context designed to enable discourse. The best example for this is **mathematics**. We all have the **same** mathematics. It was logically constructed in the same **way** in all the different **worlds** of the different speakers. I have no problem there, and **this** is what we were talking about. But there is a difference in nature, in **essence**, between the objective notion of 'the number *Five*', and the objective notion of 'this sea shell'. The sea shell is extending, **physical**. It has **spatial coordinates**, whereas the number *Five* has none. Where did this **physicality**, these spatial coordinates come from? In short, how did the 'convention' of **three dimensional objects** come about? Where from came the idea of **matter**,[90] extended in three directions? And why not **two** directions, or four? Why **three**?"

Gaya sighed. "I see. This is a **really** difficult one. I am not even sure I want to go into it." I was very surprised. She never said anything like this before. But before I had the chance to express my astonishment, she spoke: "On the other hand, I'm

---

had), but did not. Locke is often criticized for not accepting the consequences of his own empiricism, but evidently could not completely discard the well established Aristotelian tradition.

[90] This was the question posed by Locke's successor (and fierce critic), George Berkeley.[123] He rejected Locke's distinction between primary and secondary qualities, claiming that primary qualities are as 'observer dependent' as the secondary ones. Berkeley maintained that Locke's epistemology, taking perception as a causal process, is incoherent. In *The principles* he defines two 'kinds' of **existence**: of *spirits* (perceivers) and of *ideas* (perceived); The former **active**, the latter **passive**. The former capable of **causing** the latter.

Berkeley didn't take his view as revolutionary, or hard to swallow, as many of his contemporaries did (or even many present-day philosophers). To them he writes: *"The only thing whose existence we deny, is that which philosophers call **matter** or corporeal substance... If any man thinks this detracts from the existence or **reality** of things, he is very far from understanding what hath been premised in the plainest terms I could think of. Take here an abstract of what hath been said. There are spiritual substances, minds, or **human souls**, which **will** or excite ideas in themselves at pleasure... the sun that I see by day is the **real** sun (although not material) and that which I imagine by night is the idea of the former. In the sense here given of **reality**, it is evident that every vegetable, star, mineral... is as much a **real being** by our principles as by any other. Whether others mean anything by the term **reality** different from what I do, I entreat them to look into their own thoughts and see."* I believe the force of these words stands until present days. I believe Berkeley received much less attention than he deserved (and deserves) because he was a **Bishop**. His philosophy was interwoven into his belief in a Christian God, who was already in decline.

an old woman. I don't know when, or **if**, I'll have the chance again to share my **beliefs** with someone who is as eager to be exposed to them.

Gaya kept silent for a few seconds, probably thinking how to begin. Then she seemed to have reached a decision, and started: Here is a science fiction story. Suppose that it will be possible, at some point in the distant future, to digitally record all the physical events in the world. A huge network of computers, that will contain all the information regarding the physical position of all the particles in the universe. Seems farfetched, but certainly not impossible. Let us say that this huge super-computer has five or ten thousand years of history recorded in its memory banks. And let us further suppose, that virtual reality technology has advanced to the extent of including **all** human senses, including even smells and tastes. Maybe a direct link to the brain will then be possible. Now what do we have? We have a machine that can put a person at any place **and** time of the past. Just as an observer, not an **agent**, who can **affect** the events. There is no theoretical obstacle from this story becoming reality five or ten thousand years from today. Moreover: We could observe several times **at once**: We could have 'rewind', 'pause' and 'fast forward' buttons to control the experience, and could therefore observe a sequence of, say, ten 'real' minutes in just ten seconds; Just as you can now, in a short glance, see the whole **height** of this tree here, you **will** be able, in a short glance, grasp 'ten minutes' at a short glance. Maybe they will not be called 'minutes' but 'virtual minutes', but still, the analogy is clear. You will not be able, maybe, to grasp a whole **year** in one glance, but, just as well, you **now** cannot grasp ten miles in one glance either! If you just take a glance at a ten mile spread, you hardly **notice** anything, just as you will not grasp much if you 'fast forward' a whole year in a few seconds. You will get some basic picture, but no **details**: Just like your **present** spatial perception. Let me summarize this part: It is conceivably possible that technology will reach a stage when the coordinate of time will be just like the coordinates of space. It will take some getting used to, but thousands of years are a long time for humanity."

"This technological vision demonstrates how the dimension of time may gradually "solidify" and become similar to a spatial coordinate. Quite a few thinkers, philosophers and scientists alike, have recognized the similarities between the time coordinate and between the three spatial ones. Parmenides and Spinoza are the two most famous philosophers to have made this observation, and Einstein gave it the theoretical backing. If we agree to adopt, for now, a completely **deterministic** *worldview*, then **time** can be perceived as **just** a forth spatial coordinate. Theoretically, it works. We may perceive our universe as consisting of a **four** dimensional space, not three dimensional. But for some reason, we cannot **grasp** the fourth coordinate the way we grasp the first three."°

Gaya paused again, thinking how to proceed, then went on: "Now let's get back to our science fiction story. We are now faced with two notions of 'time': One regular and one virtual (i.e., the timeline of the recorded history, residing on the disks of our super-computer). The virtual time is not time anymore: It is **spatial**: It is possible to move **back and forth** in it, just like space. But this is still quite primitive, because we can only **observe**, not **change** anything in this four dimensional space.

° David Hume[124] was the third and probably most significant thinker in the line of British empiricists. He was the one to 'wake' Kant from his 'dogmatic' (rationalist) 'sleep'. More than anything, Hume was a **skeptic**, and a highly talented one. He did not share Berkeley's affinity with the Christian God, who was kind enough to provide Berkeley with the multitude of sense data, the 'raw material' for creating 'ideas', and could think of no other explanation. It is not clear whether Hume was a realist (like Locke) or an idealist (like Berkeley). But the **materiality** of reality wasn't his main concern. He was the first to fully realize that we have no direct access, in principle, to **whatever** there is. In a nutshell, Hume found empiricism **self refuting**.

Until now I have used the word 'object' for a **property** which is a member of the objective subdomain. 'Objects' are 'objective', as in 'intersubjective'; not necessarily **material**, or **extending**. Hereafter, I shall limit my usage of the term 'object', to extending, material objects only. The following discussion will not focus on the existence or inexistence of objects, whereas objects **exist** by definition. Rather, I shall concentrate on what **characterizes** them, as opposed to other existent properties that are not objects (immaterial). Let us assume that some speaker S1 has been completely paralyzed all his life. He can, nevertheless, see, hear and speak. His vision does not grant him three dimensional perception, whereas he has no understanding of depth or perspective. He can see colors, but does not associate them with **objects**. It is as if he sees a constantly changing two dimensional picture. There is no reason to deny the possibility of S1's learning to speak sufficiently well to conduct a normal conversation. Moreover, the language S1 speaks may very well be an **objective** language, loaded with names of objects. (Just as a blind man's language includes 'sun', 'light' and even 'see'). After having established the circumstances, let us ask S1: "What **is** an object?" S1's answer will no doubt be 'something that is seen'. He would have no other criterion. Similarly, a blind man would say 'something that is felt'. Neither of them would refer to the sense of **hearing**, although they both posses it. **Why?** because hearing **does not persist in time**. It 'goes away', so to speak. If it **doesn't**, it must be an object (like a constantly buzzing bee, or ticking watch). **Objects are things that persist in time**.

I consider this point extremely important when discussing the nature of **substance**. Substance is defined in terms of **time**. As such, it is the only 'means' to bridge time gaps: To be conceivable **both** in the past and in the future. We could say 'I **had** a feeling' (in the past), but it is **gone**. The only thing that can **remain**, is objects (regardless of the number of directions they extend into).

Consider a property which is a member in the objective subdomain **and** is an object; e.g., a particular gray sea shell. I decided to keep it as a souvenir from Edam. I can imagine myself showing it to my professor next week. I can even visualize the (future) event. I am showing her **the** sea shell. The situation I am imagining does not belong in the objective subdomain, as it has not (yet) happened. Nevertheless, some objects **participating** in the event do belong in it.

153

We could advance the technology further: Let us say that it is possible to **interfere** in the 'script': The giant computer handling the whole thing is **interactive:** It has **history** in its memory banks, but advanced society enables its members to change the contents of this memory bank. You could change the **facts** of history. Needless to say, this may create great problems, like the famous paradox of killing one's own grandfather before he got married. So some things will be **impossible** to change. But this is no serious limitation: We have similar limitations **now**, with our **three** dimensional space: It is impossible to break the

---

° The terms 'extending' or 'spatial' or 'material', what I call 'objects', are a certain class of properties, all sharing the characteristic of being **fixed, unchangeable** when in the **past**, and also 'portable' into the 'free zone' of time: Into the future. When related to in the future, they are 'allowed' (lingually) to **change**, and even disappear (like in 'get lost').

Science sees the picture the other way around: It maintains that objects are composed of something it calls **matter**, and **matter** is something with the property of **existence**. And here science is stuck, because it cannot figure out what existence is! Science **investigates** matter, to find out what it **is**. But the project is futile, because science **determines** things, not 'discovers' them. Science has to **decide** what it starts from, what it posits; And **these** entities cannot be 'investigated', as they were **constituted** by science itself! If science **posits** 'matter' (as it does), it cannot 'find out' what it is by closely looking at it and bombarding it in a variety of ways in billion dollar laboratories. Science should decide what it **wants** matter to be, and then find a way to make the theory **coherent**.

I suspect that the colossal failure of physics to 'uncover' the 'real' structure of matter lies in the astonishing fact that **nobody cares**. If it was really important to humanity, if there were **moral** questions involved (not just for the physicists, but to humanity in general), an idea would have come up. Finding out about quarks and the big bang **does not really make a difference**. The research is made in the name of 'truth' and 'knowledge' alone, and these have no **value** in themselves. For a human project to succeed, it needs to be **important**, it needs to contribute something to society. That is why **technology** flourishes, while pure theoretical research is dying out.

What is wrong in assuming, for example, that matter is **infinitely divisible**? Why can we accept **infinity** in mathematics, and not in nature? Because it is hard for us to **grasp**? Then we need **grasping** exercises, or to investigate the nature of the interesting concept 'infinity' (from an epistemic point of view). Who whispered on humanity's ear that matter has some 'basic structure' that science works so hard to uncover? Is the hypothesis of some 'basic structure of matter' a **necessary** one to keep the physical theory intact? I believe science is completely blinded by **realism**, coupled with (what started as British) empiricism. For science to make any sense, it requires reasonable **motivations**: Human motivations. Science should not only know **what** it is looking for (which it doesn't), but, more importantly, **why** it is looking!

I believe the best manifestation of the absurdity of science's investigating its own premises and tools, is the fuss over what is called *The problem of induction*.[125] I shall be very brief here, whereas this topic received way too much attention than it deserves. The problem is something like this: What (logically) **justifies** inferences from the **past** to the **future**? The answer, of course, is this: The **definition** of 'past' and 'future'. What I mean is this: Language **defined** 'object' as something that **persists** in time. Now, science investigates 'why do objects persist in time?' Because they are **objects!**

rules of **geometry**! It is impossible to build structures such as the ones appearing in M.C. Escher's drawings, for example. A two dimensional creature will never understand **why** it is impossible, but to us it seems completely intelligible that the 'laws' of geometry are **universal**. Similarly, there will be a 'new' geometry, making it just as impossible to cause certain effects in the chain of events.

But regardless whether we take this four-dimensional history to be "frozen" or "interactive", the problem with the whole story is not so much the technical part. Look how far we've got in the last fifty years, and the rate of change is constantly increasing. What makes this story pure fiction is the simple fact that there **is** no 'objective world'. There are only private, individual worlds, that have artificially created for themselves a **social**, shared world, held together by **language**. I started the story with a premise that I totally **reject**: The premise of **determinism**, of radical objectivism, or materialism. I do **not** share Parmenides' and Spinoza's worldview, which is the basis of the story. Humanity's **joint, objective artificial** world is constantly growing. Meanwhile, people's belief systems are constantly **converging**. They speak more and more **the same language**. This is the point where my fiction really takes off: I insinuate it is possible, even conceivable, that at some point in the distant future people will be in **complete** agreement; A utopian 'pre *tower of Babel*' state of complete homogeneity and mutual understanding. Everything will be shared; There will be no conflicts of interests. No more arguments about the 'Good'. If and when this *Utopia* is achieved, my science fiction story will have become **possible**, because there would finally be **The world**, the one and only. And **this** completely 'agreed upon' world could be saved in the memory banks of the super-computer. I also think that in this ideal state of affairs there would be no potential problem of conflicting changes in the past, because the notion of 'conflict' will have become obsolete, maybe even hard to understand."

○

°The same applies to 'laws' or 'principles': These **terms** were defined as something that **lasts** (through time). It is nothing but absurd to wonder **why**. It is as if the inventor of the game of chess would wonder, after teaching everybody the new game, **why** should the game end when the king is captured, or why does the bishop travel diagonally.

Philosophers **could**, of course, raise the question whether the very principle of regularity is **good**. Weather it should be introduced as a **public** principle, to be incorporated in every speaker's belief system. This question would be legitimate. And it also has an answer: It is **good**, if **communication** between speakers is taken to be good (which is a separate question I hope to address before too long). But if we accept communication to be desirable, if we believe that the **convergence** of speakers' belief system has **value**, then the regularity postulated by the principle of induction is inevitable. Regularity is what enables speakers to hang on to their beliefs; It keeps certain parts of the objective world **still**, so it can be grasped. Without this **postulated** regularity (postulated, not 'assumed') there is no objective subdomain, without which there is no language. **Induction** came

155

Gaya did not smile. For some reason, it was hard for her. She seemed to be awaiting my questions. I asked: "Why did you describe the way from three dimensions to four? Would it not have been simpler to describe the passage from two to three? "[91] Gaya smiled for the first time since this episode started: "I preferred to tell you about the future, because it is **open**. It is easier for you to accept a story which is admittedly fictitious, than to **believe** me that things actually happened the way I describe them. But I am afraid you are taking me too literally. It is just a science fiction story – a sort of "thought experiment" designed to demonstrate how, in principle, a spatial coordinate can be created. I am not claiming that it will actually happen this way, nor do I claim that historically the third spatial coordinate was in fact created in any similar or analogous way."[92]

I thought I got the picture. I said: "So when the number of spatial dimensions increases by one, like in your story, then the past (what **used** to be the past and is now a spatial dimension) suddenly becomes changeable?" "Good point" she replied; "The future four dimensional society I invented can "change the past", but this means that the past **changes over time** (it takes **time** to change...). There are two "pasts" here, and one of them, again, is unchangeable. It is a kind of an 'infinite series'[93] of time, each such 'time' viewing its predecessor as a **spatial** coordinate. Imagine you are in this 'four dimensional society': Today you visit the year 1995, tomorrow you visit 2995. This 'today' and 'tomorrow' are, again, **time**: If you visited a certain point in 1995 **today,** you cannot change this: You

---

into the world together with **past, future** and material **objects**. They are all inseparable, and together they **constitute** (and are constituted by) **language**.

[91] Two dimensional mathematics, i.e., **Geometry**, was already quite developed in ancient Greece. Nevertheless, **three** dimensional mathematics was **not**. Plato (or was it Socrates) noticed this point, and strongly urged (his contemporary) science to take it up.[126] It was no less than two millennia later, that **n** dimensional mathematics was developed.

[92] Why did Einstein posit 'C' as a **fixed** entity in his theory? Because he considered it to be the maximum 'speed of information': This is a perfect example how epistemology 'influences' the structure of reality. If Einstein was a **bat**[127] I don't think he would have picked the speed of light. Einstein **decided** to make it **inconceivable** that this speed should be exceeded, and by doing so, he managed to 'turn' the coordinate of time into another coordinate of space. He thus determined the 'conversion factor': How units of time are 'converted to' (or, rather, 'conceived as') units of length. The important point being, that Einstein didn't **discover** relativity: He **invented** it. Science **creates**, not **uncovers.**

[93] An infinite series of 'time within time' has often been presented as an argument **against** viewing time as a spatial coordinate. The argument goes something like this: If time is but a spatial coordinate **perceived** differently than space, then there must be **another**, 'new' time, within which the preceding four dimensions are **observed**; And the same applies to the 'new' time, and so on *ad infinitum*. The flaw of the argument is the reference to an **observer**. Under an objectivist premise, no 'observer' is required.

can only manipulate spatial coordinates, not the **past**. It's a bit confusing, I know".

I still had the little sea shell in my hand. I looked at it and asked: "So this is what the **past** is all about: a parmenidean physical four dimensional object. This is what the 'project' as you called it is all about: 'Creating' a **past** occupied by things like **this**." Gaya laughed. The hard part was over: "You make it seem not very worthwhile. I prefer to think of it as creating the **set**, the **arena** where it can all happen. Socially, I mean. By creating a richer and richer 'past', humanity has more and more to 'play with', to relate to, to enjoy, to discuss. As I said before: The objective world constantly becomes **richer**. Not only with **things**. Also with **dimensions**. But I think that for now three dimensions is more than enough. For me, anyway. The three dimensional objective world is far from complete. The debate is still open, what it **ought** to be". The word 'ought' triggered my moral instincts: "So that is what **ethics** is all about? Collectively **deciding** what the objective world **ought** to be?" Gaya nodded; "This is what ethics is all about. Reaching agreement regarding the structure, or, rather, **contents**, of the collective project. Only in recent years, it seems, such an agreement starts to seem at all **possible**. World peace is but the first stage, although a most important one. **The** most important, I would say."

World peace seemed a most proper topic to end this conversation with. We walked back in silence. I was engulfed in deep thought. When I sat at my computer the conversation with Gaya just wouldn't leave my mind. So I decided to get it out of my system. If you believe it is unintelligible, you are probably right. My apologies.

I spent most of the day doing **foot**work. It is now after dinner, and I just read the last few pages again, trying to make up my mind whether they should be left or omitted from the text, before I print today's crop. What finally made me decide to leave it as it is, was Gaya's emphasis on the importance of **objects**, an importance that I was not aware of. Having an experience is one thing, and introducing it into the objective, **public** world, is another. Cutting it out somehow seemed **immoral**, keeping something **hidden**, just because it seems a little obscure (or a lot). So I disobeyed Gaya's advice; But it was she who taught me: Rules were made to be broken.

June 29 - Health

Three more days; Thirty more pages. It's getting hard. I miss home. If it weren't for Gaya I would probably go crazy; or just shorten my stay, which would have an adverse impact on the reason for which I came: To write. I wonder if she realizes the extent of her significance. Probably yes. I have yet to find something she is **not** aware of. Edam is still as beautiful, but I am now **used** to this beauty. Like the locals. They don't **see** it any more. We humans need **change**; variety. Or do we? Many people **love** routine. Even if nothing happens: "No news - good news", they say. Maybe it's just me. Maybe I got used to having **many** moments. Maybe routine **grows** on you: The more you have it, the more you like it; And the same probably applies to the opposite: If one is **used** to variety, to frequent change, it becomes a **need**. Like an **addiction**. So the answer is probably what most people actually do: Fall in and out of routine. Have a routine, and break it every once in a while. But the **breaks** are a routine in themselves: Like my routine here. Maybe I should take a canoe and paddle in the canals for a while. People do it all the time now, since I made it possible. But I don't **feel** like it. I want to go home. Three more days.

Gaya looked tired when I met her at breakfast. "Good morning" I said. "How are you? did you sleep well?" She released a faint smile: "Good morning". She didn't answer my question. She seemed a bit **down**. I decided not to ignore it. I felt close enough to her to show a bit more interest than a polite rhetoric question. I really cared for her. I said: "You look a bit pale. Do you feel all right?" My concern was audible; and visible. Her smile brightened a bit, and this time she replied: "I don't feel so well. But it's normal. I'm an old woman, you know. One bad day in two weeks for a woman my age beats the odds."[94] Her

---

[94] This is a good opportunity to discuss 'odds', or **probability**. Let us start with a simple case. Say speaker S believes that out of every 10 occurrences of events A and B will simultaneously occur 4 times. S will then say that the probability of the occurrence of B simultaneously with A is 4 out of 10, or 40%. If this probability **were** 100%, S would say that B is **entailed** by A. However, in this case the probability is only 40%, so B cannot be said as being 'completely' entailed by A; It is somehow 'partially' entailed.

How can this belief of S be 'coded' into her belief system? How can entailment be 'partial'? Well, for this to be possible, S needs another property (besides A and B), that we shall call '0.4B/A'. While property B is **not** entailed by A, property '0.4B/A' **is**. As far as the remaining relations with every **other** property in the system, 0.4B/A has the same ones as B. In this way, S may have a variety of probabilities coded into her system. All properties that have such a form, are hereafter termed 'probability properties'. How does S acquire a 'probability property)'? Naturally, she could be **told** that B's probability out of A's occurrences is 40%, and she could decide to believe, if she considers the source credible. Or she could form such a belief all by herself, provided her system is sophisticated enough. Say S decides to **calculate** (by herself) the probability of B out of A's occurrences. All she has to do, is search her memory for all the **particular** occurrences of A, and count how many of those were concurrent with B.

158

openly admitting something was wrong got me real worried. I guess I expected her to reassure me that she was Ok. That she would give some **explanation**. I tried humor: "I could have sworn that you **cannot** feel unwell". To this she already gave an answer that was typical to her: "**Cannot**? There is nothing I **cannot** do." It was my turn to smile: "Can you make yourself feel better?" Her answer seemed genuine: "Yes I can. But I **don't want** to. There is always a price, you know. There are several things I **can** do about it. Take certain medication, for example. But in the specific case it would do me more harm, later on. I'd rather feel a bit unwell. Like willingly suffer the pain at the dentist." I wondered if she was **ill**. If she had some sort of medical problem. But I didn't dare get **so** personal. Instead, I tried a roundabout approach: "You mean that sometimes there is absolutely no escape from feeling bad, even if you do everything **right**?" It seemed like a flaw in her philosophy. Gaya answered, patiently: "You use the word 'bad' ambiguously. You must distinguish between a bad feeling and feeling bad." I raised my eyebrows, and she explained: "I admit that I almost **forgot** what it is to **feel bad**. I'm beyond this stage, for many years already. But I sometimes have 'bad feelings': I have headaches, I sometimes don't sleep very well, like tonight. It was too hot. They have no air-conditioning here. It is only as hot two or three times a year here. I sometimes have a bad **physical** feeling. But it is something completely different from **feeling bad**. You know what 'feeling bad' is. We have discussed it."

I pursued the subject. I wanted to pull her into a lecture, maybe distract her from her body. Besides, I was genuinely interested. I didn't feel so great myself. I said: "So when this happens, you just wait for it to pass?" She replied: "Of course not. I do everything that **should** be done in the circumstances. I **care** for myself. But nevertheless, medical science, at least in **my** world, has not yet succeeded in eliminating medical problems altogether. It hasn't even found a cure for the common cold, which I also happen to posses right now. Occasional bad physical sensation **goes with** being alive. That's the way it **is**. And I wouldn't have it any other way. Without **sickness** there would be no **health**. Health is a wonderful thing thanks to sickness. So when I am ill, I care for myself the best I know how, **and then** wait for it to pass. It doesn't make me angry or frightened. At the most I can become a little depressed, that's all." She made a short pause, and then decided to continue: "People associate the **lack** of health with **dying**, and **this** is a big mistake. A very big mistake. Some people

---

So S constantly **computes**. She revises the probability **with every new occurrence of A**, and the probability **changes** with every such occurrence. At some point, S notices that the computed result has not changed significantly over the last n occurrences of A. If and when this happens, S may decide she had enough, and stops counting, thus arriving at a 'fixed' probability property such as '0.4B/A'.

are ill most of their **long** life, others die young and **very** healthy." Now the conversation started to become **really** interesting. I am one of the people that associate good health with a long life, and poor health with a short one. I asked her to explain: "Let me get this straight: You are saying there is no **correlation**[95] between one's health and the length of her life?" Gaya started to become her old self. I succeeded in dragging her into another of those conversations. She started to explain: "No correlation **whatsoever**. The time of one's **death** is something completely unrelated to the phenomena of health and sickness. I think it is obvious. People **happen** to die of diseases as they happen to die from bullets, cars, rocks, trees and bridges. None of those have anything to do with **death**. Death can come at an infinite variety of circumstances. But there is no necessary **causal** connection.[96] People recover from the most horrible diseases, and others

---

[95] If and when S realizes that the computed probability of B out of occurrences of A has not significantly changed in the last n occurrences of A, she says that she has found a **correlation** between A and B. She has identified a **regularity**: She managed to construct a property such as 0.4B/A, which **does not change anymore** with every occurrence of A. It is like a sort of game: Pick two properties, and **compute** until the probability ceases to change. Obviously, there remains the question of what is **significant** and what should 'n' be. But this is already a matter of taste, of motivation (of **context**). It depends what S wants to **achieve**. If it is just **truth** that she is after, she must compute forever.

Let us now turn to a 'real life' example. It is claimed, that there is a correlation between smoking cigarettes and having lung cancer. What is the meaning of this claim? Following the above reasoning, it means that someone (some scientist, or a group of them) made the computation described above: Starting at some point in time, it examined every smoker, and out of those, counted the cases of lung cancer. This is obviously **not** what was done. What was done was something quite different: It was calculated, out of all the occurrences of lung cancer, how many of them smoked. The basic, **empirical** result, was (initially) the reverse of what we were looking for: Not how many cases of cancer out of smokers, but how many smokers out of cancer cases. Still, scientists are not so stupid. They found that the probability of being a smoker out of occurrences of cancer is **significantly higher** than the probability of being a smoker out of occurrences of being a **person**. Let us assume that the first probability was 50%, i.e., 0.5S/C, while the second was 20%, i.e., 0.2S/P. This result indicated, that the correlation cancer⇒smoking was significantly higher than the correlation person⇒smoking. This is where statistics completed its task, and other considerations entered the picture. It was **further** assumed, that there is a **causal** connection between the first pair. Note: not in the direction cancer⇒smoking, but in the opposite direction: smoking⇒cancer. This was an **assumption**, a premise without which the whole calculation wouldn't make sense. **However**, with such a premise in place, who needs probabilities? If the causal connection is considered as having been established, the statistical calculation is redundant! To this the scientists might reply: True, the causal connection is a hypothesis. But statistics **substantiate** it! Well, it cannot substantiate it, **without** begging the question. The most that can be said in favor of the claim that smoking causes cancer, is that it is **not incoherent**. Probability calculation does **not** refute the hypothesis.

[96] Causal connections are tricky things, as Hume[128] rightly pointed out. I believe causality to have an important role in our *worldview*, although not quite in the sense science takes it: As something that **is** in the world. Let me outline how I believe causality 'works' for us. A group of people decided (rightly, I believe) that smoking is **bad**. This is the **first** stage. Unfortunately, the prevailing

160

die while having their teeth fixed. But I'd rather not talk about **death** today, if you don't mind. Yesterday was a big enough strain for me. I am willing to talk about sickness and health, if you want." I felt a strange **relief** in Gaya's complete dissociation between being sick and **dying**. An old woman admitting she is ill makes you think of something **terminal**. Apparently there was no such danger. She's not going anywhere. And I **did** want her to tell me more about sickness and health. I asked: "So what **is** 'being sick'? besides the obvious definition, I mean". "What, in your opinion, **is** the obvious definition?" She inquired. I tried to phrase a short and clear one: "It is the **malfunction** of the apparatus that we call 'the body'. A deviation from its normal mode of operation." I already understood why Gaya started every discussion with 'what do **you** think it is'. It provided her with a starting point, one that **I** supplied. This way she was sure we were talking about **the same thing**. Sort of 'entering **my** world' or 'employing **my** language'. This exactly was Socrates' method. She picked it up from my definition: "You emphasized the word 'malfunction'. I take it you believe there is a **normal** mode of this apparatus, right?" I nodded and she continued: "Let us talk about this 'normal' mode. Do you consider a *Thalidomide* child, or a person who was born blind, as 'normal' in your sense of the word?" I hesitated. I could almost read her mind. If I say 'no', she would make **everyone** 'ill' in one way or another: One is to tall, one too short; one too fat, one too thin. So I said: "If they were **born** like that, I consider it **normal**. If the blind person later catches a cold, **then** I would say that he is ill; that he has a malfunction." Gaya agreed: "Fair enough. So you agree that every person has his own 'point of reference', what **for him** is considered 'healthy'. Let us make one step further. Let us now assume that a person was not born blind, but lost his eyesight at the age of twenty. Say, in an accident. What then?" I didn't think an accident qualified as 'sickness', so I said: "Why an accident? Let us suppose he had a severe **eye sickness**. He was ill for a year, his situation deteriorated, medical science couldn't help him, and finally he lost his sight. When this happened, he was not **sick** any more. He was **blind**." Gaya smiled. She didn't even look pale anymore. The conversation about sickness must have made her well. She said: "Wait a minute; You mean that **as long as he could be helped**, or **thought** he could be helped, you consider him ill, and when it is clear that he cannot be helped, when he lost his sight completely, he all of a sudden becomes **healthy**?" I scratched my head. I was

---

metaphysical paradigm takes 'bad' and 'good' as flaky, unreal and subjective. Therefore, the next step is to substantiate the claim that smoking is a **cause** of something bad. The only way to accomplish that is to find something that is universally considered bad, such as sickness and death. When an army of competent, educated people set their minds on substantiating a hypothesis, they are bound to succeed. And they have: It appears that the **objective** world of tomorrow, the world humanity **creates** for itself, will be devoid of smoking.

161

puzzled. I didn't know what to say, Gaya giggling from across the table. I said: "I give up. Just give me the whole story."

She did. "People are so **afraid** of being ill, they become completely incoherent in their understanding what illness **is**. First, we must make an initial important distinction: A distinction between '**I am** ill' and between '**He or She is** ill'. The two sentences employ a **completely** different sense of the word 'ill'. Remind me to later discuss the **source** of this mix-up. The difference between the two senses is this: '**I am ill**' means: 'I am not satisfied with the functioning of my body, and I believe it **can** be fixed. I have **hope**'. On the other hand, the meaning of '**She is ill**' is: 'She needs **care** from other people. She needs to be looked after.' Do you accept this distinction?" I did not. At least not **yet**. I tried a counter example: "Let me start with the first sense. Terminal patients at some point **accept** the fact that they cannot be cured.[97] They have no more hope. Still they are **ill**!" Gaya laughed audibly; I didn't like it. It made me feel stupid. She said: "You are talking about the **second** sense; the sense of **she**, or **they**. Think **as** a terminal patient. I am telling you, and I **know**, am **sure**. I'm not **guessing** here. If a person has no **hope**, if he accepted the fact that he is going to die, it is as if he **wants** to die. And then he does. Take my word for it: Nobody considers **herself**

---

[97] Medical science already explicitly accepts the **correlation** between a patient's **will** to live and his chances of recovery. It is widely accepted, that the patient's attitude towards his illness is a key factor. Still, medical science has absolutely no explanation to this phenomenon. In fact, if causality is taken as the universal principle that governs reality, medical science should clearly **deny** this correlation. This is a good example of an apparent **contradiction** between causality and statistics. Only in this case, it is **good** that people recover. So no effort is invested in trying to **refute** this correlation.

Death is an interesting concept, in the context of **speakers** and **language**. There is no problem when the death in question is someone else's: To say 'X is dead' is like saying 'X does not exist anymore', which is not really problematic, even if X **used** to exists. Things can 'stop existing'. The problem arises when a speaker refers to his **own** death, as in "I do not exist". Much has been said about the absurdity of this statement. Heidegger has made the death of the **self** a central motive in his thought, treating death as something which is constantly 'anticipated', always lurking in the background.

The statement "I do not exist" is indeed problematic, if 'existence' is to encompass **everything**, not leaving anything outside its scope, as the realist view essentially maintains. However, if 'existence' is taken the way I proposed, i.e., as membership in the objective subdomain constituted by language, the problem is automatically solved. When S1 says to S2 "I do not exist", he means that he is a **predicate** rather than an **object**. It is just like saying "my pain does not exist" or "**red** does not exist". The consequence of such a statement is making the concept "I" **subjective** rather than **objective; private rather than public. It is as if S1 notifies S2 that they cannot speak of S1 **and still mean the same thing**. Still, they can both use the concept S1 **as a predicate**: They can say, for example, "S1's wife", and still mean the same woman. But S1 simply ceases to be an objective **object** in the shared world.

162

ill if she has no hope. A blind person does not consider himself ill if he believes he is going to remain blind. Remember the TV series *Run for your life* with *Ben Gazarra*? No, you were probably too young. It was about a man that was terminally ill and was given a prognosis of no more than six months to live; Nothing could be done to prevent it. **He** definitely didn't consider himself ill, whereas he had no hope. He had a hell of a time, though. All kinds of adventures. The series was very successful. It ran for years. He didn't **die**, neither was he **ill**, in the first sense of the word. Such things happen all the time." I tried another direction: "Cannot one be ill and **not know it**?" Gaya laughed again. **She** was definitely not ill any more: "I don't even **understand** what could possibly be meant by that!" I explained: "The doctor decided not to tell him." Gaya explained patiently: "Again you are talking about the second sense. Do you understand the **first**? The first is only about **your, personal** illness. Better think of counter examples to the **second** sense, which is in much more common use. The second sense is simply 'She needs care'. You want to contest this one?" I tried to think of sick people who needed **no** care, or of people who needed care and were not ill: "How about 'she is alone at home, with a cold. No need to care for her; She can take care of herself'. This time it was a good one. Gaya treated it seriously. She asked: "What does **she** think? Does **she** consider herself ill? In the first sense, I mean." I started an offensive: "Who knows? What does it matter? We are now talking about your **second** sense!" Gaya said, carefully: "Let me see: You are talking about **my** situation right now: I take care of myself; I don't need anyone else's care. Right?" "Yes!" I said triumphantly. Gaya looked like a fighter preparing for the final blow: "But you **did** care for me! You were **worried**! You know what **care** means by now. Not necessarily helping me out of bed. Your way was to talk to me, be nice, show affection. When you say about **her** that she just has a common cold and can take care of herself, you would still call her tomorrow and ask her how she is, right? because you **care**. Because **she is ill**." Gaya thought I was defeated, but I still had some life in me: "This makes practically everyone **ill** in one way or another. If anyone who is 'cared for' is considered ill, then very few people are **not**!" Naturally, she had a good answer: "Think of the **difference**, in **your** feeling, between caring for someone whom you consider ill and someone healthy... Wait, you may be right. I used the wrong word. Let me rephrase my initial definition of '**She is ill**': The right word is **worry**, not **care**. Care is much broader. Sorry. It was misleading." I felt a slight childish **pride** for not being **so** stupid after all. She went on: "Look: When we say about someone that **she** is ill, it is something in **us**, not in **her**. We shouldn't look at **her** to understand what is going on; We should look at ourselves. It is something about **our** state of mind; Nothing to do with **her**. It is like the difference between '**I** have pain' and '**she** has pain'.[98] Again, two completely

---

[98] The example of **pain** has been a fertile source of discussion, particularly in the philosophy of

different things. **My** pain is something private, something that cannot, in principle, be shared. **Her** pain, on the other hand, is a different feeling all together. You have three daughters. They must have been in pain in your presence. You know what **her** pain is. It is a completely **different** sort of pain then yours! In the case of someone very close, it is much **more** painful, although in a completely different way!"

I was starting to understand. She was waiting for my reaction. I tried to phrase what I understood: "If I understand you correctly, you are saying that **I am ill** is a combination of dissatisfaction and hope.." She interrupted: "As far as the **body** is concerned. If you are broke, you are dissatisfied from the situation, and you hope to make some money soon, it doesn't make you ill." I nodded and continued: "..Which makes an **overweight** person, if he is dissatisfied with his weight, ill. or a cigarette smoker who wants to quit. Or a drug addict." Gaya nodded and remained silent. I continued: "Whereas saying about someone **else** that she is ill is a manifestation of my **own** state of mind regarding **her**. If I believe she has to be **worried** about.." Gaya interrupted again: "Not necessarily by **you**. You can say about a strange person that she is ill. But you mean that **someone** ought to care. Sorry, **worry**." Her account seemed to make sense. It was certainly **coherent** with her overall view of things. I decided to return to the first sense: "This business with **hope** and **dissatisfaction**. Don't they **always** go hand in hand? I mean, when there is hope, of **any** kind, not necessarily regarding sickness and health. When there is **hope**, isn't there also, inevitably, also **dissatisfaction**?" "Not necessarily" she replied. "Take my situation **now**, for example: I do **not** consider myself ill. I have hope to feel better tomorrow, but I am **not** dissatisfied with my situation, although I do not feel very well. Dissatisfaction is not simply another way of saying 'hope'. I **constantly** have hope. And I am always **satisfied**. I take 'dissatisfaction' to be closely connected to **guilt**."[99] Guilt. A new one. "How did **guilt** come into this?" I protested. "Guilt

---

mind. The behavioristic[129] view was the only account of internal mental states such as pain that was **coherent** with the realist premise: If **realism**, then **all the way**. Behaviorists denied the meaningfulness of '**my** pain'. They claimed that the only meaning of 'pain' is in its external manifestations. Behaviorism is the radical consequence of objectivism, just as solipsism is the radical consequence of relativism. Nevertheless, behaviorism didn't go very far, because it denied everyone's (own) **evident** subjectivity. The **real** significance of 'pain' is in **my** pain. If **my** pain is declared meaningless, so much for the whole doctrine.

[99] The importance of **guilt** was particularly recognized by the Catholic church. It served not only as an important motivator, but the institute of **confession**, designed to enable people to **rid** themselves of it, was of extreme importance. And it did help sinners to feel a lot better. Unfortunately, the 'vice list' was a bit problematic. Judaism also has its instrument of getting rid of guilt, in the Day of Atonement. Modern atheist society has no substitute (except for the prison system, or 'correctional facilities', which do everything but 'correcting').

is a key factor" she replied; "It is one of the two basic sources of bad and evil." Apparently the session was only starting; "What is the second?" I wondered. "The second is **fear**" she replied. "But guilt is more serious. More dangerous." I didn't want to move on to 'fear' and 'guilt' before we finished health and sickness. I said: "Wait. Before this you still owe me an explanation: How did the mix-up between the two senses of 'ill' come about?" "Oh, yes." She replied. "It is another product of western thinking. It is based on the assumption that 'I' and 'You' are of the same **kind**. That we are both entities of the same kind in an objective **place**. Again, like with 'pain': Western thinking takes 'my pain' and 'your pain' as of the same kind, while it clearly is **not**: My pain is a one very particular sensation, and **your** pain is another kind of (my) sensation. It hurts **in different places**. Where did it hurt **you** when your daughter was in pain? In your heart? In your brain? All over? Isn't it very **different** from your own pain?"

"Let us turn to **fear** and **guilt**" I said. "You said guilt was more **serious**. Why?" "Because guilt is **real**, and fear is not" she replied, and immediately continued: "Fear, again, is a product of western thought. Eastern thinking hardly recognizes its existence, let alone its significance. Fear is simple: It is an inevitable consequence from the belief that there are 'circumstances beyond one's control'. If you believe you are a meaningless speck in a vast objective universe, it makes a lot of sense to be afraid. So much can happen! So many things, practically **every**thing, is not under your control. You can do nothing about it. You are at the mercy of **laws of nature**, of weather, earthquakes, crazy leaders and an infinity of potential mishaps. What a miserable living! The acceptance of the objectivity of the universe has most horrible consequences. Particularly after **God** ceased to play an important part in the scheme of things. I don't think this conception will last for long. At least with God, there was **grace**. There was divine supervision. Now there is only blind nature and coincidence. Fear is the product. That is why I said it is not **real**. It can be **completely** eliminated, simply by changing one's 'point of view', as you call it. I believe that people who turn to religion, do it chiefly to eliminate fear. It works. Believe it or not, I was never afraid. Maybe as a child, but I don't remember. I can **speak** about it, but I really don't know the feeling. It sounds horrible to me. **frightening**." She laughed while saying the last word.[100]

---

[100] Footnote 100 seems a good point to discuss a concept that necessarily occupies **every** conceptual scheme, every belief system: The concept **I**. It is safe to assume that it is never missing from a speaker's system (except, perhaps, in severe cases of autism). What can be said about it? Well, in my case, I am the **owner** of my belief system. It **belongs** to me. It **depends** on me. Therefore, it will not be unreasonable to claim, that all the concepts (properties, beliefs) in my system are **included** in it: All properties **entail** this concept **I** (for every P, if P then I).

Wait a minute: I already **have** one such concept! One property, which was found to be entailed by all others. It is the property G: The Good. I have already identified G as synonymous (equivalent) to

"And in what way is **guilt 'real'**?" I asked. Gaya resumed a serious facade.
"Guilt is serious business. It is **real**, because people often feel guilty, **for good
reason**. In fact, some people live with it their whole life. Like *Cain*." It didn't
take much explaining. I knew exactly what she was talking about. Just to make
sure: "You mean if someone realizes that he did **wrong** and has to live with it?"
"Yes" she replied. "But I think guilt somehow appears even if he does **not**
completely realize it. More often than not, people who have done wrong (By
their own standards!) sort of 'cover up from themselves'. Let me think of an
example. Say a beggar asked you for a dime and you refused. You tell yourself
you did **right**: He should get a job. If it is **really** your **belief** that it is better **for
him** not to get your dime, then you are ok. No guilt will emerge. But if you were
just lazy and didn't want to be bothered by him, if you didn't exercise the **care**
required from a human being, although it is your belief that compassion is in
order, than your system is disrupted. Your **system** has a problem. After all, the
beggar is in **you**, it is a part of you. Small and insignificant maybe, but still part
of you. And you denied it something it deserved: Your dime. I don't have to tell
you about **guilt** in the clear cases in which you are fully **aware** of the wrong.
Then it can be amended. Sometimes. But the situation is really grave, **for you**, if
you manage to suppress it. If you manage to 'convince' yourself that the wrong
was right." I understood, in principle. But I didn't know **how** the mechanism
worked. I asked: "Say I did exactly that. What will happen to me afterwards?"
"Then," she said, "You are a little **angry** at the beggar. After all, he **should** get a
job! Why is he begging? He becomes a small target for your **anger**. And anger
has a tendency to spread: You are also angry at the circumstances that made him
a beggar. And the anger 'joins your system'. It doesn't diffuse. It has no **reason**
to diffuse. The case with the beggar is trivial, so the consequences are hardly
visible. But an accumulation of such trivial instances, and some less trivial ones,
can completely distort your *worldview*.[101] The **world** that you create becomes a

---

D; If **I** includes all the concepts in my system, it must also be synonymous with G: I≡G. Does this
make any sense?

What is "I" doing? It is seeking the good for myself (my world, my system). Identifying the concepts
Good and *I* as synonymous reduces the never ending quest for **good** to a question of self
determination; of **finding oneself**. Of defining one's own **meaning**, or **place**, in the system. The
equation I≡G is a **logical** consequence, not an ethical or lingual one. I am **the** Good, and the
negation of contradiction; 'The other side' of contradiction. No wonder contradiction is hard to
understand: It is **my** mirror image. No wonder **F** is essential: It is my 'other side'.

[101] It is not impossible for people to say (or think) "I am bad", which is a consequence of acting in
a way that is 'bad' by their own standards. In such a case, the equation I≡G seems not to hold. But it
also makes the whole system **logically incoherent**. This is why Kant preached **coherence**. When a
person acts in a way that is bad by his own standards, it (logically) follows that he is not entailed by
his entire belief system. If he is a realist, of course, his system is incoherent in the first place...

cruel one. Your punishment is **living in a cruel world**.[102]" These words reminded me of something: "I think I have a little story you'll like. I was once criticized for the permissive upbringing of my daughters. Someone said to me: 'The way you bring up your kids does not prepare them for the **cruel world**'. I was annoyed with this criticism. I am very sensitive to criticism where my daughters are concerned. I replied: '**What** cruel world?'. I was then hardly aware of what I was saying; It was more of an instinct. But it makes perfect sense now. I couldn't agree with you more. Unethical behavior simply creates an unethical world."

Gaya remained silent. She looked tired again. She did a lot of speaking. And she always put her heart into it. I said: "Do you want to do anything? A short walk? Anything I can do for you?" Gaya was touched by my sensitivity. She produced a small smile and said: "No. I'll just go and lie down. Thank you. For your concern. I know you mean it. And I'm glad you care. It's all I need."

I didn't see Gaya for the rest of the day. After dinner I went for a walk alone. I found a new bench, in a beautiful spot surrounded by trees. The sun was setting, as usual, and sent its last rays to me through the branches. I could see millions of little bugs hovering in the air, as if using up the last minutes of sunshine. They were in a frenzy, chasing each other at random. Or is it at random? Could their lives be **meaningless**? I doubt it. Maybe I'll ask Gaya tomorrow. I sat there on the bench until the last ray disappeared behind the trees. I walked back thinking about Gaya. I hope she's better. She said some amazing things today. Could she be right about **health**? Why **do** people get sick, then? Could they possibly bring it over **themselves** for some reason? Maybe they **need** to be sick? Maybe they **need** to be cared for? Or maybe their world needs a **change**? I wonder.

---

[102] Hell?

June 30 - Purpose

Two more days; Twenty more pages. It is getting slightly easier; I can already feel the end. Funny word, **end**.[103] Equivocal; Ambiguous. My coming to Edam was a means to an **end** (namely, this book), and it's coming to an **end**. I wonder if other languages have a similar equivocacy. Hebrew does not. In Hebrew, 'end' (the one that supposedly justifies the means) is equivocal with **reason**, which I think makes more sense. Not always is the end (or ends) achieved in the end. Sometimes a thing ends without the ends having been achieved. But the end is always the **reason** for doing something.

Gaya seemed a little better this morning, but still not her old self. (Well, she was her **old** self, but not her old self). I asked her whether she wanted to skip the morning walk again, but she said she'd go, if we'll make it short. I took her to

---

[103] The terms **'ends'**, **'purpose'**, **'reason'** and **'cause'** are often confused in ordinary language. 'Cause' is used when employing an objectivist view; It does not require reference to human thoughts or intentions; It is taken as being 'in the world'. Aristotle linked 'cause' with 'purpose' by defining *telos* as '*The purpose of a final cause*'. Although 'cause' may be used 'objectively', the principle of causation also participates, or is involved with the first three terms, which are synonymous with *telos*.

'Reason' is ambiguous: It is used both in justifying a **belief** and in explaining an **act**: "I have reason to believe" vs. "I acted for a reason". The first usage can be perceived as a special case of the second, if 'believing' or 'adopting a belief' is conceived as an **act**. In this usage, it is a manifestation of an **implication**: If A is the reason I believe (or perform) B (A being a belief I already have), I am simply stating $A \supset B$. However, if I perform **act** C for the reason R, then R is also the **purpose** of act C, or the **ends** I seek to accomplish by the act. Let us concentrate on C and R.

R is a desired **state of affairs**. It is something I **want**. As always, it is a **property**. C is also a property, but of a different kind: an act. The first observation regarding the relations between these two properties, is that C precedes R in time. Here is where **cause** enters the picture: For R to be the reason of act C, a causal connection between C and R must be assumed. Therefore, I must be holding the belief 'C is a cause of R', for R to be the reason of C. What we have now is a two-way relationship between C and R:

$$C \text{ is the } \mathbf{cause} \text{ of } \mathbf{R} \qquad \mathbf{R} \text{ is the } \mathbf{reason} \text{ of } C$$
$$\text{or:}$$
$$\mathbf{R} \supset \mathbf{C}$$

An act always has a reason, and **is** a cause. This establishes a general relation between **reason** and **cause**. The cause causes the reason, and the reason explains the cause (the act which is believed to act as a cause). Naturally, a property may be **both** a cause and a reason, such as in $P \supset Q \supset S$. Here Q is the cause of P and the reason of S. (The discussion is, of course, in the context of human **actions**[130], not 'objective' science). **Explaining** Q with S is called a **causal explanation**. Explaining it with P is a **teleological** one. This makes **G** the **primal cause**, and it makes **F** the **ultimate reason**. Whatever that means....

the spot I discovered yesterday evening, which was not far away and quite beautiful. We sat on the same bench and I asked her about the bugs. She laughed: "You think I'm a bug expert?" I looked at her and answered in a serious expression: "Yes." She laughed again and replied: "Of course insects have a **meaningful** life. They have been around for so much longer than we humans! Do you think they would have survived for so many millions of years, without significantly changing, if it wasn't worth their while? Insects are the greatest evolutionary success. It is just very hard for us to **relate** to them, because they are so small, and so different. But I think it is mainly because of their short life span. Short in **our** terms, I mean. I don't think it **seems** short to them. I guess their **moments** last split seconds. And I think their **pleasure** is much more concentrated. You know there are butterflies that live **as butterflies** for just one day. Can you imagine the **excitement** during this one day?"

We were watching the ducks in the canal next to us. There were two small groups, each consisting of a mother and several very young ducklings. Gaya said: "It is much easier for us to relate to species that seem more similar to **us**. Mother duck and five little ducklings is a picture which is completely intelligible to us. We can easily relate to it. We know perfectly well what **motherhood** is." I wondered whether Gaya was a **mother**. For some reason I didn't dare ask. It seemed she would have told me if it was my place to know. She continued: "What this mother duck is experiencing right now is probably as close to its **meaning of life**[104] as we can conceive. Can you imagine the **responsibility** she has? Those tiny ducklings are the easiest prey around here. For cats, for large birds or rats. And they have to be taught so much! She has to keep constant watch on them for the whole summer. And she has no one to **share** this responsibility with!" She made it sound unbearable. I said: "And this is the **meaning** of her life? It doesn't sound like much fun. Does she **enjoy** it?" Gaya was staring at the ducks. "Enjoy? Enjoyment can be a deceiving term. What is **enjoyable** changes so many times in one's life! What is enjoyable for a teenager seems absurd to an old man. What the little ducklings **enjoy** now is completely different from what they will enjoy when they grow up. It works the other way around: Enjoyment is achieved, or **felt**, when the 'meaning' is 'fulfilled', so to speak. Enjoyment is the **product** of fulfilling one's purpose. It is the **compass** leading to the purpose, not the purpose itself.

---

[104] On the year the United States of America declared its independence, Wolfgang Amadeus Mozart offered his version as to the 'meaning of life' in a letter directed to Padre Martini: *"We live in this world to compel ourselves industriously to enlighten one another by means of reasoning and to apply ourselves always to carrying forward the sciences and the arts."*. A year later, he congratulated his father on his birthday in the following words: *"I wish you as many years as are needed to have nothing left to do in music"*.

I smelled a juicy topic for conversation, and pursued this line: "You mean that every creature has an 'inherent' purpose? And when it is fulfilled the creature experiences the feeling of pleasure?" Gaya answered carefully: "Not exactly. The purpose is not 'preplanned' or 'innate'. Let me put it this way: The **concept** of 'purpose' is such, that it includes 'pleasure' as a side effect, if it is reached.[105] Take one of these ducklings, for instance. It is hungry. It swims after its mother, who directs it to **food**. It eats, and it is not hungry any more. It **remembers**. In time, being **hungry** becomes, in a way, **good news**: It remembers the feeling of satisfying hunger. It is the first **fulfillment** the duckling experiences. It learns that it is able to **produce** this feeling, the feeling of fulfilling a need, of satisfying it, which is what we call 'pleasure'. And as the **needs** change, the way to bring about pleasure changes as well. But the pleasure **itself** is the same. It is the same old 'Good'. Now, the stronger the **need**, the bigger the pleasure. The bigger the **suffering** before fulfillment, the more ecstatic the satisfaction, the enjoyment. This is what **drugs** are all about. The name of the game is 'find needs and fulfill them'[106]."

---

[105] If fulfillment of (ones) purpose is taken to be the cause of pleasure, then the following proposition holds: 'Pleasure' ⊃ '(Fulfillment of) purpose'. And whereas 'Purpose' ⊃ 'Good', then 'Purpose' could be perceived as the middle term, mediating between 'Pleasure' and 'Good'.

[106] The question of 'the meaning of life' has not received much attention from philosophers ever since Nietzsche[131] announced God's death. One of the more interesting attempts to address the issue at all was made by Richard Taylor in *Good and Evil*[132]. In it, he exemplifies a case of meaningless existence, and tries to add to it the ingredients which could possibly render it meaningful. For this he borrows the mythological figure of *Sisyphus*, who was condemned by the gods to an eternal task of rolling a heavy stone to a top of a mountain, from where it rolls down only to be pushed up again by poor Sisyphus.

Taylor offers two possible ways of adding **meaning** to Sisyphus' life. The first is an **objective** way: To have Sisyphus assemble the stones on the top of the mountain, to build a beautiful and enduring temple out of. This would supposedly provide Sisyphus with a **goal**, something his efforts are directed towards. The second, **subjective** way, would be for the gods to inject some magic substance into Sisyphus' veins, to make him **want** to push stones up the mountain. Taylor appears to prefer the second, subjective way; The one involving his **will**. David Wiggins, in *Truth, Invention and the Meaning of Life*[133] seems to prefer a combination of the two.

The question I wish to address based on this excellent example, is whether such 'meaning' (or goal, or purpose, or *telos*) can **at all** be viewed **objectively**. I claim that it is a categorical mistake to talk of 'objective goals'. Goals are **inherently** subjective. Even if a goal is set by a **group** of people, it is still **internal**, to the group, conceived as an entity having an (internal) purpose. If I am right, Taylor's second way of granting Sisyphus' life with meaning should be enough: If Sisyphus really **wants** to roll stones up the mountain, it should be enough to render his life as meaningful as can be. Still, it is hard to accept the claim that **any** goal, provided it is **wanted**, is as meaningful as any other. What **ethics** is all about, is to answer this problem: To identify a goal that is **transcendent**: Although **internal**, could be seen as **worthy** also observed from the **outside**. The reason this problem **cannot** be solved, is simply because we say 'outside', but we have absolutely no idea **what** **'outside' is**. We get our notion of 'outside' by analogy: Usually a **spatial** analogy. But we are

I was disappointed to hear that. I said: "This cannot be a worthy 'meaning' of life; Not even for a duck. An endless quest of pleasure, of needs to fulfill." Gaya shook her head in disapproval. "No, no. I explained pleasure and fulfillment, not the 'meaning of life'. All I described at this stage is the mechanism of producing pleasure. I told you about this Frenchman I knew, DesJardins. He used to put it this way: Most people are **addicted** to suffering. They wouldn't give it up, because it is so **pleasant** to get rid of. It is so **satisfying** to rid oneself of sorrow and pain, that people cling to it, are dependent on it." She still wasn't making sense to me. "But if **this** is how pleasure is achieved, what other option is there but to engage in an endless cycle of 'suffering-pleasure-suffering-pleasure'?" "Precisely" she replied. "If you take **pleasure** as what it is all about, that is where you end up. Pleasure is **blind**. It can be achieved in a thousand ways, and it is always the same pleasure, the same good. It is like a rollercoaster: Down-up-down-up. People who think that is what life is about are right in claiming that life is meaningless. But look at this mother-duck: What is **she** doing now? What need is **she** fulfilling? What is **her** way of finding the good?" She was waiting for my answer. I couldn't think of the duck's situation as **pleasant** in any way. I decided not to make a fool of myself, and said: "Well?" Gaya delivered the answer: "She discovered **care**. Whereas **any** fulfillment produces pleasure, it is possible to find pleasure **everywhere**. So the **purpose** she has 'posited' to herself is to bring up her five kids, to the point they become independent. She **loves** them, cares for them. **Her** need is **their** enjoyment. It is 'pleasure once removed'. Look: She knows various kinds of pleasure, all derived from one or another sort of need that is fulfilled. But there is another possibility: To 'define' her **own** need, her own purpose, as **their** pleasure. So it is like this: If they are enjoying, she is happy. If they are suffering, she is unhappy." I still wasn't **satisfied**: "What is the big deal? What is the difference between this particular way of fulfillment and any other way? What makes this way 'special', or 'worthwhile'? For the duck, I mean. Not for us, with our values and opinions regarding what is 'right'." Gaya seemed a little annoyed: "Who was talking about **us**? I am **only** discussing it from the duck's point of view. What is so **special** in this way of fulfillment, is that it **lasts forever**. It never dies out." I didn't understand why: "Why does it last forever?" "Because," she said "It is always **different**. If you pursue your **own** enjoyment, the fulfillment of your **own** need, you **must** find new things to **want** all the time, because once you have **reached** your goal, it is not a goal any more. Oscar Wilde said it explicitly: 'There are two sources of agony in life: Not getting what you want, and **getting**

---

creatures with a **point of view**, and a particular one: A human point of view. We cannot imagine what 'outside human' is. This is what ethics often tries to do. **Internally**, we know perfectly well what the human goal is: Happiness. Everyone knows it, everybody wants it.

171

it'. Suppose you want something, and get it. Now you have two possibilities: Either **wait** until you want it **again**, which means, go through a stage of **need**, of 'suffering' its **lack**, so there is a **point** in reaching it again, or you manage to find a **new** need, a new goal, a new purpose, which gets exceedingly harder all the time. **instead,** you can do something much more clever, which is what the duck did: You make it your purpose to provide enjoyment for **others**. It has the huge advantage, that you never run out of **goals**! because for the little ducklings, everything is **new**! Their goals are not yet 'used up', as it is for their mother. There is a whole world of new pleasure, new fulfillments, for every one of them. And when they are also 'used up', when they grow, she makes **new ducklings** to care for, to create pleasures for." I had a question: "How does the duck bring herself to **want** someone **else's** enjoyment as **her** need?" Gaya nodded. "Good question. This is where the ingenious invention of **love** enters the picture. She **loves** them. It is **really** her need that they will have a good life. The phenomenon of **love** makes the trick possible.[107] You see, Every year the duck loves a new set of ducklings, and it supplies her with an infinite source of satisfaction, of pleasure, if she succeeds in making **them** enjoy. She can fail, of course, and then she is miserable. But it is possible to succeed, even **constantly** succeed, and then the duck's pleasure does **not** suffer from the seemingly inevitable 'rollercoaster' effect." I kept on bombarding Gaya with questions: "Why doesn't she have **enough** of this sort of fulfillment? You said that when she enjoys **directly**, once her goal is achieved it is not desired any more. Why does the same phenomenon not occur here?" "It does occur" she answered. "The purpose she has is to care for them as long as they depend on her for their life and their pleasure. This goal lasts a whole season, and then it is fulfilled. It is **over**. That is why she makes new ones. Besides, she **also** has her own private **direct** pleasure, when she copulates, for example. She is also in a cycle, between her 'private' pleasure and her 'social' pleasure of caring for others. But what is nice about **this** cycle, is that does not necessarily involve a phase of need, pain or suffering."[108]

---

[107] Let us now enhance Sisyphus' story with another ingredient: Let us inject another chemical into his veins, this time providing him with **affection**, with loving feelings towards some species of creatures living at the top of the mountain, who happen to **feed** on stones of the kind Sisyphus rolls up. Now the story receives a whole new dimension: Sisyphus still **wants** to roll stones up the mountain, he **enjoys** satisfying his will, but in addition, he provides food to a whole colony of creatures he **loves**. Does this make a difference?

[108] 'Bad' was often described as the **lack** of good (mostly to justify bad's existence in God's creation; e.g., Leibniz). If so, isn't 'Good' the **lack** of 'bad'? The problem with this possibility was widely discussed throughout history, mostly by the Church. Although 'Good' and 'Bad' **seem** symmetric, they are not. What determines the asymmetry, the directionality, is the human intentionality, pointed like a compass towards the **God**.

I had enough about ducks. I wanted to talk about **people**. I said: "Are you saying that raising children is the only purpose that is worthwhile?" "Not at all!" She exclaimed. "We were talking about **ducks**, and just to demonstrate the **principle**. Still, raising kids is a paradigmatic example of the **smart** way of deriving pleasure out of life. But it is just an example to demonstrate the principle." I was slow in understanding today. "What **is** 'the principle'? Would you phrase the principle, as it applies to humans?" Gaya smiled: "But of course! Here it is: People have the ability to define their purposes, their goals. Achieving these goals makes them **happy**. Once this happens, the goal is 'used up', so to speak. Therefore, goals have to be constantly **sought**. The trick is to 'hitch-hike' on **other's** goals. Ten people have ten times as many goals as one person. The phenomenon of **love** makes it possible. If there are ten people you **love**, their goals become **your** goals. So you enhance your 'happiness potential' by ten-fold. If you have ten children you love, and you care for them in a way that they all achieve **their** goals, you've got it made! Ducks are simple creatures. They just love their children. I guess. But people can also love other people. They can love **animals**. They can love their spouse, their friends, sometimes even strangers. It is even theoretically possible for them to love **everybody**. So the happiness potential can theoretically be **infinite**." Now things started to make sense. I said: "But it is also **dangerous**: If you have ten kids and they are all miserable, you become ten times as **un**happy!" Gaya agreed: "True. Like the Hi-Tech business. High risk and high return. But it's not **really** dangerous, because it is **really** only up to you. If you do the **right** things, nothing bad can happen to the ones dependent on you. There is no 'fate' or circumstances 'beyond one's control'. You are the **master** of your world, and as such, you can love everyone you know, and to the extent that you are involved in their life, they will not let you down if you do not let them down. If (another) person is **bad**, he may very well be unhappy. But then, it is unlikely that you will **love** him. So, in a way, he brought it upon himself. Still, he can be helped, if you want to help him. And then you can also grow to love him." I remained quiet for a moment, then said: "Love thy neighbor". Gaya smiled: "Sounds tacky, but there is a lot of wisdom compressed in these three words. But it is taken the wrong way. People understand it as a **commandment**, not as a piece of **advice**, for their **own** happiness".

I got the picture. Then a question crossed my mind: "You make it sound as if, after all, the meaning of life is happiness; enjoyment. It somehow sounds as a lowly thing: 'The meaning of life is enjoyment'." Gaya hesitated before replying. Then she said: "The word 'enjoyment' has bad connotations. It has been abused. Better use 'happiness'." I still wasn't happy with this answer: "Still. Even 'Happiness' sounds cheap." Gaya tried again: "Then, how about 'happiness for the entire world?' If you take it all the way, that's what you **end** up with. Look:

173

'Happiness' or 'enjoyment' are just **words**. The important thing is what they **denote**. We have discussed the 'Good' at great length. You know the feeling. Like your 'magic moments'. Now, take this feeling, and give it to everyone. Everyone and everything. **All the time**. Does it seem worthwhile now? This is what I take 'Happiness' to mean, in its ideal sense." I was willing to accept that, but I was in an argumentative mood: "Suppose it was **achieved**. It is an **ideal**, I know, but suppose it **was** achieved. What now? It will get a bit **boring** after a while, don't you think?"[109] Gaya sighed. It must have been a good question. She answered it: "You are both intelligent and quite educated. But you still have a **limited** *worldview*. Don't misunderstand me: The same applies to **me**, or to anyone else. There are many things that you have not yet **invented**.[110] Not yet **thought of**. Not like a fourth or fifth dimensions. I mean much more **far out**. Things that may **evolve** out of your **present** world. The possibilities are, of course, limitless. So, based on your **present** world, what you can **now** conceptualize, I would say that complete happiness for everyone all the time is just about it[111]. I cannot think of anything **beyond** this. **However**, I know one more thing: I know that in the future, your world will expand. It has a potential to go anywhere. So here is **another** goal that could be set: To **think up** a goal that is even **more** worthy than the one we were able to think up based on our **present** knowledge. Does this qualify as a goal **beyond** absolute universal **Good**? All you have to do, is acknowledge the **possibility** of finding one; Of **making one up**. Goals can be invented, you know. So you can have the goal of finding an even better goal than the previous one you had." This answer was a bit **circular**, but I left it at that.

---

[109] The phenomenon of boredom seems to be a significant obstacle in considering everything **eternal**, even if it is eternal **good**, or eternal happiness. As **intentional** beings, we have an *extatic* tendency (Heidegger again): We **exceed** the present situation, strive for something **else**, something **more**. The concept of **change** is, for us, essential. This may be the reason we find it difficult to grasp **infinity**. Heidegger (and Gaya) believed that **time** (or *Duree*) and **change** are (in) our **essence**. This is also the view of *Tao*.[134] We **are** 'change', which explains our fear of death: It is so **static**.

[110] This also coheres with the *Existentialist* view, that humans have no **essence**, but **being**. Human existence determines its own essence; Every **particular** human being is sovereign to 'invent' her own personal 'meaning of life'. Everything that can be 'thought up' is therefore possible. However, the (syntactical) structure of the (human) conceptual scheme imposes a **logical** constraint. New concepts can be created indefinitely, but only sequentially, always based on the previous state of the system: step by step. Concepts are built (using the '⊃') **sequentially**, like building blocks: The third cannot be erected before the second. This is what we do with (in) **time.**

[111] Utilitarianism:[135] The most happiness for most people. If Gaya's solipsism is accepted, utilitarianism coincides with radical **egoism**: The most happiness (just) for **me** (meaning, the entire world).

We walked back. I was thinking of **love**.[112] I never viewed it as a **trick**, a tool employed to multiply happiness. But it certainly does that. I asked Gaya: "Do you think love was **invented** for the purpose you described? As a **means** to an end? As a way to overcome the inherent problematic of satisfying needs?" Gaya breathed a little heavy. Maybe we were walking a little too fast. I slowed down, and she replied: "Invented by **whom**?" I knew what she meant. I said: "You tell me". She smiled: "Love and language go hand in hand. Language is **socializing**. Overcoming the basic **solitude** which is the basic human situation. We start **alone**. Without language, love would be impossible, inconceivable. And without love, there is no **reason** to speak, to **add** someone else to your private world. Love and Language are each other's **condition**." We arrived at *De Fortuna* before I had the chance to exploit the subject. Gaya didn't look so well, and I didn't want to impose.

I was **worried** about Gaya. So as far as **I** was concerned, **she** was ill. (Regardless of the question how **she** defined her situation). I was therefore very happy to see her in the dining room when I came to have dinner. She was having desert. I considered it a good sign. She waived at me, inviting me to sit at her table. She usually didn't eat so early. She explained: "Mr. Dekker is picking me up at eight o'clock. I have to go somewhere. How was your day? How is your writing?" I smiled: "So so. I am writing more about **you** than about anything else". I'm not sure I should have said that, because she wasn't very pleased to hear it: "Writing about me won't get you a degree. Don't get carried away." It was my turn to smile: "**Now** you are telling me? 'Carried away' is a grand understatement. I cannot even remember myself before I met you. **Philosophically**, I mean." Again, she didn't look very pleased: "Come on, you know better than that. It has nothing, **absolutely** nothing to do with me. You studied hard for years, you planned this trip for months, you brought a hundred kilos of books with you; Don't lay it on me. You **summoned** me, remember?" She opened her little purse that was lying on the table, and retrieved and old, shabby watch. She glanced at it, and said, while winding it: "Mr. Dekker should be here any moment." I gathered she wanted to change the subject, and followed suit: "You have to manually wind your watch every day?" She smiled: "This watch is over fifty years old". It did look old. I asked: "Why do you keep it? Sentimental value?" "Not at all" she replied; "I bought it myself. It was new then". "You don't say!" I exclaimed. "And it still works?" Gaya laughed: "Yes. I must be taking good care of it. To tell you the truth, I wish it broke already. It's time I joined civilization.

---

[112] **Love** is another concept that was neglected by (non-religious) western philosophy, to an almost unbelievable extent. A phenomenon so common, and still so significant. It simply does not **fit** in the realist metaphysical paradigm; This in itself is a good reason to quickly replace it. Love needs to be **explained**. It is way too important to ignore.

As far as **watches** are concerned, I mean". "So why don't you just throw it away and get a new one?" I wondered. "I'll tell you a story" she replied. "Once an old *Guru* gave a private lesson to one of his pupils. The pupil was sitting on a shabby old rug, facing the master. When the lesson was over, the pupil stood up, bowed to the master, and before he left, he threw the rug he was sitting on to the corner. The master called the pupil back and scolded him fiercely: 'How **dare** you treat the rug this way! This rug made the lesson **comfortable** for you! It protected you from the cold, hard ground! Don't you have any respect? Shame on you!' Then the master took the rug from the corner, and carefully folded it, gently placing it in the same corner. It's an old story. You never heard it before?" I didn't. I asked: "And the moral of the story?" Gaya looked at the watch again. "The moral is obvious: Exercise **care**. Even towards inanimate objects. I take care of my stuff. I don't even think about it; I just do." She laughed again: "The problem is, I am stuck with all this old stuff." She reminded me of my mother. I said: "My mother is like that. She never **replaces** anything. She also has fifty year old things." Gaya was impressed: "Really? She must be quite a woman, your mother. Any news about your *Deja vu* in Berlin?" I almost forgot about it; apparently she didn't. "No" I said; "Why is it **important** to hang on to old things?" She laughed again, glancing at the watch for the third time. "It's not important to hang on to old things. What **is** important, is show **respect**. Treat everything around you with care. Everything and every**one**. Not for the sake of the **things**. For the sake of **you**." I was interested, but before I had the chance to say anything, we saw Dekker outside the window. He spotted us, but before he had the chance to come in, Gaya said: "I have to run. Sorry. Bye!" and left.[113]

I remained at her table, thinking of what she said. I never thought **things** mattered. That is, if you see **things** as **outside**, as something **else**. For her, things were a part of her. By being 'nice' to things, she was just being nice to herself. I thought of the way people treated their homes here in Edam. Some of the houses here were two, three and even four hundred years old. Back home, they last fifty. I thought of my mother again. Her conduct suddenly seemed praiseworthy, while until now it was just an oddity. I have to talk to her more.

---

[113]   Heidegger (whom **I** consider a solipsist, although he would probably object to the classification) explained **object** in an exactly **opposite** way from the scientific realist approach. For him, the objects **themselves** were not primary. What he considered primary was the **attitude** of a person (a *Dasein*), the **purpose** that could be served: A 'hammer' is a secondary conceptualization of my need to drive a nail. **First** comes my **need;** then I conceptualize the **tool** (to drive nails): A hammer. Only **afterwards** the hammer 'becomes' a physical object. Our perception of reality is, thus, **value laden**: We 'see' (conceptualize) the things we **need**, and not the other way around; We do not 'pick' out of 'everything there is' the things that can accommodates our needs. Our needs 'create', so to speak, the **tools** for satisfying those needs, and the 'objects' in general are a **product**, a further conceptualization of the tools.

July 1

I am shocked and shaken. I just returned from breakfast, and am as confused as I ever was. What happened was this: I got up early, this being my last day here. I'm flying home tomorrow. I had breakfast, and waited for Gaya to arrive. At ten o'clock I suspected something was wrong. I went to look for Mr. Dekker, but he wasn't there. There was someone else at the reception desk. I asked him for Mr. Dekker, and he said: "I am Mr. Dekker". I must have looked puzzled, because he smiled and said: "Maybe you mean my brother. He went on vacation. I'm his brother". When he said that, I noticed the resemblance. I said: "Oh, yes. He said you were on holiday". It is the first of July. Dekker said his brother was returning at the end of June. I added: "I wasn't aware that he was going when you return. I wish I could say good-bye to him. I've been staying here for the last three weeks. I'm in room 28". He smiled again and said: "I'll tell him. You are checking out tomorrow, right?" He was as nice as his brother. I nodded and said: "In fact, I was looking for Gaya. Do you know where she is?" Now things started to go wrong. He said: "For **whom**?" "For Gaya" I replied. "Who is Gaya?" He asked in a wondering tone. I was very surprised. She was an old friend of the family. I said: "She's a guest here. An elderly oriental lady". This didn't help. He said: "There is no one here by that name. What is her last name?" It never occurred to me to ask. But it didn't make sense. I opened my mouth to explain, to say that he **must** know her, that she's been a regular guest here for many years, that she is a close friend of his family, but the words were stuck in my mouth. I managed to utter "Never mind. Thank you" and literally ran away from there. I went straight to my room, my head spinning. I sat on my bed, my mind working like crazy. I took a deep breath, and tried to concentrate: What is the **meaning** of this? I tried to calm down, forcing myself not to panic, not to run out again and start an investigation. What would **Gaya** say? How **should** I act now? 'Think straight' I said to myself. What would **she** do?
°

°Time to wrap up. In the time I have left I shall try to answer the following questions:

(1) Why do the preceding 113 footnotes qualify as an MA thesis in philosophy?
(2) Why did I find it impossible to limit its scope to one of the traditional philosophical domains?
(3) Why did so many great thinkers express so many different, seemingly contradicting views?
(4) Why is philosophy today considered so unimportant by the general public?

These questions are, of course, in ascending order of **importance**. Therefore, I shall address them in reverse order. (The discussion will, of course, be limited to **western** philosophy).

(4) Why is philosophy today considered so unimportant by the general public?

This has not always been the case. In fact, throughout most of recorded history, the situation was exactly the reverse. Ever since *Thales*[136] said 'everything is water', and for the following two

I tried to relax. Thoughts were racing in my mind. What is the meaning of this? Was she **lying** to me? The idea seemed unbearable. No. It's absurd. Why would she? Maybe it's a misunderstanding. Maybe 'Gaya' is a nick-name the brother doesn't know. I got up from my bed to speak to Dekker's brother again, explain the whole story. At the door I changed my mind. I tried to read Gaya's mind, although she wasn't there. **Why** am I in such a panic? I was going to leave here anyway. What did I expect? To exchange phone numbers? To invite her to my home? To kiss her goodbye? I carefully reconstructed yesterday evening's events. She was apparently going away **then**. She left with Dekker. Is that why

---

thousand and five hundred years, 'philosophy' was synonymous with 'wisdom', and was considered a trade suitable for the most talented and respected of all people. However, this is clearly not the case in the twentieth century. On the contrary: 'Philosophy' turned synonymous with empty hairsplitting, suitable for those who have nothing **better** to do. In the few cases where philosophers **were** (or are) respected (in this last century), it was due to their personal virtues, and **despite** their choice of philosophy as their field of interest. It is safe to assume, that those few would have been equally respected and admired, had they chosen another. (Albert Einstein could have been [was?] a great philosopher, and would probably have received public acclaim as one, although, I would suspect, not to the extent that he did as a scientist).

What happened? **How** did it happen? How did philosophy's status deteriorate so badly, and so **quickly**? How could its supreme status, the one it held for two and a half millennia, be completely shattered in a single century? What is even harder to understand, is that the decline of philosophy was simultaneous with the decline of **God**, while one might have thought that the opposite would occur: That the absence of constraints over freedom of speech imposed by the church would enable philosophy to **flourish**.

What I believe happened, was a phenomenon known as 'over correction': Philosophy **brought it over itself**. It caused an effect that went **too far**, to the extent of self destruction. Philosophy was **so** successful in achieving its 'goals', that this very success, so to speak, 'turned against' the cause that brought it about, like the story of the *Golem of Prague*, which turned against its creator. It all happened very quickly, and philosophy 'lost control' over the circumstances.

Here is how I believe it happened: Ever since *Descartes*[137], philosophy had a feud with the church. For sixteen centuries, the church had a monopoly over the **good**, over the well-being of (western) humans. Philosophy (often without fully realizing it, as was the case with Descartes himself) undermined this monopoly. It took the side of **science**. In fact, philosophy **was** (natural) science. The sciences, so to speak, were **born** from it. Philosophy **and** science, combined, were winning the battle (against the church). The basic implicit claim of philosophy was: Between religion and science, **science is better for people**. Therefore, if a choice has to made, it should be science, not religion. This was an **ethical** claim to abandon one **metaphysical** position and adopt another: The metaphysical position employed by science to this day: (Scientific, or common sense) **Realism**. (I will not define the term here again. You know what I mean by it). Philosophy advocated realism, and claimed it was not only 'the truth', but, more importantly, that it was **better**. And it worked. Realism 'caught on', science flourished, and really brought **good** to the people, as philosophy claimed it would. Now, who got the credit? Philosophy? No. Science got the credit. Science and **realism**, which go hand in hand. Not the **free thought** that brought it about, philosophy, but the *Golem*: Science and realism. So, as things turned out, it is more respectable to be a **scientist** than to be a **philosopher**. As simple as that.

178

she ran out? Why didn't she **say** she was leaving? Maybe she hates **goodbyes**? Still, what kind of **behavior** is this? Gaya is the most **ethical** person I ever met! I tried to think straight: Gaya is beyond question. Her motives cannot be doubted. I was sure of that. Apparently, she thought she was doing the right thing. She **always** does the right thing. What if what she did **was** the right thing? But how could **this** be **right**? Disappearing like that! And we've become so close! Or have we? Yes! We have. I was positive she was very fond of me. I can't be wrong about this. If so, she must have thought she was doing the right thing **for me**. Maybe. Wait a minute - That's impossible! How come **he** says he doesn't know her? Did she use a false name? Whatever for? From the beginning? Is this some kind of **game**? A test? I was trying to think whether Dekker ever called her 'Gaya'. I can't remember. She used **his** name, but did he mention hers? Maybe there's a completely logical explanation to all this.

I finally calmed down. The way I managed that was to convince myself that there is no rush. I can conduct an **investigation** just as well later, or tomorrow, or at any other time in the future. I know the place, I know Dekker. I can always get in touch with the other Mr. Dekker when he returns and clear everything out. Besides, I shall definitely return to this beautiful place anyway. There is no rush. I felt better. No immediate action is **required**.

°

°So what's wrong with that? What is so important in keeping philosophy's status? Well, it is very wrong, and it is very important. Because philosophy is **still** free thought. And it **still** has to seek the **good** for people, as it always took itself as doing. But philosophy got so overwhelmed by its own success in building up science, that it became its **servant**. It started to worship the *Golem*. It **forgot** that it still has work to do: To **improve**. Science doesn't need philosophy's help anymore. It is strong enough. Much stronger than philosophy itself, the one that brought it into power. But philosophy's interest in science in the first place was only as **means** to bring about **good**. Now that science **is bringing** the good that it can bring, **philosophy must move on**. And it doesn't! It sticks to its old success, trying to share a bit of the glory.

What do I mean in "philosophy must move on"? I mean it has to resume its **primal role**: Seeking the **good** for humankind. This good will not be enhanced anymore by supporting science and realism. They are strong enough, and need no help anyway. If philosophy will continue to blindly advocate realism, it would achieve nothing and continue to deteriorate, **and it should** deteriorate, if it continues to do what it is doing: The general public is **right** in denouncing the value of philosophy, because it **achieves nothing**. It did in the past, but not anymore. The core of philosophy **was** always **ethics**. But in the last century it is not ethics any more. At most, it is 'meta ethics'[138] or other kinds of lip service to what should have been the most important issue. It is the primal role of philosophy **to investigate the good**. To find out what it is, find new ways to enhance it, to bring it about. The attitude of Analytic philosophy to ethics is a **disgrace** to philosophy. The positivist claim regarding the meaninglessness of ethical propositions is an extreme manifestation of philosophy's problem nowadays: It **forgot what it is**.[139]

Any philosophical paper, book, or discussion that consciously disregards the issue of **the good** is not philosophy. It is what the public takes it to be: empty verbiage and lingual hairsplitting

179

Then a second wave of thoughts arrived. I couldn't get her out of my mind. It was as if she was **speaking** to me, although she wasn't there. She said: "What's gotten into you? Have you forgotten **everything**? What are you **doing**? I am gone for a few hours, and already you completely lapse into your old, conventional, **western** way of thinking? **Where** are you looking for explanations? **Where**? In 'the world?' You should know better. Something **strange** happened to you? So you immediately look for a **scientific** explanation?" And I answered, as if she was **really** there: "**You** taught me: Do the **right** thing. And what is **right**, according to **my** *worldview*, is not to **lose** you. Not to lose **touch**. I care for you." She laughed. Well, not **she**. Her image I had in my mind did. I knew **exactly** how she would argue if she were here: "It is good that you care. But don't fool yourself. You care for **yourself** now. In fact, **care** is always basically for **oneself**. But the question is, what is the right thing to **do**: Is it right to go and **search** for me? What purpose would it serve? How exactly will **you** benefit, how will your world become better, even slightly, by **finding** me, by 'keeping in touch'? You are going home tomorrow **anyway**. When you needed me I was **here**. Do you really **need** me now? What exactly are you trying to accomplish?" And I replied: "I still have a lot to learn from you. I have a clear interest in having **access** to you." She laughed: "You know that isn't true. Look at the conversation you are having right now! You are doing just fine. Do you really need my **physical** presence? What **is** physical presence? Is there any question you need an answer for right now? A question you need my **body** to answer? You are just acting out of **reflex**. And a **western** reflex it is!"

It was spooky. This conversation, I mean. It got to a point that I needed to convince myself that she really **existed** at all. Maybe it was just a strange hallucination, triggered by the special circumstances I created for myself, conditions of voluntary solitary confinement? Am I going **crazy**? Well, if it **was** a hallucination, it was certainly **fruitful**. I feel so much more **whole** after spending two weeks with her. I would recommend such a hallucination to anyone. No. I'm not crazy. It was **real**. But if it was **real**, then she was telling me a whole lot of nonsense! This whole thing is completely self refuting: If she is **real**, then what she taught me is **false**. If she was **right**, then she was never **real** in the first place! My mind was beginning to boil again. I felt I was running a fever. I washed my face and sat at my computer to write the last few pages.

---

performed by people who have nothing better to do. This is why philosophy is (rightly) considered so unimportant by the general public.

° **(3) Why did so many great thinkers express so many different, seemingly contradicting views?**

Writing helped. I typed these two last pages in a frenzy, without stopping for a second. I feel better. Now, let me see. Let me analyze the situation **calmly**. Let me start this way: Let's assume that all she told me was **true**. That 'reality' is something which is **my** creation. If this is the case, then it is up to **me** to explain the situation. Not up to 'the facts', the **objective** facts. On the other hand, if I assume that it is **not** up to me, then she was not telling me **the truth**. Just some lunatic mystic ideas. But in **this** case, why do I want to **find** her so badly? If it

---

If philosophy is what I take it to be, namely, the employment of **reason** in quest of the **good**, then this phenomenon seems genuinely inexplicable. If it is just the quest of the **truth**, then it is possible that many thinkers should say completely different things, because there may be many truths, in a variety of areas. But even if we limit the discussion to the (many) cases where philosophers explicitly discussed the good, there are still as many opinions as there are philosophers. How is this possible? Is **one** of them right and all the others wrong? Most improbable. Another possible answer could be "there **is no such thing** as 'the good'". **If** this is the case, then philosophy has reached the end of its lifespan. I sincerely hope that this is not the case, and am operating under the assumption that it is not. That the good can be sought.

Many (most?) philosophers throughout history shared this view: There **is** something there to look for. It **used** to be God, whom philosophy helped overthrow. Now it has the responsibility to find a substitute (besides science, which makes its contributions, but nobody thinks that it **is** the answer). Many thinkers have claimed they **know**, and have written books about it, but they all disagree with each other. Could **they all be wrong?** A mystery.

I propose to assume that **they were all right**. I know this sounds strange, but isn't it worth a try? I propose that all the philosophers who wrote about it, from Plato, through St. Augustine and St. Aquinas, Spinoza and Leibniz to Kant and Hegel, were all **right**. They all offered **correct accounts** as to the nature of **the good**. Sure, there is a slight problem: They seem to **contradict** each other. So? What of it? Do we clearly understand what **contradiction** is? We do not. So let us investigate it! Isn't that what philosophy is all about? They all wrote in one **language** or another. The (alleged) contradictions between what they all said are manifested in **language**. So let us investigate language! There is a lot of work to be done. But at least there is a **hypothesis** in place, something to chew on: "What if they were all **right?**"

And there is, of course, the question of **non-western** philosophy. Of eastern thought, for example. I have limited my discussion to western thought, just because I know next to nothing about the alternative. But doesn't it need an **explanation** too? Even from a western point of view: Could these billions be all wrong? Or is their 'good' different from ours? Shouldn't they be included in the project?

The same applies, of course, to a genre in philosophy known as 'continental'.[140] Many Anglo-saxon or 'analytical' philosophers (e.g. Searle[141]) consider them unintelligible. I even heard people claim that they do not understand their own statements. This allegation cannot be treated seriously. Many of the continental thinkers are extremely intelligent and learned and obviously know exactly what they are talking about. Shouldn't their claims be reconciled with all others into a total coherent picture? I claim they are also **right**. I claim that all (or at least most) of the great philosophers are **right**. The task is to explain, in line with the critical tradition, **how it is possible**. At least I have a **hypothesis** in place, which is more than can be said about many others. What philosophy needs is a **synthesis** between all those seemingly contradicting views.

was all a piece of rubbish, **I shouldn't care**! This is an **interesting** situation. There are only two possibilities: The first, to **accept** Gaya's philosophy, to accept that she is an exceptional human being, which makes her a **part of me**. There is no sense in looking for her **outside**. The second, to **reject** Gaya's philosophy, in which case there is no **point** in looking for her (outside). So, whichever it is, **it makes no <u>sense</u> to look for her anyway**! This just about settled my dilemma. Then I heard her voice again. She was unmistakably **proud** of me: "See? What did I tell you? Do you really need my old **body**? If you do, I should be flattered. Nobody has been interested in my **body** for decades.." She laughed again, as she had so many times: "Look: You **summoned** me. Or I **found** you. Is there a real difference between the two? You have everything in your book. Practically every word. It is **objective**. You have transformed me into **language**. To ask if it **really** happened is a manifestation of complete **misunderstanding** of everything we talked about. People will no doubt ask you if you **really** met a woman called Gaya. And if my name is not 'Gaya'? Does it make a difference? Does anything make a difference, one's my **ideas** are safely recorded for anyone who is interested?"

°

° **(2) Why did I find it impossible to limit its scope to one of the traditional philosophical domains?**

I **could** have written a thesis in epistemology. Or in the philosophy of language. Or in logic. Or in ethics. Or in metaphysics. Or in the philosophy of science. But in writing about each of these topics, I would need to employ **presuppositions**. Premises of the discussion, which belong in the other fields, the ones I was **not** writing about. As should be completely obvious by now, I am not a realist. This view has implications on each and every one of the abovementioned fields. As should also be obvious by now, I am a holist. This also effects each of them. What I **could** do, is say: Let us **presuppose** solipsism, and then take up a specific subject. I believe it would have been absurd. If I want to **advocate** solipsism, explain how it can be both coherent, intelligible and with great explanatory value, I am **compelled** to touch on each of the different subjects. I need to explain, first and foremost, why it is **good**, so I have **ethics**. I have to show how it is coherent, hence logic. I must explain how (and with whom...) a solipsist **speaks**, which belongs in the philosophy of language, and so on.

Every discussion has its **context**. Some contexts are more limited than others. Most theses employ a deliberately limited context. I could, for example, write a thesis about Hilary Putnam, whom I greatly respect. But then I would be limited by my own context. One cannot argue against the context from within which he argues. I summarized the claim this thesis tries to defend as the motto which appears one page after the title. It is phrased as belonging to the philosophy of language: *Language does **not** employ a moral vocabulary to describe an objective reference; It does precisely the reverse: It employs an objective vocabulary to describe a **moral reference**.* This is as **compressed** as I could make it. But this single sentence already involves the philosophy of language, ethics ('*morals*'), metaphysics and logic.

It could be argued, that spreading over so many fields, practically the whole spectrum, will result in inevitable superficiality. That it is better to pick a small subject and dig **deep**, rather than scratch the **whole** surface. Says who? This view is **imported** from science, from the era of specialization. It has

182

I have reached a decision. I am **not** looking for her. Even if I could find her **right now**, I still wouldn't. I underwent a complete transformation in half an hour. I entered this room in a state of panic, trying to think of ways to recover the loss, and half an hour later I don't even **want** to find her. Finding her suddenly seemed a way to **refute** everything she stands for. And I didn't **want** it to be refuted. I **wanted it to be true**. And if I **want** something to be true, this precisely is what **makes** it true. It is **good** that it should be **true**. It is **good** that she **should not** be 'real'. Not in the **common** sense of the word, anyway.

°

---

value, in specific places; In technology, for example. But I am not a scientist. I have (originally) a scientific education, but I turned to philosophy, not to 'copy' scientific principles such as 'specialization'. One of philosophy's most basic characteristics is its **generality**. It applies to **anyone**. It discusses the interests of anyone, at least if 'anyone' is **human**. There is nothing wrong with being superficial, provided you don't **pretend** to having done otherwise. Sometimes superficiality is **in order**. It all depends what one is trying to achieve. And what **I** was trying to achieve is explained in the following answer to the last question:

° **(1) Why do the preceding 113 footnotes qualify as an MA thesis in philosophy?**

I didn't turn to philosophy to get a job at the university. I turned to philosophy because I believed it is the most **worthy** activity one could engage in. Having been lucky enough to disregard economical considerations, I took it up **to find out**. To find out what the most intelligent people in human history said about the most important things for humans. I did this not just for the sake of 'knowing', of being in possession of some sort of 'truth', but mostly for practical considerations: To **form an opinion**. My own opinion, as to the most basic questions: What is the meaning of life? Is there a universal Good? Does God exist? What is 'existence'? What is 'death'? and most important of all, how should I conduct my life; my everyday life. I know this sounds strange, but it is the simple and plain truth. I had the time, the energy and the patience to accumulate a substantial amount of knowledge so my **opinion** could be formed based on the most **data**. I read practically every philosopher from Plato to Manor (my professor, whom I am trying very hard not to flatter, for obvious reasons). Not nearly **everything** each of them wrote, but a representative sample from every single one. And after more than two years of extensive (and extremely pleasant) studying, literally seven days a week, I **formed an opinion**.

I believe that is what an MA thesis is all about. And if it is not, that is what it **should** be about, which is what I believe counts: What things **ought** to be, much more than what they **are**. So I formed an opinion, one that satisfies three important conditions: It is **coherent**, it is **explanatory**, and it is **prescriptive**. I went into solitude, in *Edam*, in the company of about a hundred books I carefully selected, and wrote constantly for three weeks. I tried very hard to make it **intelligible**, because that is what writing is all about: **communication**. Effective communication. I didn't try to **prove**, I tried to **convince**. I did the best I could, with only one **purpose**: To outline the **opinion** which I formed as a direct result of my studies. And this is what turned out.

A word of explanation is in order regarding the unusual **format** of this work. I already explained my motives in the beginning of the 'non academic' part, but will briefly repeat it here. I don't think I have the energy to write **two** books. This one was strenuous enough. I had an obligation; An obligation to many people who 'suffered' the consequences of my sudden 'change of career'. It is just as important for me to explain to them, the ones devoid of a philosophical education (just as I was until not long ago) what this was all about. I was told by many people that the task is

As I said, it is my last day. Time to wrap up. Time to summarize. She did right in disappearing one day before the end. Today's writing will be my **own**, not hers. What this book was all about was, of course the 'meaning of life'. I know it sounds bombastic and pretentious, but this doesn't bother me one bit. I didn't know this would be the subject. But this is how it turned out. Of **my** life, I mean. It is a long description and justification of the way I am going to lead my life, and what I recommend to anyone who asks my advice.

Some people find peace in God, by 'returning' to religion, others find it in the teachings of some *Guru*. Some don't find it at all, and die in misery, which for them is a happy end. Some people are lucky enough to have **problems** all their life; problems to keep them **busy**, and even **happy** every once in a while, in times of **relief** from their standard suffering. Nevertheless, there is another possibility. Quite a few people have discovered it: Gaya, Kant, Socrates, Lao-tsu, and, I believe, quite a number of people who didn't need to **advertise** their **way**, their *Tao*. I do have a need to advertise. Really: Not to become famous or important. Not to the 'general public', whom I don't **know**, and whose **objective existence** I deny anyway... I mean my wife, my children, my teachers, my friends. I think it is simply **unfair** to keep it to myself. Immoral.

The **beauty** of it is, that it requires **no sacrifice**. Not to observe 613 commandments, not to join an *Ashram*, not to worship anybody. It requires no money, not even extensive study. It just requires one thing, accessible to everybody: It requires **care** for one's own life. Job (Ayub) remained happy and content, because he **wanted** to be happy and content. All it takes is to really believe that it is possible. Others have phrased it differently, in other times, in other languages. 'Love thy neighbor' or 'It is **you**'. But those articulations are in different languages, hence not understood by many. I tried to write in the language that the people I know speak. And in **this** language, it is simply this: If you treat your world well, your world becomes a wonderful place. Your world is the mirror image of yourself. Be **good**, and your world will follow suit. Don't believe the people who tell you that there **is** a cruel world out there. It is a **lie**. Or at least, a grave **misunderstanding**. There is no coincidence. Nothing **bad** happens by **accident**. There are no accidents.

---

impossible. That an MA thesis in philosophy cannot be intelligible by 'ordinary people', and that what **is** intelligible, would not qualify. I tried to beat the odds. Maybe because I don't **really** need the degree. It is important to me, of course, but mostly because I may one day proceed to a Ph.D. (I had the possibility of going directly for a Ph.D., but I preferred the long way. Long ways are always preferable to short ones). In any case, I didn't want the degree at the expense of leaving my friends and family in the dark regarding my 'findings'.

What is **odd**, is that I arrived at these conclusions **logically**. The people who know me know how **rational** I am. I have been often accused of being **too** rational. It was said that I need less brains and more emotion, more intuition. I disagree with them, but I think in this case all three are on my side. If you want to believe me because of **emotional** reasons, so be it. There are very good emotional reasons to accept what I am saying. If it appeals to one's basic intuitions, that's good too. But the whole thing is also extremely coherent; Or at least I find it extremely coherent. It happens to be the only logical explanation. The only explanation which does not refute itself.

Still, there is a good chance I will not be understood. It has happened before. If this will be the case, I will not be disappointed. Not at all. Because I did the **right** thing. I did my very best to **share**. I believe my *worldview* offers a **synthesis** between the western objective **realist** metaphysical paradigm and the eastern subjective solipsist one. I believe **both** are valid: We are solipsist creatures who invented **language** to create a **real** reality. It is **completely** real, as real as can be, only it is **our** creation. It is not 'out there' all by itself. **We** created the big-bang; We are not its **product**. We created evolution. We created everything that is **objective**, shared by all of us. The eastern view does not work by itself. It leaves everyone in **solitude**. The western view does not work by itself. It makes humanity **insignificant**. Only the synthesis works. It is time for a **change**. a paradigm shift. Maybe this is what *New age* is all about. I believe it is.
_o

One last word about the way this book was written. It is very similar to the painting made by the Japanese amateur painter here in Edam: I simply recorded everything that happened in the last twenty days. I tried not to miss out anything. Maybe some will find it a bit boring, but I wanted it to be a **genuine picture of reality**. It is as accurate a picture of **me** (or my world, which is the same thing) as possible, in those twenty days. I was in ideal conditions for reflection and for recording these reflections. It is as if I 'transformed myself' into words and sentences, the best I knew how. It was exhausting, but a unique experience. I hope to have the chance to do it again. Provided I find anything to **say**, of course. Bye.

°So here you have it. An unorthodox, unconventional MA thesis, which indeed failed to grant me the title 'Masters in Philosophy'. It is a summary of all I learned, the answers to the important questions I investigated. Needless to say, I also derived great pleasure and satisfaction in the process. And now, maybe the time has come to rejoin the **real** world, and move from **theory** into **practice**.

Endnotes

June 12

1. In the simile of **the cave** (Plato, *The Republic,* Book VII, 514a-521b) Socrates models the human epistemic situation as of prisoners locked up in a dark cave, watching shadows that are screened on the wall of the cave opposite them. The prisoners are under the illusion that these shadows are what (or **all**) there **is**. The philosopher who frees himself from the chains and exits the cave, not only realizes the hallucinogenic nature of the experience the prisoners (ordinary, unenlightened people) consider **real**, but also discovers the **real** world that is outside the cave.

2. *Analytic Philosophy* has dominated Anglo-American philosophy for the best part of the last century. Although Russell is considered one of its forefathers (if not **the** one), its roots clearly trace back to the writings of **Frege**. Frege contributed the widely accepted distinction between sense and reference, as well as quantified predicate calculus, which (supposedly) simulates the structure of **natural language**. *Analytic Philosophy* considers **language** as the key topic philosophy should concentrate on. For more on what characterizes *Analytic Philosophy*, see endnotes 13, 32 below.

3. Benedict (Baruch) de **Spinoza** (1632-1677) is one of the three great 17th century rationalists (the other two being Descartes and Leibniz). He was a metaphysical **monist**, who discussed **ontology** and **ethics** as inseparable. He started on his most famous book, *Ethics*, in 1663, but it was published only on the year of his death. His two other books are *Treatise on the correction of the understanding* (also published only in 1677) and *Treatise on theology and politics* (1670).

June 13

4. Samuel Hugo **Bergman**'s *History of Philosophy* is one of the few original **Hebrew** texts offering a wide, comprehensive account of the history of modern western philosophy. It was brought to print by the Bialik Institute (The first edition of the first volume, in 1970, and the fourth and last volume, in 1979). There is no English translation.

5. Spinoza's *Ethics* is a book about **the structure of reality**. On **what there is**. Still, he called it **Ethics**. This fact alone is enough to substantiate the claim I have been reiterating throughout the thesis: That **what there is** is **ethical**, moral.

Spinoza's **first** reference to the term *Good* comes only on the **fourth** (out of five) section of the book, in which he **defines** *Good: What we clearly know as beneficial to us*.

6. Willard Van Orman **Quine** is a logician and a philosopher of language. He treats the term **'being'** or **'existence'** from a logical, lingual perspective, not an ontological, metaphysical one. Quine maintains that when we say '**a** exists' (or '**a** is'), we **mean** that **a** is a value of some variable **x**. A variable has a **range** over which it ranges, some **set**, S. Therefore, the statement '**a** exists' is true iff there **is** such a set S. By defining **being** as 'being a value of a variable', Quine simply reduced being, or existence, of an **object**, to **another** existence, that of **sets** (and to the primitive notion of **participation**). But in doing so, Quine again relies on some primitive notion of existence, only this time it is the existence of **sets**. When, in turn, may we say that **S exists**? When it is a value of a variable; namely, when it **participates** in some 'higher' set, S_1.

7. In a lecture he gave at TAU in spring 1995, **Burton Dreben** said this about Quine: That he has no metaphysical bone in his body. He meant that Quine does not **consider** his views as metaphysical. In my view, this is the only thing that separates Quine from **Plato** in this context: **Had** Quine been a metaphysician, he would be **Plato**.

8. *Holism, a shopper's guide* by **Fodor and Lepore** is a book about holism written by non-holists. (Jerry Fodor is a self-proclaimed **anti** holist, and Ernest Lepore is skeptic, although sympathetic). In line with (one of) the consequences of my thesis, this is a good example of two people writing a book about something they **do not understand** (whereas they do not **agree**).

9. Aristotle carries most of the responsibility for the (still prevailing) divorce between ethics and ontology. According to him, what there **is** is independent from what is **good**. His *Nikomachean Ethics* maintains (roughly) that what is **good** is what is **average**. Although I have an intuitive antipathy to Aristotelian views, even **he** must be interpreted in line with the principle of charity (to show **how** he was right): Aristotle was a conservative thinker. He advocates (in principle) the **prevailing** paradigm(s): The good, or the **right** (behavior), is what **most** consider as commonly **agreed**; What **is** good is what is **considered** good by the people: 'The "law" of the land' ("law" in a broad sense - the prevailing ethics), in line with my claims on **June 27** (and footnotes 83-86).

10. Karl Popper entered the philosophical canon as a philosopher of science, and is best known for his proposed demarcation between **science** and what is **not** science. In line with the tradition he was part of, he was also a realist. His version of the Platonic 'world of ideas' is **world three**, the realm of **meanings** (beside the first two: The **'real'**, inaccessible reality, and the subjective, personal *worldview*). Popper maintained that science **constructs** this 'world three' employing the scientific methodology: The construction of an (artificial, man-made) **theory**, constantly checked experimentally for **coherence**. Science tries to **refute** the theory (find **inconsistencies** in it). A short account of Popper's views on the subject can be found in *Science: Conjectures and Refutations, 1963*.

11. Thomas Kuhn, on the other hand, is everything **but** a realist. I read the Hebrew translation of his *The Structure of Scientific Revolution*, in which he disagrees with Popper's view that *successive scientific theories reach closer and closer to the truth, or provide a better and better approximation of its description (p. 163)*. Nevertheless, Kuhn does not take himself as a solipsist: *"... and we assume the fixed nature of* (our stimuli, the external reference), *to avoid personal and social solipsism alike. (p. 153)*. He even denies that he is a **relativist**: In the epilogue he added in 1969 to this book (originally published in 1962), he answers his critics (e.g., Popper and Shapere) who accuse him of relativism. But **while** denying this "allegation", he says: *"Maybe there is some other way to save the notion of 'truth' to apply it to whole theories, but the present way won't do. I think there is no theory-independent way to reconstruct terms such as 'is really there'; The idea of correspondence between the ontology of a theory and its 'real' correspondents in nature, now seems to me as essentially misleading". (p. 163)*.

I cannot resist bringing several more quotations from the same epilogue: *"And let us now pay attention, that two groups whose members have systematically different sensations when exposed to the same stimuli, in fact live, in a certain sense, in different worlds." (p. 153)*. This is certainly **relativist**. And if this view is taken on a **personal** level, rather than on the level of **groups**, or lingual (or scientific) **communities**, then it is **solipsist**. On dialectics, he says: *"Consequently, one theory's superiority over another is something that cannot be proven in an argument. Instead, I claimed, must every competing group try to convert the other's beliefs by **persuasion**... Arguments for choice of theory cannot be phrased in a way similar to a logical or mathematical proof... If there is a controversy over the consequences, the parties to the discussion may retreat their course, step by step, while checking each step against what was established before. In the end of this process must one of the parties admit he has made a mistake, has ignored an established rule previously accepted... Only if, instead, the two discover that they differ on the meaning or jurisdiction of the established rules - discover that their previous consent provides no sufficient basis for proof - only then the discussion continues in its inevitable form of an argument of a scientific revolution. This argument is over premises, and it*

189

requires **persuasion** *as preliminary to the possibility of proof. (p. 157).* This **persuasion**, the argument typical to scientific revolutions, is an **ethical** process: What **should** the premises (of the theory) be. Kuhn admits explicitly: *"... it follows from my claims that such arguments function as **values**...".* In the next page he says: *"There is no **neutral** algorithm for choice of theory... This process is one of persuasion, but it manifests a deeper problem. Two persons perceiving the same state differently, while employing the exact same vocabulary in discussing it, necessarily use words in a different way. I.e., they converse out of what I have termed **distinct points of view**. How could they even **hope** to converse, let alone be convincing. (p. 158).* Kuhn limits his observation to the context of science and scientific communities and theories, but the significance of his claims transcends this limited context; *"In short, what the participants of a **communication break-down** may do, is recognize each others as members of distinct lingual communities, and become **translators**. (p. 159).* In "translators" Kuhn means, of course **radical** ones. Needless to say, it is **my** claim that this is exactly what happens in **every** conversation. Kuhn labels the experience of **conversion**, of the adoption of a new **language**, a new way to use words, as the central experience of the revolutionary process. He compares it to the replacement of a *Gestalt* scheme.

Kuhn is an extreme relativist, a holist, a radical translator. Like Quine, he is not a metaphysician, whereas he limited his statements to the narrow context of science. Although he realizes he is on the borders of **both** ethics and metaphysics, he touches neither. The above quotations are free translations from the (Hebrew) translation of the above mentioned book (and all bold-print mine). Kuhn contributed several important terms to the philosophical jargon, e.g. *normal science* and *paradigm* (in the context of scientific theory), the latter extensively used by me throughout the thesis in a broader context than intended by him.

12. Plato didn't need **three** worlds. He thought two were enough: One 'half-real', the 'common-sense' world of phenomena, and one **real**, eternal, unchanging **world of ideas**. Many of his dialogues make reference to this **reality**. (E.g., *The Republic, Book VII*). The only things that enjoy **real existence** is *ideas*, which are all 'folded into' and illuminated by a 'super-idea' (super-predicate!): *The idea of the Good*.

13. As I have already mentioned, **Gottlob Frege** may be perceived as the forefather of Analytic Philosophy. He brought **logic** and **language** closer together, in claiming his **predicate calculus** to model the natural language. He introduced the quantifiers into logic as notations for what he considered the **primitive** notion of **existence** prevailing in language: If **language** takes 'being'

190

or 'existence' as primitive, irreducible, so is the status of the "super predicate" 'existence' (symbolized by the quantifiers) in predicate logic. A basic premise in set theory is **the empty set exists**. No explanation is provided (or required) as to the **meaning** of this 'exists'. This is the *existential import* (**from** ontology, as constituted by language, by the 'meta-theory', **to** logic).

Frege took propositions as **names,** and their reference as twofold: It is either 'T' or 'F', these two being (?!) in the **world**. This dichotomy divides the set of all (?!) propositions into two: The true ones (referring to 'T') and the false ones (referring to 'F'). This dichotomy is equivalent to the dichotomy advocated in this thesis: That the first set (true propositions) is the set of **beliefs,** and the second set is the set of propositions that are **not** beliefs. Another way of explaining propositions as names, is to see 'Truth' and 'Falsity' simply as predicates. Indeed these predicate apply to a specific **class** of objects ('propositions'), just as the predicates 'Red' and 'Not-red' apply only to the class of **visible** objects. Thus conceived, 'The table is true' is simply a category mix-up, as 'The walk is red'. Now, the rule in the language game is: *Construct propositions that are synonymous with 'True'. As such, they may be **understood** by your fellow speaker: He **also** has a 'True' in his system (the distinction between his beliefs and their negations).*

Frege's doctrine that the reference of a proposition is its truth value is based on his slingshot argument: The inference from "Logically equivalent propositions are co-referential" to $\Rightarrow$ "Materially equivalent propositions are co-referential". This inference has been contested, claiming it is circular. But even if this claim were true, it still does not refute the validity (the truth?) of Frege's doctrine. The dispute centers on the question of the difference between "Logically equivalent propositions" and "Materially equivalent propositions"; or, even more specifically, on the difference between "Logical" and "Material". Is this not the distinction between "analytic" and "synthetic"? I believe it is. And if it is, everyone accepting Quine's arguments against the analytic/synthetic distinction, must take Frege's slingshot argument as circular indeed. Still, this does not refute it. There is nothing **incoherent** in Frege's view, provided the term 'existence' is taken as of no need of explanation. The exclamated question marks (?!) from the previous paragraph were meant to emphasize precisely this point: (a) What kind of "existence" do 'T' and 'F' enjoy? The same as the existence of particular tables and trees? or maybe that of universals? and (b) What is the meaning of "**all**" in 'all propositions'? How does the universal quantifier apply to propositions? Existence must be **presupposed** to make sense of Frege's account. The number of propositions in propositional calculus (as well as in predicate calculus) is traditionally taken as infinite, due to the **possibility** of constructing an infinite number of distinct wffs. I prefer the intuitionist (or, rather, **finitist**) approach, in considering the number of distinct wffs in a given language as **finite**, although an infinite variety of wffs **could** be constructed. This **potential** does not **require** language to contain an infinite number of wffs.

June 14

14. *The Meaning of Meaning* is the title of a number of different books or articles, such as by Hilary Putnam (1975), or C.K. Ogden (1923).

15. **Molyneux's problem** (whether a blind person who gains his sight will be able to visually recognize objects that he was previously familiar with through feeling) was traditionally considered as important in the debate between empiricism and rationalism: A negative answer supposedly supporting empiricism. Molyneux himself, as well as Locke and Berkeley, bet on the empiricist view, which was later empirically substantiated. However, I believe that Molyneux's problem can be presented in a 'lingual' version, from the perspective of the philosophy of language, and in this presentation, the question is much harder to answer (and accordingly, much more interesting): *When a blind person says 'square' or 'round', what is <u>common</u> between the reference of these terms, and the reference of the same terms uttered by a seeing person?* And in what way do the two persons **mean** the same things by these terms? Or **do** they?

I first realized that the world a blind person lives in **is in fact** very different from my own, in reading *Denis Diderot*'s ***Lettre sur les Aveugles a l'usage de ceux qui voient*** *(A letter about the blind for the use of seers).* This essay was published in 1749, more than twenty years after Molyneux's problem was empirically answered, and rather than advocating empiricism, it revolves around the essentially different *worldview* of the blind. The seemingly smooth communication between a seer and a blind person in the employment of a natural language, **in spite** of their very different *worldviews*, led me to the understanding that smooth communication cannot act as evidence for **shared reference**.

16. Stephen Schiffer's 1987 *Remnants of Meaning* is a divorce document from the prevailing paradigms in semantics and pragmatics. Although I consider it Schiffer's greatest achievement, *Remnants of Meaning* was not well accepted by the philosophical community, and is often treated as evidence for Schiffer's lost sense. I believe this book will be rediscovered before long.

17. Schiffer's *Meaning,* on the other hand, is still considered an important text in the objectivistically (realistically) oriented philosophy of language. I could never understand how *Meaning* could be still accepted, after *Remnants* so clearly showed that the doctrines it supports are self refuting.

18. *Meaning and Thought* is a very compressed version of the conclusions of *Remnants*. It was first published in 1985, two years before *Remnants*, in **Hebrew**, in a collection edited by Kasher and Lappin, *Modern trends in Philosophy, Vol. II.*

19. Before Schiffer 'lost his (pragmatic) senses', he was considered the successor of *H.P. Grice* and *P.F. Strawson* in the line of pragmaticians started by *Austin*. **Grice** emphasized the speakers' **intentions** in the meaning of an uttered sentence. He distinguished *utterer's meaning* from *sentence meaning* and *word meaning*, corresponding to pragmatics, semantics and syntax, respectively.

20. Quine's *Word and object (1960)* is considered the classic source of most aspects of **translation** (particularly of the **radical** kind).

21. Quine's **deflationary** notion of truth is evident throughout his writings, particularly *From a Logical Point of View (1953)* and *Philosophy of Logic (1970)*.

22. Quine's view on the *en block* referential relation between language and "the world" (and in particular, "sense data", expressed in "observation statements"), his **holism**, as opposed to Carnap's **atomism**, is particularly visible and explicit in *Two Dogmas of Empiricism (1951)*.

23. Carnap's atomistic referential relation, in line with Frege's, underlies his thought. E.g., *On Concept and Object*, first published in the quarterly *Wissenschaftliche Philosophie, 16 (1892)*, pp. 192-205.

24. John Dewey is considered by *Rorty* amongst the three most important 20th Century's thinkers, alongside *Heidegger* and *wittgenstein*. Out of the three, *Dewey* being the only Anglo-Saxon representative. I have learned about Dewey mostly from Rorty (see endnote 33 below), and from *J.E. Tiles' 'Dewey'*.

25. I first encountered **William James** through a short article in what would nowadays be labeled 'the philosophy of mind': *Does 'Consciousness' Exist?*. I was amazed to discover that James denies what I considered indisputable: The existence of consciousness, of Descartes' 'I'. It was only later that I understood what James was actually denying: **Dualism**. Like Spinoza, James combined a strong religious conviction with implicit monism. His celebrated *Principles of Psychology (1890)* is considered a classic text in psychology, although it is a perfect manifestation of the inseparability of psychology from philosophy. Together with *Pierce*, James is considered the forefather of *Pragmatism*, and it was he who made the first clear connection between what is **true** and what is **good**. (See endnote 70 below).

26. An idea that **'pays its way'** is *Richard Rorty's* non-representationalist version of a **true** one. In this he is an explicit follower of James, who used the same monitary metaphor in asking "What, in short, is the truth's cash-value in experiential terms?" See endnote 33 below.

27. **Yaacov Klatchkin** translated Spinoza's **Ethics** from Latin into Hebrew, and added an illuminating introduction on **language** and **translation**. He claims that the Hebrew language is particularly suitable for expressing Spinoza's thoughts, more than other western languages. He even claims that it is sometimes even more suitable than the original Latin in which Spinoza (probably) wrote. Klatchkin speculates that Spinoza's fluent Hebrew and his Jewish philosophical roots affected his ideas (his *worldview*).

28. In the same introduction Klatchkin points out the fact that in his first reply to Belinberg (letter 19) **Spinoza** says: "How I wished to write in the language I was brought up on (*Land* assumes he meant Hebrew, but he probably meant Spanish), so I could express my opinions more clearly". And in a letter to Oldenburg (letter 13) he says about his book on *Descartes' philosophy*, that he relied on others to mend his poor Latin style.

29. Not much was left of **Parmenides'** writings, and the little that remained is rather enigmatic. Most of what I know about Parmenides (and Heraclitus) is out of *Heracliti et Parmenidis*, by Samuel Scolnicov.

30. Fragment 8 (G.S. Kirk, J.E. Raven and M. Schofield, *The presocratic philosophers,* 2nd edition, pp. 248-9). The Hebrew version is from Scolnicov's translation (pp. 207-9), from H. Diels and W. Kranz, *Die Fragmente der Vorsokratiker*, 6th edition.

31. Towards the end of his introduction to the first edition of his *Critique of Pure Reason (1781)*, **Kant** says: *"And finally, regarding **clarity**, the reader may expect... **intuitive** (aesthetic) clarity, i.e., examples or other material explanations... I could not satisfy* (this) *requirement, which is not so strict, but still justified. Throughout my work I almost always contemplated, how to treat this requirement. Examples and explanations always seemed to me necessary, and indeed they were included in the first draft in the appropriate places. But immediately I saw the size of my task and the multitude of issues I shall have to* *treat. And when I realized, that these in themselves, in a dry, scholastic discussion, will lengthen the text substantially - I arrived at the conclusion, that there is no place to lengthen it further with examples and explanations, which are required only for popular purposes."* (My translation from Bergman and Rotenstreich's translation into Hebrew. I preferred this over one of the many available English translations, because my understanding ('interpretation') of Kant is **based** on the Hebrew text, and it is what **I** understood that counts, not what was **written**, or **translated**).

32. **Peter Hylton** received his Ph.D. in Philosophy from Harvard University. His chief area of interest is in understanding, interpreting, and "coming to terms with the history of analytic philosophy"..

33. **Richard Rorty** could be labeled a "non-representationalist pragmatist". On one hand, he clearly follows the pragmatist line (Rorty considers **Dewey** as the most significant 20th century Anglo-Saxon philosopher!), and (alongside *Davidson*) is the leading figure in contemporary pragmatist thought. On the other hand, he is anti-dualist, rejects the notion of **representation**, of the subject-predicate dichotomy. In fact, Rorty rejects **dichotomies** in principle, and is thus close to continental (Heideggerian?) views. In many respects, Rorty acts as a "bridge" between two alien *worldviews*: The Anglo-Saxon, analytic, vs. the continental, subjectivist one. He is one of the few who understand the post-modernist's **language** although he is not in their ranks. He thus acts as an **interpreter**, a position similar to that of *Putnam*. Rorty **understands** *Derrida*, unlike many others (e.g., *Searle*). His affinity with continental thought is particularly visible in ***Essays on Heidegger and others***, and with Derrida in particular, in *"Is Derrida a transcendental philosopher?" (pp. 119-128)*.

34. **Hilary Putnam** is also an interpreter between paradigms, but much less radical than Rorty. Although he is (already) an anti-realist, he is nevertheless still considered (like *Dummett*) well within the analytic tradition. Putnam is a **mobile** philosopher, and deserves much credit (not unlike *Schiffer*) for the courage he displayed in changing his views over the years. Putnam is a brilliant epistemologist and a marvelous writer, and his *'Brains in a Vat', 'Why is a Philosopher?'* and several other essays are considered textbook material. It is my bet that Putnam's long journey is far from completed.

35. **Leibniz** is an under-estimated philosopher. I believe this is not only due to his less-than-perfect personality, but also because he had the misfortune of losing his quarrel with Newton. I believe that if he and Spinoza had spent more time together, a wonderful **synthesis** would have emerged. If I ever have the time and energy, I will compose such an imaginary synthesis, based on the short (and

195

futile) encounter they had. Leibniz never offered an explanation to the apparent contradiction between the **plurality** of isolated worlds (monads) and the **singularity** of the (best!) world God created. (Corresponding to *Kripke*'s infinity of **possible** worlds vs. the one **actual** world).

36. **Hegel** is the origin, the source, of the 'continental' tradition, continued by *Husserl, Heidegger*, followed by (French) Existentialism, out of which contemporary *post modernism* evolved. On the other side of the ocean, William James was highly influenced by Hegel's thought, and his traces are clearly visible even in contemporary pragmatism. No wonder that it is pragmatists like Rorty who take continental philosophy seriously.

37. The question whether **Derrida** is a "philosopher" is addressed by Rorty in the abovementioned article (endnote 33 above). The abyss lying between Derrida's postmodernism and traditional analytic philosophy is particularly visible in the exchange (of articles) he had with Searle. It seems Searle really does not **understand** Derrida's thoughts. On the other hand, it seems that Derrida **does** understand Searle. This puts Derrida in a superior position in the debate. Still, Derrida refuses to use Searle's language. He clings to his postmodernist jargon, which is Chinese to many analytic philosophers. Derrida does seem to have the upper hand, but this only makes him seem **smarter**; At the same time, he turns out as the **villain**: He **could** be a great **interpreter** between paradigms (like Rorty, and to some extent Putnam), but he refuses the role. He'd rather be **clever** than **good**. The criticism directed towards Derrida from analytic circles centers on the wrong claim: The problem is not that his ideas are **nonsense** - they are not. It is his immoral indifference to making himself **understood** by many who do not speak his language that is **wrong**. On **Derrida vs. Searle** see: Gary B. Madison (ed.) *Working Through Derrida*, pp. 170-188, and Christopher Norris, *Deconstruction*, ch. 7.

38. **Umberto Eco** became famous as a writer specializing in medieval history. His *The name of the rose* turned into an extremely successful motion picture. But like many other writers, he is also a philosopher. His *On the possibility of generating aesthetic messages in an edenic language* was originally published in Italian in *Strumenti Critici 5, no. 11 (1971)* and translated into English by Bruce Merry in *Twentieth Century Studies 6, no. 7 (1972)*.

June 15

39. *An Experiment with Time* was first published in 1927. I read the third edition, which was substantially revised, and published in 1958.

40. I read *Introduction to the Study of Logic* in Hebrew. I don't believe it was ever translated into English. In his short introduction Bergman points out the inappropriate separation between *philosophical logic* and *symbolic (mathematical) logic*, a dichotomy of which he does not approve. He claims that in recent years mathematical logicians perceived their field as independent from the historical roots of the study of logic. I strongly identified with Bergman's criticism, whereas my own initial logical education, acquired throughout my studies in computer science, was completely devoid of any philosophical considerations. I was not even aware of the philosophical implications until I returned to school, twenty years later. On the other hand, some important logical studies performed by *phenomenologists* almost completely ignored modern (post-Fregean) symbolic logic, and **were** ignored by authors in contemporary symbolic logic. Bergman states that in his book, he attempts a **synthesis** of the two approaches.

41. The figure of **Moses** is an example of a **name** whose **meaning** is **not** derived from its **reference**. This example is provided by Hilary Putnam in *Why is a Philosopher? (p. 108)*. He points out that *The reference of our words is often determined by other members of the linguistic community... There is a **linguistic division of labor**...* (which) *extends to the fixing of reference of proper names.* When we refer to (the prophet) *Moses*, we cannot provide an appropriate identifying description. The **meaning** of the (proper) name *Moses* has nothing to do with an 'object' in the 'real' world, or, at least, does not **depend** on it (as is the case with *Hamlet*).

42. Language is considered (as) a **game** ever since *Wittgenstein*. A condition to participation in **any** game is the acquaintance with some set of **rules** of the game. Wittgenstein's conception of the rules of the language game is folded in his notion of **certainty**. In his *On Certainty*, published (post humously) in 1969, he distinguishes between what is **certain**, what is the **substratum** of our *worldview*, thus acting as **rules**, and between what **can** be true (or false), what can be **known**. The former **constitutes** the language, while the latter is its **content**. There is no sense in **doubting** what is constitutive. It is beyond 'doubt'. For two people to engage in a game (of **language**, in this case), they must have some pre-agreed set of rules. **This**, in itself, is already a rule: A requirement for the possibility of the game.

43. The question regarding the ontological status of mathematical concepts (and in particular, of **numbers**) has nowadays converged into two main doctrines: **Platonism** (also known as 'realism' regarding mathematical entities. I prefer 'Platonism', whereas I use 'realism' in a different sense, that of 'objectivism') and **Formalism**. (E.g., D. Hilbert's proof theory ('metamathematics'), intuitionism, finitism).

44. In *Phaedo, The Republic* (books V-VII), *Parmenides*.

45. Most of Frege's writings are somehow connected to his distinction between sense and reference. But the classic article dealing in this distinction, *On Sense and Reference* ("Uber Sinn und Bedeutung"), was first published in 1892, in *Zeitschrift fur Philosophie und philosophische Kritik*. It is until this day considered the most important and influential article in the philosophy of language.

46. Language is designed to describe **states of affairs**, static 'snapshots' of reality, while reality itself is **ever changing**, it is a constant flow of change. A well known Indian *Guru*, **Bhagwan Shree Rajneesh**, who had quite a substantial western following, said in *The Discipline of Transcendence* (pp. 283-4): *Eddington has said that in the English language there are a few words that are absolutely false: for example,* **rest**. *Nothing is ever in rest, the very word is wrong, because there is no equivalent in reality.* But language **assumes** that 'rest', immobility, staticness, is 'possible'. At least as far as the (fixed) **meanings** of the words are concerned. As long as the language game is in process, this fixed domain is constantly assumed, 'posited'.

47. Kant's famous simile of the hundred pounds (*Critique of Pure Reason, 627)* demonstrates that **existence** is **not** a (regular) predicate. Saying about something that it **exists** provides no (new) information about it. Kant makes this claim in his criticism of the *ontological proof for the existence of God*. This understanding of 'existence' already appears in one of Kant's pre-critical publications, *The only possible argument for proving the existence of God (1763)*. Nineteen years before the first critique, Kant already attacks the prevailing proofs of the existence of God. He rejects the ontological proof (which he calls 'Descartes' proof') and says: *"Take any object, say Julius Caesar. Posit all his possible attributes, including those of time and place, and discover that with all of these, he can still* **exist** *or* **not** *exist. The Lord, who created this world and this figure inside it, could have known all these attributes without exception, and still consider it just as* **possible**, *although inexistent, until he decided to create him... Existence is an absolute* **positing** *of a thing amongst things, and in this it is distinct from any other attribute... When I imagine that God said about some possible world* **"Be!"**, *he did not grant the wholeness he created with new properties, he did not add a new* **attribute** *to it, but "**posited**" this world including all its attributes in an absolute way"*. How enlightening!

48. Zeno was an Eleathean logician, who used language and logic to support Parmenides' claims regarding the deceiving nature of the sensory, phenomenal world. According to *Proclus*, Zeno produced some forty paradoxes (or 'attacks'), eight of which survived. Zeno's paradoxes attack the (illusory) notions of change, motion and plurality. Zeno's character appears in Plato's **Parmenides** *(128b)*, in which he says: *"...these writings of mine were meant to be some protection to the arguments of Parmenides against those who attack him... My writing is an answer to the partisans of the **many** and it returns their attack with interest, with a view to showing that the hypothesis of the **many**, if examined sufficiently in detail, leads to even more ridiculous results than the hypothesis of the **one**.*

49. Russell's paradox is considered a turning point in set theory: He showed that if a set is 'allowed' to include itself, problems arise. He offered no **reason** for the problematic of self-reference, he just pointed it out. His solution was simply to **forbid** it. A set **should not** include itself. But what about **the empty set**? On one hand, it cannot be avoided; On the other, it cannot be denied that it includes itself, whereas **every** set includes it! Therefore semantic theory requires the domain not be empty.

50. The objectivist perception results in **antinomies**: In conflicting claims about (the structure of) the world. **Kant** *(Critique of Pure Reason, 454-489)* listed four great antinomies: (1) The world is finite **and** infinite in terms of its extension in time and space. (2) The world is composed of atoms (indivisible units) **and** is infinitely divisible. (3) The world is subject only to causality (deterministic) **and** it is subject to free will. (4) There is a necessary entity (God) **and** there is no entity which is necessary. The very **concept** of **the world** as a 'complete entity', and (objective) object, is **contradictory**.

51. Chomsky claims that it is **empirically** observable, that all human **speakers** share a basic **syntax**, which he therefore considers **innate**. I am not an expert on Chomsky, but it seems to me that his basic claim is simply: "What all speakers have in common is the fact that they were born **speakers**"...

June 16

52. I discovered *Heidegger* **after** I have read Rorty, Derrida and Sartre. I believe that for people (like myself) with an empiricist, western *worldview*, this order is the easiest route to understanding him.

53. The Dictionary of Philosophy edited by D.D. Runes defines **Deontological ethics** as *"Any ethics which does not make the theory of obligation entirely dependent on the theory of value, holding that an action may be known to be right without a consideration of the goodness of anything, or at least that an action may be right and be known to be so even though it does not flow from the agent's best motive (or even from a good one) and does not, by being performed, bring into being as much good as some other action open to the agent."* Kant would probably turn in his grave had he read this "definition". Many people understand Deontological ethics as **divorced** from, or at least irrelevant to, the **Good**. Their understanding of the terms "Good" and "value" must be very different from Kant's (and mine).

54. **Alonzo Church**'s *Introduction to Mathematical Logic* is considered a classic textbook. Although Church considers it a mere introduction, I believe it is rather comprehensive and covers a wide domain. About half the text (and most of the interesting and significant parts) is in **footnotes**, and it was this book that gave me the idea for the format of my thesis.

55. After **W.V.O. Quine**, *Word and Object*, pp. 26-30.

56. I first became interested in conditional propositions in Ruth Manor's seminar bearing that name, particularly counter factual propositions and the paradox of material implication.

June 17

57. Conventional **predicate calculus** is **extensional**. A logical expression is extensional, when every one of its constituent expressions can be substituted with an equivalent one, while preserving the truth value of the expression. A language composed of extensional expressions only, is called an **extensional language**. But natural language is clearly not extensional: "Creatures with hearts" is clearly different from "creatures with kidneys". Hence, predicate logic **cannot** be taken as a model of natural language. A different, **intensional** interpretation is required for a formal language to properly model what is going on in natural language. Early logical positivism argued for the 'extensional thesis', which claims that our intensional natural language is reducible to a formal extensional language. But Carnap himself admitted in his later writings (e.g., *Meaning and Necessity, 1947*) that this reducibility is but a conjecture (a conjecture the late Wittgenstein explicitly rejected).

58. The empty set <u>exists</u>. This statement has a subject-predicate structure, while (in itself) providing the basis for predicate logic. I take it as an **axiom** and a **definition** at the same time: The positing of two terms (a 'super object' and a 'super predicate') **and** the relation prevailing between them, rendering the **truth** of the statement. One must **have** the concepts *'empty set'* and *'existence'*, **and** believe that the empty set exists, as the foundation of (any!) language.

59. 'Real' or **'realistic'** was used throughout the history of philosophy in many senses. My common use of the word throughout this thesis is as in 'common sense realism' or 'scientific realism' (as in Michael Devitt's *Realism and Truth*). In this particular case, though, I mean 'realism' in the sense of 'belief in the **independent** existence of mathematical entities'.

60. Modal logic deals in propositions which contain the concepts of **necessity** and **possibility** (and their opposites, **contingency** and **impossibility**). Modern modal logic was initiated by *C.I. Lewis* due to his dissatisfaction with Russell's **material implication**. It was *Saul Kripke* who offered a semantic interpretation to quantified modal logic, in his **semantics of possible worlds**. My understanding of 'possible worlds' vs. 'the actual world' is simply this: **The** actual world is **my own**. All (other) possible worlds are those of other (speakers).

June 18

61. Just for the record - Kant's twelve categories are: Unity, Plurality and Totality (categories of quantity); Reality, Negation and Limitation (categories of quality); Inherence/subsistence, Causality and Community (categories of relation); Possibility, Existence and Necessity (categories of Modality).

62. Isomorphism: "Two mathematical structures A and B are isomorphic when there is at least one bijective function f which maps each element a of A into a corresponding b $(=f(a))$ of B". (The *Fontana Dictionary of modern thought*). I.e., when there **exists** a one to one correspondence between the two mathematical structures. Isomorphism is as close to **identity** as any two systems can get. I would say that **isomorphism** is nothing but **identity** (when discussing **systems**).

63. *"Il n'y a pas de hors-texte"* (There is nothing outside **text**). Jacques Derrida, *Of Grammatology*.

64. This last sentence in **Wittgenstein**'s *Tractatus Logico Philosophicus* is not only **mystical**, but also (like many other significant philosophical questions or statements) both **trivial** and **deep** at the same time. Wittgenstein himself considers it mystical: *"Not **how** is the world is mystical, but **that** it **is"** (6.44); "Observing the world as eternal is observing it as a limited whole. The perception of the world as a limited whole is the mystical" (6.45)*. It is **trivial** because it means "What **cannot** be discussed **shouldn't** be discussed". But it is also **deep**: In 6.5 Wittgenstein writes: *"To an answer that cannot be expressed, the question is also ineffable... If a question can at all be phrased, it can also be answered."* Wittgenstein considers the question "Why does the world **exist**?" a question that cannot be answered. Therefore, the corresponding question must be meaningless; And it **is** meaningless: What could possibly be **meant** by this question? We don't even know what **sort** of answer to seek; We do not **understand** our own question "Why does the world exist?" It is a **senseless** question, in Wittgenstein's own terminology. 'The world' is here understood as 'everything', while existence is an attribute which **by definition** applies only to **parts** of it (whereas we constantly discuss things which do **not** exist).

I don't think Wittgenstein substantially revised his philosophical *worldview* throughout his life, despite the prevailing distinction between 'the early' and 'the late'. He just **rephrased** it. The later Wittgenstein harshly criticized the *Tractatus*. But so did the early one, in the next-to-last clause (6.54): "...My propositions are... senseless, when he has climbed out through them, on them, over them. (He must so to speak throw away the ladder, after he has climbed up on it.)"

65. **Tarski**'s *Der Wahrheitsbegriff in den formalisierten Sprachen*, Studia Philosophica, vol. 1 (1935), pp. 261-405, is devoted to the problem of finding a definition of semantical truth for a logistic system L, not in L itself but in a metalanguage which defines the syntax of L.

66. As Godel showed, truth cannot be defined in terms of the language to which the (particular notion of) truth applies. Hence, as far as a (particular) theory is concerned, it has no **meaning** ('explanatory value') in its terms - only in the terms of the metalanguage. Therefore, there is no 'external' ('transcendental') **explanation** to the (general) notion of truth - it is for ever 'internal'. In **my** terms, the 'ultimate' metalanguage is simply **the speaker** himself; The **meaning** of truth thus being 'what he believes'.

202

67. **Aristotle**'s *Organon* (his wider logic, considered as the **tool** for practicing science, for the acquisition of knowledge) is comprised of six books: *The Categories*, providing the epistemic/ontological foundations, *Topica*, which acts as a reservoir of premises, of presuppositions which are (apriori) true, from which inferences may be made, *De Sophisticis Elenchis*, which lists (sophistic) 'fallacies', claims which Aristotle considers false, and warns against, *De Interpretatione*, his hermeneutics, dealing in truth and falsity of propositions, and two books of *Analytica, priori* and *posteriori*, outlining Aristotle's logical theory itself.

June 19

68. A comprehensive account of **correspondence truth** from a realistic point of view can be found in **Michael Devitt**'s *Realism and Truth,* pp. 26-107.

69. In my paper *The Truth about Truth (1995)* I claim there is no conflict between the three doctrines; That they differ only in their **emphasis** on various **aspects** of truth.

70. Although it was *C.S. Peirce* who coined the term **pragmatism**, he did not explicitly link truth with the **good**. He described pragmatism as *a method of determining the meanings of hard words and abstract conceptions*; His pragmatism was essentially **epistemic**. Peirce's famous pragmatist maxim states: *"Consider what effects, that might conceivably have **practical** bearings, we conceive the object of our conceptions to have. Then, our conception of these effects is the whole of our conception of the object."* ('*How to make our ideas clear*', *Popular Science Monthly,* vol. 12, 1878). This article made no significant impact. Peirce was only concerned with **meaning**, not with **truth**. It was William James who turned pragmatism into what it is. James borrowed Peirce's term, but loaded it with enhanced and new meaning. In 1905, Peirce tried to separate his own theory from James', renaming it 'pragmaticism', a word which he decided was 'ugly enough to be safe from kidnappers'. Peirce succeeded: It was so ugly, no one remembers it.

71. The term **'intentionality'** was used throughout the history of philosophy in a variety of senses; e.g., Frege's *aboutness* and Searle's *Intentionality*. However, I take it here in the sense of *conatus*, of the **willing, desiring** human nature.

72. Neil Wilson. *Substance without substrata*, 1959.

73. Quine is, of course, a devoted self proclaimed empiricist. The dichotomy between empiricism and rationalism seems quite outdated, but I believe it is not; It just carries new names: Contemporary empiricism is known as 'scientific realism', and contemporary rationalism can be identified in various versions of relativism.

74. A good introduction to Davidson's philosophy is offered by Simon Evnine in *Donald Davidson (1986)*.

75. "A Nice Derangement of Epitaphs", "A Coherence Theory of Truth and Knowledge" and "Empirical Content" were all published in Ernest Lepore (ed.) *Truth and Interpretation, 1986.*

76. Bjorn T. Ramberg, *Donald Davidson's Philosophy of Language (1989)* p. 103.

77. Ibid., p. 107.

78. Ibid., pp. 108-113.

79. *The Journal of Philosophy*, vol. LXXXVII, no. 6, june 1990, pp 279-328.

80. John Dewey, *Experience and Nature (1958)*, p. 410.

June 20

81. The requirement that the domain not be empty is one of Russell's significant set-theoretical contributions to logical theory.

82. This polemic against my contention of truth as 'a belief' was raised by Ruth Manor, who rightly claimed that my kind of belief system does not leave room for the notion of 'false proposition' at all. And she was right: In my book, 'False proposition' are a species of 'true propositions' (beliefs).

June 21

83. My interest in the 'definition' of rationality was aroused in a Ruth Manor's seminar *Logic and Rationality*, during which I was exposed to M. Fisch's *Towards a Rational Theory of Progress*, which offers a view of rationality based on **progress**, a view which seemed to be lacking the most important characteristic I believed rationality involves: **Morality**.

84. This is the basic claim I make in a short paper titled *Logic and Morality (1994)*.

85. G. E. Moore, *The Subject-Matter of Ethics; Principia Ethica* (1903).

86. Plato, *The Republic,* Book VI, 505a-509c.

87. Ibid., Book I.

88. Gottlob Frege, *Logical Syntax of Language,* §§ 17, 44.

89. Bertrand Russell, *Human Knowledge: Its Scope and Limits* (1948).

90. Solipsism: "(a) *Methodological*: The epistemological doctrine which considers the individual self and its states the only possible or legitimate starting point for philosophical construction. (b) *Metaphysical*: Subvariety of idealism which maintains that the individual self of the solipsistic philosopher is the whole of reality and that the external world and other persons are representations of that self having no independent existence." (*Dictionary of Philosophy,* D.D. Runes).

91. Hilary Putnam, *Realism with a Human Face, (1986)*, p. 106.

June 22

92. Ruth Manor, ***Simulating Imagination,*** *Logos*, vol. 7 (1986).

93. *LDG, Language for the Description of God* by Alon and Graves, a book summarizing the LDG seminar, is currently in editing stages.

94. B. Spinoza, *Ethics*, Part II, Prop. XLIII.

95. Maimonides' great masterpiece, *The Guide to the Perplexed (1190)*, transcends **Jewish** thought, although it was **meant** for a Jewish audience. In the introduction to the first part, Maimonides says: *The object of this treatise is to enlighten a religious man who has been trained to believe in the truth of our holy law, who conscientiously fulfills his moral and religious duties, and at the same time has been successful in his philosophical studies.*

96. St. Thomas Aquinas, *Summa theologiae* (Eyre and Spottiswood, London, 1963-80).

97. Rene Descartes, *Meditations on First Philosophy*, 3rd and 5th meditations.

98. St. Augustine of Hippo (354-430 AD) was a (neo) Platonist. His major writings are the *Confessions* and *City of God*.

June 23

99. The first article I ever read about paradoxes was Ruth Manor's *What is Paradoxical in Paradoxes?*, published in Hebrew in *Israeli Philosophy (1983)*, as a collection of papers presented in a conference of the Israeli Philosophical Society in Bar Ilan University.

100. Immanuel Kant, *Fundamental Principles of the Metaphysics of Ethics (1783)*.

101. Plato took 'The Beautiful' as an *Idea*, on par with other 'high' ideas such as 'The Big'. However, 'The Beautiful' deserves special treatment, whereas it is the object of *Eros*. We Become acquainted with The Beautiful first by our attractions to beautiful **things**, or **people**, but in time, it is The Beautiful **itself** that becomes the object of attraction. (Plato, *Symposium*).

102. **Husserl**'s *Cartesian Meditations (1929)* was his last and most comprehensive book, providing an overall account of his phenomenology.

103. **Heidegger**'s most influential book is also his first: *Being and Time (1927)*.

104. **Franz Brentano** was an interesting and original thinker, who receives little attention from contemporary philosophers. (Bergman is one of the few who considered him important). Brentano identified three modes of intentionality (of 'psychic activity'): Representation, judgment, and attraction ('love and hate'). The latter two correspond to 'truth' and 'rightness' (goodness), and together they compose (construct?) the representation. Brentano considered himself an Aristotelian, and had significant influence on Husserl.

105. Edmund Husserl, *Ideas for a pure phenomenology*, chapter 1, §27.

June 24

106. Gottfried Wilhelm **Leibniz**, *Monadology*, para. 59.

107. A.M. Turing defined his 'machine' in 1936, as a model onto which any deterministic algorithm is reducible. A Turing machine allegedly cannot pass 'Turing's test'; I.e., it cannot produce (lingual) behavior indistinguishable from that of a ('real') human.

108. By Ronald Knox. (Bertrand Russell, *History of Western Philosophy*, p. 623).

June 25

109. Aristotle followed Plato in loading the term **'sophism'** with a negative connotation: *"An eristic or contentious syllogism; distinguished from paralogism by the intent to deceive"*. However, I believe that the important characteristic of sophism was its **relativistic** perception. In a sense, the sophists were the first **pragmatists**, whereas for them the **true** was "what worked" (for their students, politically).

110. **Henri Bergson**, *Time and Free will: an essay on the immediate data of consciousness (1889)*, translated into Hebrew by J. Ur (Who also translated Bergson's *Creative Evolution, 1907*).

111. *"Thus defined, God has nothing of the ready-made, he is uninterrupted life, action, freedom. And the creation, so conceived, is not a mystery; we experience it in ourselves when we act freely."* **Bergson**, *Creative Evolution*, quoted in L. Kolakowski, *Bergson*, p. 61.

June 26

112. L. **Wittgenstein**, *Tractatus Logico-Philosophicus*, **7**.

113. J.M.E. **McTaggart**, *The Unreality of Time*, **Mind**, 17 (1908), pp. 457-74.

114. I became interested in **Dummett**'s anti-realism about the past thanks to Anat Matar's presentation on this topic to the philosophy department colloquium at TAU in 1994.

115. Both in Dummett's *Truth and Other Enigmas, 1978.*

116. Grene, Marjorie, *Introduction to Existentialism, 1948.* A good introduction in Hebrew also by Jacob Golomb, *Introduction to Philosophies of Existence, 1990.*

June 27

117. The speech act *'command'* was taken as constituted by one preliminary condition, that the command**er** is in a position of **authority**, and three basic conditions: (a) The content of the command must be taken as constituting a **norm** in the particular context. (b) It must be **possible** to carry out the commanded action. (c) It is impossible to refuse the command.

118. John L. **Austin**, *How to Do Things with Words*, 1962.

119. John **Searle**, *Speech Acts, an essay in the philosophy of language, 1969.*

120. On questions as epistemic requests, see Jaakko **Hintikka**, *Answers to Questions*, and Ranier **Lang**, *Questions as Epistemic Requests*, both in Henry Hiz (ed.), *Questions, 1977.* Also, J. Hintikka, *Interrogative Model of Inquiry As a Logic of Discovery,* and J. Hintikka and I. Halonen, *Semantics and Pragmatics of Why-Questions.*

121. A detailed account on my reduced 'speech act theory' (reduced to questions and assertions only) is provided in my paper *A Different Look at Questions and Answers* (1994). Also, see Asa Kasher's *Minimal Speakers, Necessary Speech Acts.*

June 28

122. John **Locke**, *An Essay Concerning Human Understanding (1690).*

123. George **Berkeley**, *A Treatise Concerning the Principles of Human Knowledge (1710).*

124. David **Hume**, *A Treatise of Human Nature (1739-40).*

125. On the problem of induction, see Karl **Popper**, *Objective Knowledge, 1972* ch.1: *Conjectural knowledge: My solution of the problem of induction*), and Richard Swinburne (ed.), *The Justification of Induction.*

126. Plato, *The Republic, 527d-528e.*

127. Thomas **Nagel**, *What is it like to be a bat?*, appeared in *The Philosophical Review,* Oct. 1974.

June 29

128. D. **Hume,** *A Treatise of Human Nature*, Book I, Part III.

129. G. **Ryle**, *The Concept of Mind, 1949*, ch. 2.

June 30

130. The various doctrines in the philosophy of action differ from each other, first and foremost, over the basic question of what an action **is**. Most of them (e.g., Danto, Hornsby and others) address this issue from an apriori realistic point of view. However, in the present context, the term 'action' should be understood in its common usage, as something that is intentionally performed by a rational human being.

131. Friedrich **Nietzsche**, *Also Sprach Zarathustra*, Part IV.

132. Richard **Taylor**, *Good and Evil, 1970.*

133. David **Wiggins**, *Truth, Invention, and the Meaning of Life*, first published in *Proceedings of the British Academy LXII (1976).*

134. Allan W. **Watts,** *Tao, The Watercourse Way (1975).*

135. John Stuart **Mill**, *Utilitarianism (1861).*

July 1

136. Kirk, Raven and Schofield, *The Presocratic Philosophers*, pp. 1-6.

137. Descartes meant to **support** Christianity. The way things turned out, it was his (methodological!) skepticism that started the snowball which eventually crushed it.

138. Meta-ethics deals in the question "what is ethics?" Does ethics deal in the **good**? In the **pleasant**? In the **right**? The problem with meta-ethics is that it is purely **lingual**: It essentially discusses the **meaning** of the word "ethics".

Bibliography

Aquinas, Thomas, 1963-80, *Theological Summary*, Eyre & Spottiswood.

Aristotle (W.D. Ross, ed.) 1908-52, *The Works of Aristotle*,
Oxford University Press.

Austin, John L. 1962, *How to Do Things with Words*, Oxford University Press.

Ayer, A.J. (ed.) (A. Pap, trans.) 1959, *Logical Positivism*, Free Press.

Berkeley, George (A.A. Luce & T.E. Jessop, ed.) 1948-57,
The Works of George Berkeley, Thomas Nelson.

Bergson, Henri (F.L. Pogson, trans.) 1971,
Time and free will: An essay on the immediate data of conciousness,
Allen & Unwin, Originally published in 1889.
- - - - -   (C. Brereton & F. Rothwell, trans.) 1911, *Laughter*, Macmillan.
- - - - -   (A. Mitchell, trans.) 1976, *Creative Evolution*, Greenwood Press.
Originally published in 1907.

Carnap, Rudolf (R.A. George, trans.)1967, *The Logical Structure of the World,*
Routledge. Originally published in 1928.
- - - - -   1937, *The Logical Syntax of Language*, Harcourt, Brace.
- - - - -   1956, *Meaning and Necessity*, 2nd edition,
Chicago University Press. 1st edition: 1947.

Cavell, Stanley 1994, *Philosophy's Recounting of the Ordinary*,
Clarendon Press.

Chappell, V.C. (ed.) 1962, *The Philosophy of Mind*, Prentice-Hall.

Church, Alonzo 1956, *Introduction to Mathematical Logic*, 2nd edition,
Princeton University Press. 1st edition: 1944.

Cross, R.C. & Woozley, A.D.
1964, *Plato's REPUBLIC - A Philosophical Commentary,*
Macmillan.

Daniel C. Dennett, 1978, *Brainstorms*, Bradford.

211

Davidson, Donald 1980, *Essays on Actions and Events*, Clarendon Press.
- - - - -   1990, "The Structure and Content of Truth",
            The Journal of Philosophy, vol. 87, no. 6, pp. 279-328.

Deleuze, Gilles (Tomlinson & Habberjam, trans.) 1988, *Bergsonism*, Zone.
- - - - -   (Paul Patton, trans.) *Difference and Repetition*, Athlone Press.
- - - - -   (M. Lester & C. Stivale, trans.) *The Logic of Sense*,
            Columbia University Press.

Derrida, Jacques (David B. Allison, trans.)1973, *Speech and Phenomena*,
            Northwestern University Press.
- - - - -   1976, *Of Grammatology*, John Hopkins University Press.
- - - - -   1982, *Margins of Philosophy*, University of Chicago Press.

Descartes, Rene (Cottingham, Stoothof, Murdoch, trans.)
            1984, *The Philosophical Writings of Descartes*,
            Cambridge University Press.

Devitt, Michael 1991, *Realism and Truth*, 2nd edition,
            Blackwell. 1st edition 1984.

Dewey, John 1958, *Experience and Nature*, Dover.

Dummett, Michael 1978, *Truth and Other Enigmas*, Harvard University Press.
- - - - -   1982, "Realism", *Synthese 52* pp. 55-112.
- - - - -   1991, *The Logical Basis of Metaphysics*, Duckworth.
- - - - -   1992, *The Seas of Language*, Clarendon Press.
- - - - -   1993, *Origins of Analytical Philosophy*, Harvard University Press.

Dunne, J.W. 1958, *An Experiment with Time*, 2nd edition,
            Faber and Faber. 1st edition.: 1927

Eco, Umberto (Bruce Merry, trans.)
            1972, "On the Possibility of Generating Esthetic
            Messages in an Edenic Language", *20th Century Studies 6*, no. 7.

Evnine, Simon 1988, *Donald Davidson*, Polity Press.

Fisch, Menachem 1994, "Towards a Rational Theory of Progress", *Synthese 99*,
277-304

Fodor, Jerry, 1981, *Representations*, MIT Press.

Fodor, Jerry & Lepore, Ernest 1992, *HOLISM, a shopper's guide*, Blackwell.

Frege, Gottlob (P.Geach & M. Black, trans.) 1952,
     Translations from the Philosophical Writings of Gottlob Frege,
     Blackwell.
- - - - -   (A.M. Quinton & M. Quinton, trans.)
     1956, "The thought: A logical inquiry", *Mind, vol. 65* pp. 289-311.

Grene, Marjorie 1948, *Introduction to Existentialism*,
     University of Chicago Press.

Grice, Paul 1989, *Studies in the Way of Words*, Harvard University Press.
- - - - -   1941, "Personal Identity", *Mind 50*, pp. 330-350.

Guthrie, W.K.C., *A History of Greek Philosophy*, Cambridge University Press.

Haack, Susan, *Deviant Logic - Some philosophical issues*,
     Cambridge University Press.

Happold, F.C. 1966, *Religious Faith and Twentieth Century Man*, Penguin.

Hegel, G.W.F. (J. Sibree, trans.) 1956, *Lectures on the Philosophy of History*,
     Dover (A.V. Miller, trans.) 1977, *Hegel's Phenomenology of Spirit*,
     Oxford University Press.

Heidegger, Martin (Macquarrie & Robinson, trans.) 1962,
     Being and Time, Harper & Row. Originally published in 1927.

Hiz, Henry (ed.) 1977, *Questions*, D. Reidel Publishing.

Hornsby, Jennifer 1980, *Actions*, Routledge.

Hume, David (L.A. Selby-Bigge, ed.)
     1978, *A Treatise on Human Nature*,
     Oxford University Press, Originally Published 1739-40.

Husserl, Edmund (J.N. Findlay, trans.)
    1970, *Logical Investigations*, Routledge. Originally published in 1900.
- - - - -   (W.R. Boyce Gibson, trans.) 1962,
       Ideas for a Pure Phenomenology,
       Allen & Unwin. Originally published in 1913.

Hylton, Peter 1990, *Russell, Idealism and the Emergence of Analytic Philosophy,* Clarendon Press.

James, William (F.H. Burkhardt, ed.) 1975,
    The Works of William James, Harvard University Press.

Kasher, Asa, "Minimal Speakers, Necessary Speech Acts",

Kornblith, Hilary (ed.) 1994, *Naturalizing Epistemology*, MIT Press.

Kant, Immanuel, (N. Kemp Smith, trans.) 1933,
    Critique of Pure Reason, 2nd edition, Macmillan. 1st edition: 1929.
    Originally published in 1781, 2nd (original) edition in 1787.
- - - - -   (Paul Carus, ed.) 1949, *Prolegomena to any future metaphysics*,
       Open Court. Originally published in 1783.

Kaufman, Walter 1958, *Critique of Religion and Philosophy*, Harper & Bros.

Kirk, G.S., Raven, J.E. & Schofield, M 1983, *The Presocratic Philosophers*, 2nd edition, Cambridge.

Kuhn, Thomas 1970, *The Structure of Scientific Revolution*, 2nd edition, Chicago University Press. 1st edition: 1962.

Leibniz, Gottfried Wilhelm (P. Lucas & L. Grint, trans.) 1961,
    Discourse on Metaphysics, Manchester University Press.
- - - - -   (H.T. Mason, trans.) 1967, *The Leibniz-Arnauld Correspondence*,
       Manchester University Press.
- - - - -   (P. Wiener, ed.) 1951, *Leibniz: Selections*, Scribner's.

Lepore, Ernest (ed.) 1986, *Truth and Interpretation*, Blackwell.

Levinas, Emmanuel (Michael B. Smith, trans) *Outside the Subject*,
    Athlone Press.
- - - - -   (Alphonso Lingis, trans.) 1978, *Existence and Existents*,
       Martinus Nijhof.

- - - - -   (Richard A. Cohen, trans.) 1985 *Ethics and Infinity*,
              Duquesne University Press. Originally published in 1982.
- - - - -   (A. Lingis, trans.) 1987, *Collected Philosophical Papers*,
          Martinus Nijhof.

Locke, John (P.H. Nidditch, ed.)
          1979, *An Essay Concerning Human Understanding*,
          Oxford University Press.

Madison, Gary B. (ed.) 1993, *Working Through Derrida*,
          Northwestern University Press

Maimonides, Moses (Schlomo Pines, trans.)
          1963, *The Guide of the Perplexed*, University of Chicago Press.

Manor, Ruth 1986, "Simulating Imagination", *Logos, vol. 7*, pp. 69-81.

McTaggart, J.M.E. 1908, "The Unreality of Time", *Mind* 17 pp. 457-74.

Mill, John Stuart (J.M. Robson, ed.) 1963-86,
          The Collected Works of John Stuart Mill,
          University of Toronto Press.

Moore, G.E. 1959, *Principia Ethica*, Cambridge University Press.
          Originally published in 1903.
- - - - -   1963, *Philosophical Papers*, Allen & Unwin.

Nagel, Thomas 1974, "What Is It Like to Be a Bat?",
          The Philosophical Review, October 1974.
- - - - -   1971, "Brain Bisection and the Unity of Conciousness",
          Synthese 22, pp. 396-413.

Nozick, Robert 1981, *Philosophical Explanations*, Clarendon Press.

Ogden, C.K. & Richards, I.A. 1972, *The Meaning of Meaning*,
          10th edition. Routledge. 1st edition: 1923.

Otto, Rudolf (John W. Harvey, trans.) 1950, *The Idea of the Holy*,
          2nd edition, Oxford University Press. 1st edition 1923.

Parfit, Derek 1971, "Personal Identity", *Philosophical Review, vol. 80*, 1971.

Peirce, C.S. 1878, "How to make our ideas clear",
   Popular Science Monthly, vol. 12.

Plato (Desmond Lee, trans.) 1974, *The Republic*,
   2nd edition, Penguin. 1st edition 1955.

Popper, Karl 1969, *Conjectures and Refutations*, 3rd edition,
   Routledge. 1st edition: 1963.
   - - - - -   1972, *Objective Knowledge*, Clarendon Press.

Putnam, Hilary, 1982, *Reason, Truth and History*,
   Cambridge University Press.
   - - - - -   1983, *Realism and Reason*, Cambridge University Press.
   - - - - -   1990, *Realism with a Human Face*, Harvard University Press.

Quine, Willard Van Orman 1951, "Two Dogmas of Empiricism",
   Philosophical Review, 1951.
   - - - - -   1953, *From a Logical Point of View*, MIT Press.
   - - - - -   1960, *Word and Object*, MIT Press.
   - - - - -   1970, *The Philosophy of Logic*, MIT Press.

Quinton, Anthony 1962, "The Soul",
   The Journal of Philosophy 59, no. 15, 393-409.

Rajneesh, Bhagwan Shree 1978, *The Discipline of Transcendence, vol. 1*
   Rajneesh Foundation.

Ramberg, Bjorn T. 1989 *Donald Davidson's Philosophy of Language*,
   Basil Blackwell.

Rorty, Richard 1980, *Philosophy and the Mirror of Nature*, Basil Blackwell.
   - - - - -   1988, *Objectivity, Relativism and Truth*, Cambridge U. Press.
   - - - - -   1989, *Contingency, Irony, and Solidarity*, Cambridge U. Press.
   - - - - -   1990, *Essays on Heidegger and Others*, Cambridge U. Press.

Russell, Bertrand 1905, "On Denoting", *Mind 1905*.
   - - - - -   1973, *The Problems of Philosophy*,
         Oxford University Press. 1st ed.: 1912.
   - - - - -   1950, *Mysticism and Logic*, 9th edition, George Allen & Unwin.
         1st edition: 1910.
   - - - - -   1945, *History of Western Philosophy*, Allen & Unwin.

216

- - - - -   1948, *Human Knowledge: Its scope and its limits*,
            Allen & Unwin.

Ryle, Gilbert 1949, *The Concept of Mind*, Oxford University Press.

Sartre, Jean-Paul (H.E. Barnes, trans.) 1958, *Being and Nothingness*,
            Methuen. Originally published in 1943.

Scharfstein, Ben-Ami 1973, *Mystical Experience*, Basil Blackwell.

Schiffer, Stephen 1972, *Meaning*, Oxford University Press.
- - - - -   1987, *Remnants of Meaning*, MIT Press.

Searle, John R., *Intentionality - An essay in the philosophy of mind*,
            Cambridge University Press.
- - - - -   1969, *Speech Acts - An essay in the philosophy of language*,
            Cambridge University Press.

Spinoza, Benedict (R.H.M Elwes, trans) 1956,
            The works of Benedict de Spinoza, Dover

Stace, W.T. 1961, *Mysticism and Philosophy*, Macmillan.

Strawson, P.F. *Introduction to Logical Theory*, Methuen.
- - - - -   1970, *Meaning and Truth*, Clarendon Press.

Swinburne, Richard (ed.) 1976, *The Justification of Induction*,
            Oxford University Press.

Tarski, Alfred 1956, *Logic, Semantics, Metamathematics*, Clarendon.

Taylor, Richard 1970, *Good and Evil*, Macmillan.

Tiles, J.E. 1988, *Dewey*, London, N.Y: Routledge.

Tomlin, E.W.F. 1961 *R.G. Collingwood*, 2nd edition, Longmans, Green.
            1st ed.: 1953.

Watts, Alan 1957, *The Way of Zen*, Pantheon.
- - - - -   1975, *TAO - The Watercourse Way*, Arkana.

Wiggins, David 1976, "Truth, Invention, and the Meaning of Life", *Proceedings of the British Academy 62.*

Wilhelm, Richard & Baynes, Cary F. (trans.) 1967 *The I Ching (Book of Changes)*, 3rd edition. Princeton University Press. 1st ed. 1950

Wilson, N.L. 1959, "Substance Without Substrata", *Review of Metaphysics* 12, 521-539.

Wittgenstein, Ludwig (D.F. Pears & B.F. McGuinness, trans.) 1963, *Tractatus Logico-Philosophicus*, 2nd edition, Routledge. 1st edition: 1961. Originally published in 1921.
- - - - - (G.E.M. Anscombe, trans.) 1967 *Philosophical Investigations*, 3rd edition. Blackwell. 1st edition 1953.
- - - - - (Anscombe & Wright, ed; Paul & Anscombe, trans.) 1974 *On Certainty*, 2nd edition. Blackwell. 1st edition 1969.

www.ingramcontent.com/pod-product-compliance
Lightning Source LLC
LaVergne TN
LVHW011225080426
835509LV00005B/323